**Australian &
New Zealand Edition**

Marketing Your Small Business

FOR

DUMMIES®

T0339292

**Australian &
New Zealand Edition**

Marketing
Your Small
Business

FOR

DUMMIES®

by Carolyn Tate

WILEY

Wiley Publishing Australia Pty Ltd

Marketing Your Small Business For Dummies®

Australian & New Zealand edition published by
Wiley Publishing Australia Pty Ltd
42 McDougall Street
Milton, Qld 4064
www.dummies.com

Copyright © 2010 Wiley Publishing Australia Pty Ltd

The moral rights of the author have been asserted.

National Library of Australia
Cataloguing-in-Publication data:

Author:	Tate, Carolyn.
Title:	Marketing Your Small Business For Dummies/Carolyn Tate.
Edition:	Australian & New Zealand ed.
ISBN:	978 1 74216 852 4 (pbk.)
Notes:	Includes index.
Subjects:	Small business — Marketing. Branding (Marketing). Advertising.
Dewey Number:	338.642

Cover image: © khz, 2010. Used under licence from Shutterstock.com

Typeset by diacriTech, Chennai, India

Printed in China by
Printplus Limited

10 9 8 7 6 5 4 3 2 1

About the Author

Carolyn Tate (previously Stafford) is different from other marketers. She has a no-bull approach and a passion for making marketing real for small-business owners.

After 18 years in marketing roles with the big corporates, Carolyn decided to jump ship in 2002 and became the founder of her own small business, Connect Marketing. She is now well recognised as a leading small-business marketing expert. Her first book, *Small Business Big Brand*, was published in 2007 and she has run workshops for over 2,000 people all over Australia and New Zealand. She speaks regularly at major conferences on branding and marketing, and is a sought-after media commentator on the subject.

Hundreds of small-business owners have sought her advice and mentoring to help them put in place a real marketing plan. Often a critic of mainstream marketing and advertising tactics, Carolyn directly challenges business owners to get out of the rut of the old ways of marketing, which often treated it as an afterthought, and to put marketing at the heart of their business. She believes that brilliant and clever marketing is the key to business success.

Coogee, Sydney, is Carolyn's home base, where she particularly loves spending the summer seaside season with her son, Billy, and walking her dog, Dash. She travels internationally every year (for work and pleasure), loves reading a good book, yoga, swimming, movies, live music, surf lifesaving, helping out at school and travelling all over Australia to spend time with her family.

Carolyn is currently working towards her goal to live and work from anywhere in the world — doing what she loves — writing books, working on various creative projects, and teaching and inspiring audiences on a whole range of topics, including marketing. Contact Carolyn at carolyn@connectmarketing.com.au or visit her website at www.connectmarketing.com.au.

Dedication

To my son, Billy, who inspires me to be the best I can be ...

To the millions of small-business owners who have taken the plunge to create their own destiny in business and life ...

Author's Acknowledgements

Writing this book has simply been a joy!

My first book, *Small Business Big Brand*, was self-published, which meant I had to manage the whole process, from writing to editing to design and printing. And then came the huge task of marketing the book to get it in the hands of small-business owners across Australia and New Zealand. It was a great experience, if not a tough and tedious process.

Writing *Marketing Your Small Business For Dummies*, on the other hand, has been a simple and focused process. No editing or production processes to manage. No printing and distribution to look after, just free-flow creative writing on my part, coupled with the comfort of knowing everything is being handled by the wonderful team at Wiley.

So a big thanks must go to Bronwyn Duhigg, who recruited me to write this book and guided me through the process of structuring the contents of the book to make sure it would hit the mark with you, my audience. A big thanks also to Kerry Davies, my editor, who, with wit and humour, sharpened up my writing and gave it more punch. Every author should have an editor like Kerry!

A big thanks also to the thousands of small-business owners and my clients who, over the years, have shared their war stories with me. Your willingness to share with me has, in turn, allowed me to share real-life inspired stories and brought this book to life.

Thank you also to the featured entrepreneurs for allowing me to interview them and tell their stories.

Writing is really a solo pursuit. To make it happen I needed big chunks of time set aside, many cups of coffee, no disruptions, a computer, access to the number-one research tool (the internet) . . . and a lot of will and determination.

The will and determination came not only from an inherent belief in myself, but also from the support and encouragement of those who care about me and love me. So a huge bouquet of thanks to you — my family and friends — for not only encouraging me to keep writing, but also for supporting me as a woman, mother and entrepreneur.

Publisher's Acknowledgments

We're proud of this book; please send us your comments through our online registration form located at www.dummies.com/register/.

Some of the people who helped bring this book to market include the following:

Acquisitions, Editorial and Media Development

Project Editor: Kerry Davies

Acquisitions Editor: Bronwyn Duhigg

Editorial Manager: Gabrielle Packman

Production

Graphics: Wiley Art Studio

Cartoons: Glenn Lumsden

Proofreader: Marguerite Thomas

Indexer: Karen Gillen

The author and publisher would like to thank the following copyright holders, organisations and individuals for their permission to reproduce copyright material in this book.

Images

- © Carolyn Tate: **page 37**
- Tribe Research: **page 49**
- Kidstuff: **page 55**
- © Justin Herald: **page 98**
- Catch: **page 103**
- New Zealand Companies: **page 106** New Zealand Companies Office, Ministry of Economic Development
- ABC: **pages 111 and 116** © Australian Broadcasting Corporation Library Sales
- © The Tap Doctor: **page 122**
- Advertising Standards Bureau: **page 193**
- Media Monitors Pty Ltd: **page 195**
- PRIA: **page 226** Public Relations Institute of Australia (PRIA)
- Experian Hitwise: **page 286**
- Sensis Pty Ltd: **page 287**
- © NetLingo: **page 290**
- DSBN: **page 302** DSBN . . . Dynamic Small Business Network
- © SafetyCulture: **page 304**
- Google Inc.: **pages 311 and 316**
- © Smart Company: **page 318**
- © Problogger: **page 324**
- © oDesk: **page 325**

Text

- McCrindle Research Pty Ltd: **page 45**
- Interbrand: **page 96**
- © Nick Bowditch: **page 233**

Every effort has been made to trace the ownership of copyright material. Information that will enable the publisher to rectify any error or omission in subsequent editions will be welcome. In such cases, please contact the Permissions Section of John Wiley & Sons Australia, Ltd.

Contents at a Glance

Table of Contents

Introduction

· ·

Welcome to *Marketing Your Small Business For Dummies*. If you are one of the two million or so small businesses in Australia or New Zealand needing a real, practical, no-nonsense guide on how to market your business (without spending thousands of dollars in the process), then you've come to the right place.

I understand that for many business owners, marketing can be a minefield. You may be asking yourself questions like: Where do I start? What marketing tactics will work best for my business? How much money should I spend on marketing? What return on investment can I expect? How do I find the time for marketing? Who can help me market my business? And more.

I reckon pretty much any business owner is capable of being brilliant at marketing. You just need to get the know-how and discover the techniques that work best for you and your type of business. Marketing is not rocket science. But neither is there a 'silver bullet' for solving marketing issues. Marketing, like any other discipline in your business, requires a good plan and the willingness to dedicate time and energy into implementing it. And, of course, a healthy dose of conviction and belief in what you have to offer helps!

About This Book

If you're just starting out in business or are already in business and barely have the time to manage the business, let alone market it, this book is for you. Whether you want to know how to package your services, run an advertising campaign, get your business online, get your message out via direct mail or be a better networker, it's all here.

In this book, I share real-life stories from business owners who've had real marketing success. I explain what marketing really is (and no, it's not advertising or selling) and how to integrate it into your everyday business life. The tables, hypotheticals and checklists used in the book give you practical and actionable lists of things you can try in your business straightaway.

The tone of the book is light and friendly, making this a down-to-earth book suitable for MBA graduates or people just leaving high school and venturing into the world of small business.

This book is your first port of call for all things marketing. It'll become well loved, dog-eared, scribbled on and battered — and never given away! That's because I am simply passionate about giving you the knowledge you need to be brilliant at marketing and to help you make it happen.

How to Use This Book

Marketing Your Small Business For Dummies is split into 21 chapters and two appendixes across seven parts, and is designed so you can pick it up and read any part at any time, with no rules on how to use it. However, if you're new to business or the world of marketing, I strongly recommend you read Parts I and II before venturing into other parts of the book. That's because these parts cover the basic knowledge you need around marketing before getting into more tactical activities, like building a website or hosting an event.

If you've been in business a while you can read the book from cover to cover or simply close your eyes and open to a page at random (I find this a really fun way to read by the way). If you're looking for a specific marketing topic, check out the table of contents at the front or the index at the back of the book and head straight to it.

What You're Not to Read

A Buddhist proverb says, 'When the student is ready, the teacher will appear.' Your marketing teacher could be me (through this book), a friend in business, your TAFE or university lecturer, authors of other marketing books you choose to read, or an online newsletter you subscribe to. Each one of these will impart pearls of wisdom and knowledge on how to market your business. From each, you will take what you need.

Bookshops are full of big theoretical books on marketing that use a lot of marketing jargon like 'above-the-line advertising' and speak very much in the corporate tongue. If you happen to come across one of these in your local bookstore, open to a page at random and, if it doesn't talk to you directly or you don't understand it, put it back! You won't read it and you probably won't use it. What not to read is just as important as what to read — and this *For Dummies* book is a must-read for all small-business owners. I understand you don't want technical talk, and I promise you don't get it here!

A few spots in this book are optional reading. Sidebars, which are stories in grey boxes, are a little tangential to the main action, so you can skip them if you like, but I'm sure you'll find them interesting.

One last note: Getting the knowledge you need to be brilliant at marketing is one thing. Doing something with the knowledge is quite another.

Foolish Assumptions

In writing this book, I assume nothing. And I know you're not foolish or you wouldn't be reading this now. I assume nothing about you, your business, your prior experience, knowledge or area of expertise.

You could've just started a business or be running a multi-million-dollar enterprise. You could be a whiz at the finances or a master salesperson. You could be painter or a cab driver. Whoever you are and whatever business you run, I guarantee you'll discover something about marketing that you never knew. And I guarantee that if you try (and persevere with) the recommendations in this book, your business will grow and prosper as a result.

Conventions Used in This Book

I want to help you get the information you need as fast as possible. To assist you, I use several conventions:

- ✔ Monofont is used to signal a web address.

    When this book was printed, some web addresses may have needed to break across two lines of text. If that happened, rest assured that no extra characters (such as hyphens or spaces) are used to indicate the break. So, when using one of these web addresses, just type in exactly what you see in this book, pretending that the line break doesn't exist.

- ✔ *Italics* signal that a word is an important term.

- ✔ **Bold** words make the key terms and phrases in bulleted and numbered lists jump out and grab your attention. Bold words also sometimes denote something that needs to be typed into a search window.

✔ Sidebars, text separated from the rest of the type in grey boxes, are interesting but slightly tangential to the subject at hand. Sidebars are generally fun and optional reading. You won't miss anything critical if you skip them. If you choose to read the sidebars, though, I think you'll be glad you did.

How This Book Is Organised

This book is split into seven parts, with each part tackling a different area of marketing, from the basics to the more tricky stuff.

Part I: Entering the World of Marketing

In this section, you discover how to navigate yourself around the murky world of marketing. You find out what marketing really is (and isn't), why the customer must be at the heart of all marketing decisions, how the external environment can impact on your marketing efforts, how to get a marketing plan and stick to it, and how to set marketing goals and objectives.

Part II: Investing in Your Brand

This part takes a look at why branding is so important to your business. You get to understand what a brand is and how to build your brand as an asset. Learn how to create a knockout visual identity and logo, refresh a tired brand, select great brand (and product) names, and use your own personal brand to market your business.

Part III: Getting Your Business in the Media

Getting your message out in the media today means much more than running a few simple ads on the local radio station. In this part, you get to master the basics of advertising, learn how to be creative with your advertising message and choose the best media to hit your target market fair and square between the eyes. You find out if publicity (and public relations) is the right way to go for your business and how to get your story in print, on air or online.

Part IV: Relationship Marketing

Marketing is oh so much more than advertising. In fact, for most businesses with very limited budgets, relationship-marketing techniques are much more effective in building your business reputation and for finding new clients. Discover what relationship marketing is and how to build a variety of relationship-based marketing activities into your marketing plan, including how to build a client referral program, how to be a master networker, how to use sponsorship effectively to market your business and much more.

Part V: Marketing Online

Over 50 per cent of Australian small businesses don't have a website and many business owners who do have one are, in fact, not happy with the one they do have! If this is you or you just need some creative and fun new ideas to market your business online, then read this part. You'll learn what e-marketing really is, how to get a great website and drive traffic to it, and how to use social media and other online marketing tools to generate more business.

Part VI: The Part of Tens

This part leads you through three ten-step checklists that are critical for marketing success. Check out the travel business hypothetical, giving ideal responses to the ten essential questions you need to ask to create a powerful customer value proposition. Discover ten marketing do's and don'ts, and ten top marketing ideas you can use in your business right now.

Part VII: Appendixes

At the back of the book, you find practical templates you can copy and use to put together your marketing plan and budget.

Icons Used in This Book

Throughout this book you find useful icons so you can note specific types of information. Here's what each icon means:

This icon is used to indicate handy tips or advice on marketing ideas you can implement in your business quickly and effectively.

Tie a piece of string on your finger, put reminder notes on your fridge, in the car or on your bathroom mirror. Whatever you do, don't forget!

A pitfall to be avoided at all costs. Read these warnings carefully before making any marketing decisions for your business.

Learn from other business owners what works and what doesn't when it comes to marketing, by reading their real-life stories. And then get inspired to try them out for yourself.

Here you find quotes from marketing experts, business giants, and world leaders and thinkers. These are gems you'll want to remember and even quote to your colleagues.

Put yourself in someone else's shoes, with these hypothetical situations and mini case studies. You'll soon find yourself solving a problem and being able to transfer that solution to your own situation.

Thousands of great online resources are available to help you with your marketing and, best of all, most of them cost nothing. I certainly couldn't list all of them, but all the websites I do include are written in language small-business owners can relate to.

Where to Go from Here

If you're confused about marketing, don't know where to start or have already had your fingers burned trying out different marketing techniques, relax. Pour yourself a cup of coffee (or a glass of wine), grab a pen and a notebook, find a quiet creative space, sit back and take a deep breath. And turn the page. You'll be glad you did!

Whether you're a beautician in Broken Hill, a caterer in Christchurch, a mortgage broker in Brisbane or a graphic designer in Grafton, I hope this book gives you the inspiration to be brilliant at marketing so you can build a healthy, prosperous and personally fulfilling business that brings joy to your staff, customers and everyone else you touch.

Part I
Entering the World of Marketing

Glenn Lumsden

'Ms Brown, while we're waiting for word-of-mouth to spread, would <u>you</u> like to buy one of our coffee mugs?'

In this part ...

*B*eing in your own small business can be daunting. You need to wear so many hats. One minute you're head of IT, the next head of sales and the next you're the chief financial officer. If you're like me, you naturally gravitate to the areas in your business that you're good at, which means some of the important stuff like marketing can get left behind.

In this part, I show you why marketing is critical to business success, whether you're a plumber, an accountant, a consultant or you happen to manufacture innovative new technology products for global distribution. Discover what marketing really is, how to avoid the common pitfalls, how to pinpoint your target markets and analyse what they want from you, as well as set your own marketing goals and write a marketing plan.

Every business owner must be a marketer. You can't avoid it. This part helps you set the stage for marketing brilliance. Enjoy!

Chapter 1

Understanding the Marketing Process

· ·

In This Chapter

▶ Understanding the meaning and role of marketing

▶ Working on the four Ps of marketing (and a few others) for your business

▶ Fitting marketing into your business plan

· ·

Marketing isn't hard, but, to be good at it, you need a good knowledge of what marketing is and a real feel for how the marketing process should be tackled, depending on the kind of business you're in and the kind of customers you need.

If you're a sole operator selling your time as an occupational health and safety consultant, then you can only deal with so many customers at one time, so you don't need a detailed or expensive (thank goodness) approach to marketing. If you happen to own a retail store or a restaurant, your approach most surely needs to be taken up a notch. And if you operate an online business selling information products, your marketing plan bears absolutely no resemblance to that of the consultant or the retail store. Horses for courses is the name of the game.

Your marketing approach and the steps you take to market your business depend entirely on how many customers you need and how much money each customer spends with you — now and in the future.

What Is Marketing Anyway?

Depending on who you ask, the answer to this question varies greatly. Everyone agrees that marketing is a critical factor in business success, but no two people you ask give you the same definition of marketing.

A marketing professor at university would battle to agree with the head of marketing at a big bank, and I'm sure they'd challenge my definition of marketing too. In plain small-business English, marketing is the process through which you attract new prospects, acquire them as customers and keep them loyal.

In a little more detail, marketing is also about:

- Taking on a series of tasks to get your business noticed and get more customers
- Having clear points of difference from other similar operators, tailoring and packaging your products or services to meet the desires of your target audience, and having a compelling *customer value proposition (CVP)*

   The CVP is a clear and succinct statement of the value you offer your customers; that is, what they get for what they pay. Check out Chapter 2 for tips on creating a powerful CVP and Chapter 19 for a hypothetical response to the ten questions involved in the CVP model.
- Finding and then communicating directly with current and potential customers in a way that gets them engaged enough to make an enquiry and ultimately buy from you (or at the very least recommend you to others)
- Being able to generate a consistent flow of new leads (month in and month out) to fill the pipeline so you can convert a healthy dose of these leads into new business
- Achieving win-win-win — a win for the customer, a win for you and a win for all the other people you employ in the process, including your suppliers and, of course, your staff

Marketing versus sales and advertising

In a word association test I conducted with 150 small-business owners, I asked the question, 'What three words come to mind when you think of marketing?' Overwhelmingly, the top three responses were, in order, advertising, selling and branding. Quite frankly, it irks me that the common misperception of most people (not you, of course) is that marketing equals advertising or selling. It doesn't.

Advertising is but one promotional tactic in the marketing toolkit, and selling is what you do when you've generated a lead through following a sound marketing process.

You can market your business in 101 different ways (thankfully all covered in this book) and they can include anything from networking to developing

a referral program, getting publicity or taking your best customers
out to lunch.

> *More business decisions occur over lunch and dinner than at any other*
> *time, yet no MBA courses are given on the subject.*
>
> —*Peter Drucker (1909–2005), writer, management consultant*
> *and social ecologist*

Of course, for many business owners, advertising *is* one of the tactics in
their marketing toolkit. Just remember it's not the be all and end all!

Common marketing mistakes

The fact that marketing doesn't equal advertising or selling is an important
point to bear in mind when you consider how to market your business.
But that's not the only thing you need to think about. Avoid these other
common mistakes:

- **Not having a marketing plan:** A solid marketing plan is the result of
  having a well thought out (and validated) business plan in the first
  place. If you don't have a business plan, think about how you might
  get one. Checking out *Small Business For Dummies*, 3rd Australian &
  New Zealand Edition (Wiley Publishing Australia), may be a good start.

- **Taking a scattergun approach to marketing:** When business is slow,
  getting desperate and taking the 'any marketing tactic will do' approach
  is a common trap. Following a simple marketing plan will help you
  avoid grabbing for cheap one-off activities, like letterbox drops, that
  may not work for your business (though, of course, sometimes that's
  just the right tactic).

- **Slashing the marketing budget:** Successful business owners
  understand that to make money you need to spend money. Instead of
  slashing the budget, work out ways you can get a better bang for your
  buck.

- **Not spending time on marketing:** You spend time doing your accounts,
  servicing clients and managing staff, so make sure you spend time on
  marketing. I recommend spending at least four to six hours per week
  for solo operators. If you've got the dough, why not pay for a part-time
  marketer?

- **Not defining your ideal customer:** I once asked a financial planner who
  his ideal customer was. His response? Anyone who's breathing! Very
  dangerous tactics. Like anything in life, getting what you want starts
  with defining what you want. The same goes for your ideal customer.

✔ **Not using technology to support your marketing effort:** A good database is at the heart of being able to keep in touch with and market to existing and potential customers. Other forms of technology like Skype, social media such as Facebook, websites and teleconferencing can also be used really effectively in your marketing effort. More on online marketing in Chapters 16 to 18.

✔ **Not engaging your staff in marketing:** Everyone in your business should be marketing your business for you. If your personal assistant (PA) is at a barbeque on a weekend and she (or he) gets asked 'What do you do?' make sure she's giving your business a big wrap and looking out for new business opportunities. Make everyone in your business the head of marketing.

Why small-business marketing and big-business marketing are different

The same principles for marketing a business apply whether you're a one-man-band start-up or a global powerhouse like Microsoft or Cadbury. But that's where the similarities end.

Five main differences exist between marketing for a small business and marketing for a large enterprise:

✔ **Budget:** Big businesses have big marketing budgets to keep their brand in front of the thousands and even millions of current and potential customers. Consider how much money Coca-Cola would spend every year on marketing. Aren't you glad you run a small business?

✔ **Staffing:** To keep the marketing wheel turning, big businesses employ thousands of marketers. As a small business, you don't have the luxury of employing huge teams of people to do it for you.

✔ **Suppliers:** Sitting beside the big-business marketing teams are big-business suppliers such as advertising agencies, brand specialists, research companies, media booking agencies and public relations (PR) firms. Small businesses don't need and generally can't afford big agencies.

✔ **Strategy:** Big businesses spend millions on research and producing strategic marketing plans the size of this book. Your strategy can be produced on just a few pages and is much simpler and easier to follow.

✔ **Tactics:** Direct mail, mass advertising and expensive websites often feature heavily in big-business marketing plans. Your tactics may include some of these; however, you can market your business in many different ways. I'm betting the tactics you use are radically different.

Marketing a start-up business

Marketing a start-up business is very different from marketing a business that's been around for 20 years. Most start-ups have limited funds and no customers, making marketing a pretty vital ingredient to business success.

Developing a marketing plan for a start-up business is a ten-step process. You need to first establish your goals and vision for the business and yourself. You also need to do some market research to examine how your product or service sits in the marketplace and against the competition. Knowing your product works and its price point is right is also paramount. When you have all of that sorted, then you start to develop the actual strategies for promoting your product and providing ongoing support for your customers.

The process is set out in Table 1-1 (the words *product* and *service* are, of course, interchangeable — it depends on what your business is).

Table 1-1	Start-up Business Marketing Process	
Step	*What You Need to Establish*	*What You Should Ask Yourself*
1	Personal vision	Why am I in business? What are my personal goals? How will my business help me achieve my personal goals?
2	Business vision and mission	How will my business make the world a better place? How will it add value to the lives of my customers? What will this business look like in 5, 10 or 20 years?
3	Business goals and objectives	What are my specific revenue, profit, sales and income goals? What will my business model look like in the future?
4	Customer, product and competition research	Who is my target market? What product or service do they want from me? Who is the competition out there and what are they offering? How will I be different?
5	Business brand development	What will my business name be? What do I want my brand and logo to look like? What do I want customers to feel about my brand?

(continued)

Table 1-1 *(continued)*

Step	What You Need to Establish	What You Should Ask Yourself
6	Product development, testing and refinement	How will I develop a prototype of my product or service and test it on my desired target market? How will I use that knowledge to make my product the best on the market?
7	Pricing, packaging and distribution	How will I price and package my product so that it appears highly attractive to potential customers? How and when will my customers pay me? How and where will my customers purchase the product — online, by fax order or in person, and will that be through a reseller or in my shop?
8	Product or service launch	How will I tell the world (or at least my target audience) that I'm open for business? What special offer will I make to attract my very first customers?
9	Promotions and selling	How will I promote my product or service to potential customers, now and in the future? Will I use online marketing, cold calling, direct mail, letterbox drops or networking to promote my business? How will my salespeople go about selling my product?
10	Service and support	How will I service my customers and provide ongoing support? What will my ongoing communication plan with customers look like?

Marketing to grow your established business

If you've been in business a while and things are feeling a little tired, or perhaps you've hit a bump in the road, you may just need to give your marketing program a spring clean. On the other hand, you may need to give your whole business and marketing approach a complete overhaul. You need to follow the same process as for a start-up business, shown in Table 1-1. Just spend more time on the steps that are most relevant to you.

Reinventing your business

Imagine you own a public relations company and you just lost your biggest long-term corporate customer. Needless to say, you're in panic mode. You have to either lay off staff because of the huge loss of revenue or refocus the business to get more customers. Through following the ten-step marketing process, you decide to change your business vision and refocus your services to capture the small to medium (*SME*, which stands for small to medium enterprise) business market, rather than the big corporates.

After an intense planning day, you agree to refresh your brand and put together a special SME PR package (and at a much lower cost than you were charging your corporate customers!). The package includes a suite of pre-written media releases, a list of appropriate media contacts, and a training workshop on how to build relationships with journalists and how to handle a radio or TV interview. A 9 am to 5 pm PR support hotline is established for ongoing advice and creative ideas.

Talking with 12 potential SME customers you find out what your competitors are offering and decide to charge customers an up-front fee of $2,000 and then a monthly fee of $750 for ongoing advice (up to five hours per month). You then launch the new package to your past SME customers and to a list of prospective customers you have your staff create. You upgrade your website to promote the package and employ a search engine optimisation (SEO) specialist to help you get traction online (more on this in Part V). Other promotional activities include a direct mailout campaign, media coverage in small-business magazines and direct sales calls.

The result is 20 new customers in 20 days! And, most importantly, no need to lay off staff or be dependent on one big corporate customer for most of your business anymore!

Whether you have a start-up or established business, you need to revisit the marketing process every 6 to 12 months to make sure you're on top of your game and remain relevant and appealing to the ever-changing needs of customers.

The Australian government has a whole-of-government website aimed at assisting the business community. Go to www.business.gov.au and check out the How-to Guides and the Resources list to find useful marketing tools worth downloading and completing, or click on Market Research & Statistics under Business Topics. The New Zealand government has a similar website at www.business.govt.nz, with business resources, topics and tools.

The role of innovation in marketing

Today's consumers are more savvy, time-poor and discerning than ever before. They filter out 99 per cent of the estimated 3,000-plus marketing messages they get per day and they've developed an uncanny knack for seeking out the best deals and the most innovative products to fill their needs.

Coupled with this, the internet has revolutionised the way consumers look for product and service information and the way they buy.

Today's customers buy — they don't get sold to! And the best way to get customers to buy is to offer something that's different and innovative (and that, of course, fills their needs).

> *Business has only two functions — marketing and innovation.*
>
> —Milan Kundera, Czechoslavakian author, b. 1929

If you offer the same old products and services to the same old customers, you soon find your business becomes irrelevant and tired. Regular doses of creativity and innovation need to be applied to ensure you stay ahead of the game.

Here are some questions to ask yourself to see if you need a dose of innovation:

- ✔ When was the last time you did some research with customers to help you determine what new products or services, or customer service initiatives, you could develop?

- ✔ When was the last time you introduced a new service or product to your old customers?

- ✔ When did you last refresh and repackage a tired old product by introducing a great new customer benefit or by *value-adding* (improving an existing product to increase its value)?

- ✔ When did you last refresh your brand and positioning, and approach a whole new target market?

- ✔ Have you ever considered how you might generate potential new sources of revenue through marketing your products online?

- ✔ Have you developed any new customer service initiatives lately?

- ✔ Have you refreshed and updated your promotional brochures?

Don't be a 'me-too' business offering a 'me-too' product or service. If you own a café, refresh the menu regularly, offer a signature dish that no other café does, have special offers like a glass of wine with each meal or bring in a guitarist on weekends. Whatever you do, you have no excuse for not being innovative and creative — and it makes being in business much more *fun*!

The Four Ps of Marketing

When I first studied marketing way back in the 1980s, the four Ps of marketing was considered marketing's holy grail. If you didn't have a firm handle on the four Ps and university qualifications to back it up, you'd never make an A-grade marketer or get a high-flying corporate marketing job.

Today the marketing landscape has changed significantly. The four Ps are still highly relevant but many marketers are now less precious and are inventing their own five, six or even seven Ps of marketing.

To avoid talking jargon any longer, here is my simple definition. The *four Ps of marketing* are about having the right *product* at the right *price*, in the right *place* backed by the right *promotions* (shown in Figure 1-1). Throughout this section I give you a clearer definition of what to consider under each of these Ps and I give you my own special addition of a few other Ps to consider in the marketing mix.

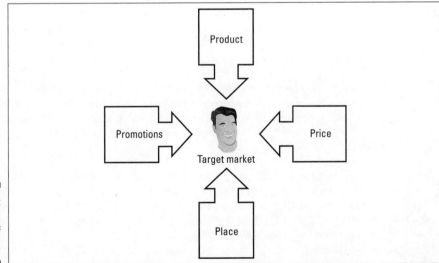

Figure 1-1:
The classic four Ps of marketing.

Many people make the mistake of thinking about marketing in terms of the fourth P, promotions. Promotional tactics may include building a website, advertising, putting inserts in a magazine, sales calls and more. The heart of good marketing is actually about having a compelling product or service on offer in the first place, so when people do respond to your ad in the paper they're keen to find out more — and spend their hard-earned cash with you!

To check out Wikipedia's entry on marketing, go to http//:en.wikipedia.org and enter **Marketing** into the search window. It includes a range of definitions on the good old favourite four Ps of marketing.

Product

Whether you offer a product or a service, the first P applies. And in a service business, service actually is the product! Having a valuable product that customers need and want is the golden key to business success. To find out more about what customers want and how they buy, read Chapter 2.

In the meantime, you need to make some decisions about these aspects:

- Brand and product name (see Part II for lots more on branding)
- Product specifications and functionality
- Guarantees and warranties
- Packaging and styling
- Ongoing support and service
- Legal and technical requirements
- Additional accessories or services

In developing a new product for your business, or refreshing an old one, it pays to do some customer research and to find out what the competition is up to before testing your product and going into full-scale launch mode. Nothing is worse than launching a new product only to find someone has beaten you to it.

Being creative and having a good understanding of what customers are looking for are really important in the product creation process. Brainstorm creative ideas with others and take all ideas on board at first — don't filter — just go with the flow and eliminate ideas down the track when you can prove they probably won't work.

Price

This P is all about how you price your product or service. And your RRP (registered retail price) isn't everything; a whole host of other pricing considerations make your product stand out in a cluttered marketplace.

You need to make some decisions about these aspects:

- Retail pricing
- Wholesale pricing
- Money-back guarantees
- Seasonal or promotional discounts
- Early-payment discounts
- Payment methods
- Volume discounts
- Up-front fees or charge on delivery
- Product-bundling prices

Developing a pricing strategy for your product or business is tricky, no doubt. Being the cheapest or the most expensive often doesn't pay, but it does pay to add value and provide attractive incentives to loyal customers.

Place

Where you sell your product — place — is really about how you distribute your product or where customers can buy it. Your distribution strategy could be complex or simple, and depends entirely on your product. The strategy for a takeaway fish and chip shop, for example, is far simpler than the strategy you employ if you sell accounting software.

In distributing your product, you need to make some decisions about these aspects:

- Wholesale distribution
- Reseller distribution
- Shopfront distribution
- Warehousing and inventory
- Ordering via websites, fax or phone

✔ Geography — local, national, global

✔ Order processing and dispatch

✔ Delivery guarantees and returns

The size of your potential market and the number of customers you want are big factors in choosing your distribution methods. If you want thousands of customers, consider multiple channels for distribution. If you only need a handful of customers, keep it simple and choose just one distribution method.

Promotion

When you've got a great product at a great price and have worked out how customers can get it, you need to promote it to your target market. Choosing the best and most accurate ways to promote your product can sometimes feel like you have a loaded shotgun in your hand but no idea where to aim it. Literally hundreds of ways you can promote your business are available, and finding the tin cans you need to hit really can be tough.

Here are just a few of the things you may consider in promoting your business:

✔ Promotional planning and budgets

✔ Product launch

✔ Brochures

✔ Promotional giveaways

✔ Personal selling

✔ Website and online marketing

✔ Advertising

✔ Public relations

✔ Direct mail

✔ Networking

✔ Events

✔ Sponsorships

Thankfully, much of this book is aimed at how to go about these promotional activities to get your business in the hands, hearts and minds of the people you want as customers. I help guide you through the pitfalls and perils of choosing the best promotional tactics for your business. Relax!

Easing the pain, and making sales gain

Over 20 per cent of Australians and New Zealanders suffer from intolerance to lactose, which is found in all dairy products. Lacteeze is a product manufactured and owned by a company in Canada, and Sheena Cole is the sole distributor of the product in Australia and New Zealand. Taken before eating dairy, Lacteeze prevents the severe symptoms of lactose intolerance such as bloating, gas, abdominal cramps and sometimes diarrhoea.

Sheena has seen sales of Lacteeze skyrocket through careful consideration of each of the four Ps, and a few others besides. Her products have been repackaged and are now far more attention-grabbing and carry a clear marketing message. She plans to rationalise her product range over the next year after doing thorough customer and market research. She holds regular sales meetings with her reps, who are responsible for ensuring Lacteeze gets stocked and distributed through the 7,000-plus pharmacies and health-food stores around Australia and New Zealand.

A detailed financial management spreadsheet is updated and reviewed weekly to ensure she is continuing to make the margins needed to fund the overheads and ongoing marketing costs of the business.

Sheena's promotional activities are aimed at raising consumer awareness of the lactose intolerance problem and Lacteeze through website marketing, advertising and publicity. Because GPs, pharmacists and gut specialists are often the first port of call for people with symptoms, she also advertises and writes articles for specialist publications these people read. Information packs, including samples, are also sent to a targeted list of these health professionals. A step-by-step approach, coupled with a high degree of passion and persistence, has given Sheena comfort she's on track to help the millions of people suffering from intolerance to dairy.

To find our more about Lacteeze, and to sample Sheena's approach, visit www.lacteeze.com.au.

Passion, people and persistency (the other Ps)

Adding a few of my own favourite and fun Ps to the marketing mix spices it up a little. And I'm sure you could add a few of your own, too, given a few creative moments to yourself.

- ✔ **Passion:** Marketing your business if you don't have the passion for what you do and what you offer is downright near impossible. I was at a mortgage-broking conference once and I asked a guy, 'What do you do?' His response? 'I'm a mortgage broker ... unfortunately.' Now, would you buy a home loan from this guy? Your passion rubs off on everyone you touch. It keeps you motivated to work on the other four Ps and focused on your customers. So, if you've lost the passion, don't waste time; find something to reignite it.

✔ **People:** As a business owner, you are first and foremost in the people business. Every person you connect with has the potential to be your greatest advocate and your own personal sales force. How you remunerate and reward your staff, thank your customers and deal with suppliers contributes to the successful growth (or serious decline) of your business. Have you got a people strategy in your business?

✔ **Persistency:** This is a personal favourite. Your desire to succeed, a belief in yourself and the will to never ever give up (persistency) ensures your marketing efforts pay off. I've seen many a business owner ditch a marketing activity that could have worked for them if only they'd made a few minor changes and persevered.

How Marketing Supports Your Business Plan

Despite the gloomy media headlines, relatively few small businesses actually fail due to bankruptcy. What is not known, however, is how many businesses choose to shut up shop for other reasons, like cash flow problems, competitive forces, product problems or legal issues.

It takes as much energy to wish as it does to plan.

—Eleanor Roosevelt (1884–1968), First Lady of the United States and human rights activist

A solid (and yes it can be simple) business plan gives you confidence that you've got all your bases covered in the event you get thrown a curve ball. And you *will* get thrown a curve ball, believe me. Now, please don't call me pessimistic — it's just the law of the universe!

How you handle the curve ball determines whether your business fails or prospers. You can drop the ball, have a dummy spit and take your bat and go home. Or you can catch the ball, hold it lovingly in your hands and throw it right back!

Many business owners dive straight into hanging out the 'open for business' sign without putting time into a proper business plan (not you, of course). Business planning can be time-consuming and often appears complicated, but putting some energy and time into it rewards you in a number of ways. Business planning

✔ Provides a contingency plan for the curve ball.

✔ Helps you remain focused on your business vision.

✔ Keeps you accountable to achieve objectives, goals and financial projections.

✔ Helps you get a loan from the bank, if you need one, and can help attract investors.

✔ Keeps business partners and staff, if you have them, on the same path.

✔ Helps keep your marketing plan in check and on track.

Call me biased, but I'm a big believer that good marketing is the biggest contributor to business success. And good marketing is the result of a solid business plan in the first place. So, if you don't have a plan, I suggest you get one.

The Dynamic Small Business Network (DSBN) offers free membership to access some great articles, tools and templates to guide you in building your business plan. A premium membership is also available for a small fee. Check them out at www.dsbn.com.au.

Business vision is everything

Creating a business you love working in, one that inspires you to bound out of bed every morning, starts with having a dream of what you want to achieve — you need a vision. And the vision shouldn't just be 'to become fabulously wealthy'. It should be inspiring and purposeful, and about how your business will make a difference to the world (or market) you operate in.

A business plan outlines the mechanics of how your business will operate. It gives you an action plan and benchmarks you can measure your success against. But it's not a document that inspires you to keep on keeping on. Your vision does this. Your vision is what inspires you to keep marketing, to keep loving your customers and to burn the midnight oil. And it's the first thing to get right, way up-front, before you even sit down to write the plan.

So what is meant by a vision? To demonstrate, Table 1-2 gives some examples of different types of business and a typical vision statement for each.

Table 1-2	Different Businesses and Their Visions
Business Type	*Typical Vision Statement*
Occupational health and safety consultant	To help Australian companies create a work environment that keeps their employees safe, happy and healthy.
Landscape gardener	To create beautiful gardens as a tranquil haven for people to feel happy and at peace in.
Kids' clothing store	To make children feel special, playful and unique with our vibrant, one-of-a-kind kids' clothes.
Children's book store	To inspire children to become lifelong readers through books that are fun and educational.
Bakery	To provide scrumptious breads and pastries that bring a smile to the faces of our customers.

One technique I recommend to all my clients is to create a vision document — a simple one-page document that is written as though your business has just won an award and is being featured on the front page of the local paper. What would the headline be? Why did you win the award? What would the journalist have written about your business?

Reviewing your business plan

Your business plan doesn't need to be as thick as *War and Peace*. It just needs to be simple and cover the following elements:

- ✔ Business vision
- ✔ Business objectives and goals, and key performance indicators
- ✔ Revenue and profit objectives
- ✔ Expenses and budgets, including a cash flow projection
- ✔ Funding and banking requirements
- ✔ Staffing requirements
- ✔ SWOT analysis (strengths, weaknesses, opportunities, threats)

- ✔ Technology and infrastructure requirements
- ✔ Target markets
- ✔ Competitor and environmental factors
- ✔ Product or service offering
- ✔ New product development
- ✔ Customer service plan and objectives
- ✔ Marketing plan and objectives
- ✔ Sales plan and objectives
- ✔ And any other things you can think of!

If you have an old plan that hasn't seen the light of day for years, it pays to dust it off and give it a refresh before you attempt any of the marketing activities I cover in this book. A change in vision and a change in the business plan definitely means a change in your marketing plan.

Identifying the role marketing plays in your business

Many business plans I've reviewed seem to have had marketing almost slapped on as an afterthought. Huge amounts of time have been spent on the mechanics and financial projections, and a mere half-page (usually mistakenly titled 'advertising') has been devoted to marketing.

Poor marketing (or no marketing at all) is the ruin of many a business. Whereas great marketing is the making of many a business. Think Richard Branson and Virgin, or Janine Allis and Boost. These two savvy entrepreneurs are marketing gurus in my books. And you can bet that marketing is given more than a mere half a page in their business plans!

Marketing is simply about finding, getting and keeping customers — as simple as that. Without customers you don't have a business. Without good marketing, how would customers even know you exist, let alone know how to buy from you?

Make a commitment to put marketing at the heart of your business and to make it the central theme of your business plan. Don't take it too seriously though. Think of it as a process, not an event. Get the knowledge (why you're reading this book, I guess), try a few things, test and measure, and try it again, but never, ever give up!

The marketing SWOT analysis

Before jumping head first into marketing your business, it pays to take a realistic look at your marketing *strengths*, *weaknesses*, *threats* and *opportunities*.

Do your SWOT analysis on the whole business as part of your business plan, but also with a specific eye on marketing. A graphic designer may see her main strengths are that she is well connected and a good networker. A threat may be that 20 other graphic designers operate in her local area. A weakness may be her limited dough to market the business. An opportunity may be that she can specialise in design for fashion houses because of her many years working in the industry.

Getting an outsider's opinion when it comes to the SWOT analysis is always beneficial. Get some customers or other business owners to give you a warts-and-all opinion. Brainstorm the list and then identify your top three to five to focus on.

Gavin Willis owns Premier Cut, the premier concrete-cutting business in the Illawarra, New South Wales, with a strong track record over 25 years. Premier Cut specialises in all areas of concrete cutting, polishing and sawing, including core drilling, floor sawing, hand and ring sawing, and wall sawing. Gavin has three staff and an excellent reputation for fast turnaround and professional service. He has grown the business steadily through a dedicated approach to business planning and marketing, and a fair amount of SWOTting too! check out Gavin's website at www.premiercut.com.au. Figure 1-2 shows an actual SWOT analysis for Premier Cut.

Don't be put off by a SWOT analysis. Being realistic and practical about these things is critical, making a real difference to how you tackle your marketing, and what messages you give your customers and your target market.

By now you should have a good handle on the basics of marketing and what's required to be good at it. Great marketing can breathe fun and life into your business (and, of course, a healthy dose of leads and new business). Bad marketing or, worse still, no marketing can be the death of your business. Be inspired to put marketing at the heart of your business!

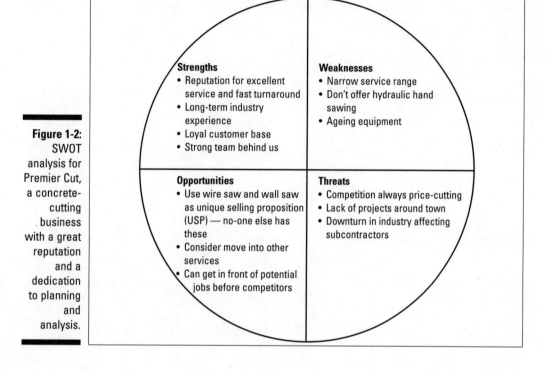

Figure 1-2:
SWOT
analysis for
Premier Cut,
a concrete-
cutting
business
with a great
reputation
and a
dedication
to planning
and
analysis.

Strengths
- Reputation for excellent service and fast turnaround
- Long-term industry experience
- Loyal customer base
- Strong team behind us

Weaknesses
- Narrow service range
- Don't offer hydraulic hand sawing
- Ageing equipment

Opportunities
- Use wire saw and wall saw as unique selling proposition (USP) — no-one else has these
- Consider move into other services
- Can get in front of potential jobs before competitors

Threats
- Competition always price-cutting
- Lack of projects around town
- Downturn in industry affecting subcontractors

Chapter 2

Putting Customers First

*Y*ou may have always been an entrepreneur and business owner, or at one point jumped ship from the corporate world to the small-business world like I did years ago. Either way, growing a business based on what you know, your history and your technical skills, rather than the opportunities in the marketplace, is tempting.

If I had my time over (hindsight is a wonderful thing), perhaps I could've used my marketing skills and knowledge to market a highly desirable widget rather than setting up my business, Connect Marketing? Not really. I love teaching and writing! But worth a thought.

And, if you've been a highly successful accountant in corporate land, perhaps you could have used your financial prowess to run a really successful property development company instead of opening an accounting practice?

My point? Business success and, of course, marketing success, is often dependent on market opportunity and being able to identify opportunities to fill unfilled (or unsatisfactorily filled) customer needs and wants.

That's why I devote a full chapter to putting customers first. No matter what business you're in, getting a handle on what the market (customers) want and why customers buy, how they like to be serviced and communicated with, and what new product and services they're desperate for is vital.

Understanding Why Customers Buy

Customers buy for many reasons and, thankfully, these decisions aren't always based on price. At a conference once, I asked the audience to call out the names of their favourite brands. One guy yelled out Cadbury, and I asked him why he loves it. His response? 'I think of Cadbury, and I dream of me and my family sharing our favourite block of Fruit & Nut while watching *Australian Idol.*' Do you think price is a consideration for this guy?

People buy for rational and emotional reasons. Rational reasons may include price, follow-up service, quality, guarantees, colour, style, flavour and more. These are what I call the 'box-ticking' parts of the buying decision. They're essential but not deal breakers. Most customers make the ultimate buying decision, however, for emotional reasons. If I buy that BMW, my friends will think I'm really successful. If I buy that creamy cup of soy coffee, I'll get an energy boost. If I go to that lawyer to handle my divorce, he'll make sure my children and I are looked after.

Consider why your customers buy from you. What rational and emotional needs does your product or service fill?

Today's customers buy for their own reasons — they don't get sold to. If you understand what motivates them to buy your product or service, then half the marketing job is done.

Price versus value

What role does price play in the purchasing decision? It's definitely a big factor in the buying process, but not the be all and end all. Sure, everyone loves a bargain but, if you've got a good handle on what else the customer values about you, then you won't find yourself constantly reverting to price-cutting mode.

Recently I changed my hairdresser. I had been going to my last hairdresser for about five years because my office space used to be near his salon, and he was recommended to me. I stayed with him when I moved offices, even though it meant an hour's drive from home. Making a switch to my new hairdresser was a painful decision. I made the switch for four reasons:

- **Relationship and rapport:** I met my new hairdresser in the dog park. We got chatting and I really liked her (and her kids and dog).

- **Recommendation:** A number of friends have been using her for years and recommended her. And, of course, I liked their hairdos too!

✔ **Location:** Her salon is only five minutes away from home.

✔ **Price:** Her prices are very reasonable and I don't have extra parking fees to pay.

In my situation, price was the least important factor in the buying decision. Price alone wouldn't have caused me to change hairdressers. In fact, I hadn't even thought about changing hairdressers until I met my new hairdresser in the dog park! What was more *value*-able to me was the relationship and her location.

Think about what your customers value most about you.

Pain or pleasure

All marketing messages are aimed at either fixing a problem or providing a pleasing benefit to the customer (also known as hitting the pain-or-pleasure button) and either one is ultimately the reason customers buy. How you make them *feel* when they read your advertisement or check out your website is what inspires them to pick up the phone with credit card in hand.

The dentist who promises to take out my wisdom teeth pain-free wins my vote. The fitness instructor who promises to make exercise enjoyable is the one I want on board. The accountant who fixes my tax headaches can call me anytime!

How does your product or service fix a problem or provide a pleasing benefit? Remember to use pain-or-pleasure buttons in all your marketing messages and headlines. It gets customers buying!

Product or service life cycle

Sadly, some people live in a material and often fickle world. One minute a product can be hot and the next redundant. So understanding where your product sits in the life cycle and how it meets the ever-changing environment and needs of the customer is important.

Think about how purchasing and listening to music has changed in the last 30 years. The industry has evolved from records and turntables, to tapes and tape players, to CDs and CD players, to iPods and iTunes. Personally, I'm quite pleased to see records and record players back in vogue.

One theory is that every product or service goes through a five-step evolution from development to introduction to growth to maturity to decline, shown in Figure 2-1.

Consider what stage you're at right now. If you're at the height of growth or have slipped into maturity or decline, I suggest you don't waste time and do some research. Talk to your customers and find out what you need to do to refresh your product, prices or packaging so they keep buying from you. Or maybe you need to bring in a whole new product.

If you're still selling the same old products and services, and not listening to your customers or keeping an eye on the competition and what's happening in the market, it's time to get a fresh perspective.

The buying cycle

Consumers are bombarded with marketing messages from the time the alarm goes off in the morning until they turn the lights off at night. Getting your marketing message through (particularly if you're not well known already) can be tough.

Understanding how a prospective customer goes from being completely unaware that you exist to becoming a customer pays off. Table 2-1 gives a step-by-step approach to how customers decide to find out more about you and actually buy.

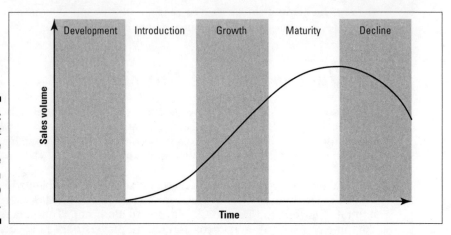

Figure 2-1:
The product life cycle can be seen as a five-step evolution.

Table 2-1	Six Steps of Customer Buying Behaviour	
Step	*What Happens*	*The Result*
1	Attention	You've got their attention at least! However, if they don't need or want your type of product or service they probably stop right here. Sorry.
2	Awareness	You've hit a pain-or-pleasure button. They're interested and have a need, so they want a bit more information on who you are and what you do.
3	Interest	Now you've really got their interest. They want to have a good chat with you to find out more. They also start talking to their friends, partners and kids to gauge their interest and input.
4	Desire	They've got the good oil on you. They know all the ins and outs of what you offer and they've weighed up the options. They're poised to purchase.
5	Action	They've made the decision. The purchase is made. They've got the goods in their hot little hands or it's on order awaiting delivery.
6	Post-purchase analysis	The product is in full use. Here's where they make the final analysis on whether their money's been well spent. Hopefully they won't need to claim that money-back guarantee!

Someone may be moderately interested in what you have to offer (Step 1 or 2) but not interested in buying right now. Your job is to keep *top-of-mind* by keeping in front of them with your marketing and promotions effort. You might need to expose yourself to these people five, six or seven times before their interest is piqued.

In Step 3, I talk about other people involved in the decision-making process. Consider how your product meets the needs of everyone who uses it. If you own a family restaurant you target the whole family. If you're a mortgage broker you want to talk to both partners in the family. If you happen to sell a kids' toy, you want to get in front of the kids so they can badger their parents to buy it!

The customer is king. By putting them at the heart of all business decisions and all your marketing efforts, you always remain relevant and appealing, and customers come back time and again.

The biggest mistake anyone can make is to focus on the competitor. You focus on the consumer and you will get it right.

—*K. B. Dadiseth, Board member of Taj Hotels, India*

Developing a Customer Value Proposition

Sorry, another bit of jargon coming up. The most important thing to get right up-front, loud and clear, with your customers is your CVP.

A *customer value proposition (CVP)* is a statement of the value you offer your customers. It states clearly what they get for what they pay you. It covers the compelling reasons for them to buy and answers the questions of who you are, what you offer, who you offer it to, how much you do it for and much more. The full model is shown in Figure 2-2. And it's written by a good copywriter in marketing language, not tech talk. Flick to Chapter 19 to check out a hypothetical response to these vital ten questions and spend some time answering them for your own business.

Think about the CVP in another way. If you were given one minute to tell a prospective customer everything he needed to know to make a decision about whether to buy or not, could you do it? Could you do it with passion and conviction, and get him asking more?

I've seen many business owners stumble over this. They've been handed a golden opportunity to tell someone about their business and they've either bored them to tears with the minutiae or been lost for words altogether. Don't let this happen to you.

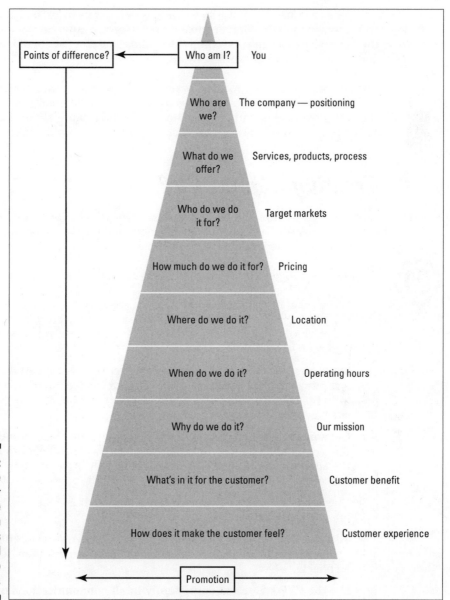

Figure 2-2:
The customer value proposition model gives you ten vital questions to answer.

Get clear on your CVP. Put it in writing — on your website, on your brochures, on your customer presentations, on a plaque on the wall and on the screen-saver of all your computers. And then practise, practise, practise and get it right in your conversations.

The customer value proposition really is 'all about the customer'. Never bombard people with a full rundown of your CVP in rote fashion. Engage them in conversation and ask questions to find out more about them and their needs, then skilfully weave your CVP into the conversation.

Creating a great CVP

Get your CVP right and you'll never stray from your purpose. It keeps your customer at the heart of your business and gives you the personal motivation you need to keep on keeping on!

Try these tips to get in the flow and build a great CVP for your business:

- ✔ **Write your CVP out of the office, in a space of creativity.** Using coloured textas and a lot of white paper, paint a picture of what this business will look like and what you want it to be, not necessarily how it looks now.

- ✔ **Say it straight then get a good copywriter to say it great!** A copywriter can put your responses into compelling words and statements that can form the basis of your sales materials, the copy for your website and even as a plaque on your wall.

- ✔ **Get someone to help.** Sometimes you can get too close to this stuff. Ask your staff, a mentor or other business owner to help brainstorm the answers to your CVP. Their insights might bring up some real gems.

- ✔ **Check out the CVPs of your competition.** What are they saying? How are you different?

- ✔ **Test the CVP on your customers.** When you have some of the answers, contact some of your most valued customers and ask them to give you feedback.

- ✔ **Use the CVP statement consistently in all communications on your written brochures and online.** Live your CVP and learn it off by heart.

- ✔ **Learn how to use your CVP verbally too.** When you're asked to give a 30-second elevator pitch on your business or if you get asked some of the questions, you'll be able to answer them articulately and in an engaging way.

✔ **In the process of defining your CVP, identify your three most important points of difference.** Points of difference are explained in more detail in the next section. Use them consistently when talking with customers, as well as in your marketing messages on your website and in your promotions. Remember to spend most time communicating at the bottom three areas of the CVP (refer to Figure 2-2).

✔ **Refine and review it regularly.** Nothing is ever set in stone. As your business evolves, so should your CVP.

✔ **Make sure everyone knows your CVP.** That means your staff, customers, business associates, friends — and your mum!

✔ **Consider how many CVPs you need.** If you have numerous target markets or stakeholders in your business, consider writing a separate CVP for each. If you have staff, get them to help you write one for them too.

Defining your points of difference

The riskiest thing in business (and in life) is to play it safe and follow the crowd. For your business to stand out among the noise and competition, you need to be different.

As you go through the CVP model, identify (and create) points of difference for your business. A *point of difference (POD)* is something that differentiates your business from other similar businesses. Creating them isn't hard. You just need a bit of creativity and to know it's something your customers really value. It also needs to be powerful enough to get people talking about you and referring you. Table 2-2 shows some businesses with a real point of difference.

Table 2-2	Points of Difference for Different Businesses
Business Type	*Point of Difference*
Personal trainer	Monthly payments and bonus sessions for weight loss or fitness goals achieved
Psychologist	Specialising in working with lawyers and their clients
Hotel	Weekly author, artist and musician showcase evenings
Financial planner	Self-managed superannuation fund specialists
Doctor	Free annual health check-ups for over-60s
Printer	24-hour printing and overnight delivery service
Electrician	Same-day service and 12-month guarantee on all work

A landscape contractor I know runs a 'do one thing different today' program. He asks each of his workers, while on a job, to do one thing different for their clients every day, like changing a blown light bulb, fixing a leaking tap or even bringing the clothes off the line or cleaning the pool. These simple things make a big difference and get people raving about his staff — and his company. This landscaper's point of difference is 'to exceed customers' expectations every single day'.

Every business should have at least one outstanding point of difference to make it memorable. Revisit the CVP model and get creative.

If you're struggling to find your POD, read *Purple Cow* by Seth Godin for some inspiration. (The title could've been *Blue Goldfish*, like this book's cover.)

Developing a fabulous tagline

A tagline is a line (from, say, three to eight words) used under your brand name, and sometimes in advertising, to tell people about your most important benefit or point of difference. It's all about what makes you special — to the customer. The idea is to create something memorable that reinforces how you want people to think and feel about your business. Taglines can be rational and practical (yawn) or emotional and inspiring (yay!).

As a marketer, I believe companies with inspirational taglines are the ones that embed themselves (over time) in the hearts and minds of people. For a small business, investing the time and money in getting a great name that works with a really powerful tagline is worth every cent. And it will set you up for the future.

A good time to think about your tagline and how it will inspire your customers is when you tackle CVP and POD issues.

Some examples of big companies with great taglines you no doubt know are:

Nike	*Just do it.*
FedEx	*When it absolutely, positively has to be there overnight.*
Avis	*We try harder.*
American Express	*Don't leave home without it.*
Burger King	*Have it your way.*
BMW	*The ultimate driving machine.*

Apple Computer	*The power to be your best.*
Cisco	*Powering the internet generation.*
Disneyland	*The happiest place on Earth.*
DeBeers	*A diamond is forever.*

When working on your CVP, POD and tagline, put your customer at the heart of each question or decision you need to make. Ask yourself:

✔ What would my customers *think*?

✔ How would my customers *feel*?

✔ What would my customers *do*?

Identifying Your Target Markets

I've had many business owners tell me their target market is any person who's breathing — with money. That's a lot of people, making it nigh on impossible to focus your marketing efforts.

Another term for target market is *ideal customer group*. In your business and marketing plan (and way before you hit the promotions trail), you need to paint a picture of your ideal customer group or groups. You need to describe them in detail according to demographics (age, sex, income and so on), industry, location, buying behaviours and stage of life. You need to work out who they are, where they are, how to get to them and, most importantly, why they need you.

Conversely, it pays to work out who you don't want as customers. When business is slow you may be tempted to take on any customer at any price. Don't fall into this trap. You may find in the long run these customers end up costing you money. A case of short-term gain for long-term pain!

Identifying your target market is an art and a science, and necessary to help you market directly to the people most likely to buy from you. Start by asking yourself some thought-provoking questions:

✔ What groups of customers have I served in the past?

✔ Which kinds of customers do I like working with?

✔ Which ones don't I like working with?

✔ Who really needs and wants my services?

✔ Who's willing and able to pay for my services?

   ✔ Who will be the most loyal and greatest advocates?

   ✔ Where are my networks and contacts already?

   ✔ How does my expertise and work history affect the types of customers I should serve?

Pinpointing the ideal customer

The single biggest contributor to marketing and sales success is the ability to pinpoint with absolute accuracy your target market or markets. You may have just one target market, or you could have three or four.

So you know where to spend most of your time, money and energy on your marketing and promotions, a good idea is to prioritise each market in terms of where you get the biggest pay-off.

The number of customers you need determines how many target markets you approach. Each target market can also be huge or tiny. For example, if you're about to launch a new toy aimed at young girls aged 8 to 12 (watch out parents), your market is huge. On the other hand, if you're a corporate leadership coach and only need a few customers, you'd do well to aim your arrow at the top 200 Australian company directors.

I like to use an archery board to help my customers prioritise their markets — with the bullseye being your number-one target market, of course! Figure 2-3 shows how an interior decorator might plot her target market.

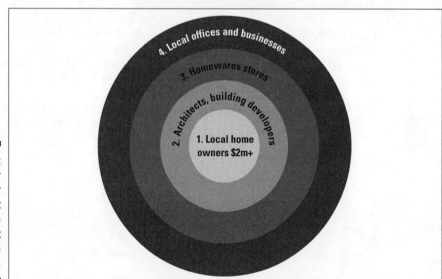

Figure 2-3: An interior decorator might prioritise her target markets like this.

Not accurately pinpointing your target markets and just launching yourself at anyone who'll listen means wasted dollars and wasted time.

Geographics

Location. Location. Location. Where is your target market geographically located? Your target market could be local, say within five kilometres of where you live and work. It could be within the city you operate in, say Melbourne or Auckland. It could be within the region you operate in, say far north Queensland, or it could even be a suburb in another city in another country!

Ponder this. Chongqing city in the western region of China has a population of more than 30 million people. Western health and beauty products and other personal services such as pet care and grooming are in high demand by the wealthy Chinese. One suburb of Chongqing alone could be all you need to target!

Never determine your target markets by geographics alone. You need to add some other vital ingredients to the mix (read on).

Demographics

Your target market mix always includes a healthy dose of demographics. *Demographics* refers to the physical and often quantifiable characteristics of a population and it helps you work out *who* to target. Some of my favourite demographic questions to consider about a target market are:

- What's the age range? (Not 1 to 99, please!)
- Male or female?
- What's the average household income?
- Single, married, widowed, divorced?
- How many people in the family?
- What's the occupation? (Professional, blue-collar, business owner, unemployed, pensioner, student and so on.)
- What industry is your market in? (Health, finance, IT, telecommunications, manufacturing.)
- What's the highest level of education? (High school, university, MBA.)
- What's the country of origin or ethnic background?

If you already have customers, pick out your top 20 and use their information as the basis of helping you determine your preferred demographics.

Now you're starting to get a clearer picture of your ideal customer, do some research to make sure your target market includes enough customers who can buy your product or service to bring in the sales you need.

Many sources of free data and statistics are available online to help you work out your numbers. The Australian Bureau of Statistics census data is very useful (go to www.abs.gov.au and click on Census Data in the left-hand menu), and Wikipedia (http//:en.wikipedia.org) is always a great source of info and stats. In New Zealand, check out www.stats.govt.nz and click on Census under Quick Links.

Psychographics and buying behaviour

Working out the demographics of your target market is actually pretty easy. On the other hand, working out the psychology behind why your target customers buy, and how their attitudes, values, religious backgrounds and beliefs affect their purchasing decisions, can be tough going.

Say you run a home-delivery pizza parlour and demographically one of your target markets is all families with two children, living within three postcodes of your business and with a household income of more than $70,000. Questions you may want to consider are:

- How many times a week do these families order takeaway?

- Is ordering pizza most often an impulse buying decision or a Saturday night family regular?

- Who is the ultimate pizza-buying decision maker — Mum, Dad or the kids?

- Are they brand followers? Do they prefer buying from the big brands like Domino's or small local businesses like yours?

- What media do these people consume? Where are they most likely to find out about the best pizza parlour in town — in the letterbox or the local paper, on the internet or TV, or do they ask their friends?

- How likely are these people to be regular customers?

- How price-conscious are they? Would they respond to family deals?

✔ What kinds of pizza do these people like — gourmet or traditional?

✔ How do they like to buy pizza — phone and home delivery and/or pick-up?

✔ Would they want a bit more than the average pizza parlour delivers? How about a DVD, soft drinks, ice-creams, salads or a bottle of wine?

Getting a handle on psychographics — attitudes, values and buying behaviours — can sometimes be tricky but, if you get it right, it can really give you a competitive edge.

Lots of great, cheap (and even free) research and survey tools are available for you to use to get savvy on customer buying behaviours. Read the section 'Customer research' later in this chapter for more.

Life stage

You've most likely heard the terms Gen X, Gen Y, Gen Z, and no doubt read about baby-boomers, retirees and so on. Advertising agencies and many big businesses love to categorise their target markets by the stage of life they're in. I'm officially a Gen X on the cusp of baby-boomer but like to think I exhibit many Gen Y characteristics. On the other hand, I can think of a few people who are Gen Xs but act like retirement is just around the corner!

Table 2-3 gives you an idea of the number of Australians within each generation.

Table 2-3   Australia's Generations: The Definitive Classification

Description	Born	Age	Pop'n (million)	% of Pop'n
Builders	Before 1946	64+	3.02	12%
Boomers	1946–1964	45–63	5.26	24%
Generation X	1965–1979	30–44	4.62	21%
Generation Y	1980–1994	15–29	4.62	21%
Generation Z	1995–2009	Under 15	4.18	19%

Source: ABS Population Pyramid 2006 and McCrindle Research Study 2006

Saying your target market is just baby-boomers isn't enough, however. Each of these generations has a lot of characteristics, and overlaying or combining them with your desired demographics and psychographics can help you create a rich picture of your ideal customers.

An excellent resource for more on life stages and the different generations, and how to market to them, is a research paper from McCrindle Research, titled *Seriously Cool: Marketing, Communicating and Engaging with the Diverse Generations*. Go to www.mccrindle.com.au, select Resources from the menu bar and scroll down to find the downloadable PDF.

Putting it all together

When you have a clear idea of what goes into defining a target market, you need to put it all together.

Use the diagram shown in Figure 2-4 to work it out. Write down a loose idea of who your target market may be, such as families, in the middle circle. Then in each of the quadrants list as many attributes as you can think of. When you've got all the attributes listed, narrow them down to the most critical ones.

Do some research to back up your thoughts using the websites I mention earlier in this chapter. It really helps to know how many people are in the market you're after, so you can work out realistic sales potential.

Figure 2-4:
Work out the attributes of your target market.

Determining What Your Customers Want

Creating demand for your product or service only happens when you have a good understanding of what your customers want. You can work out what they want and value most by asking questions, listening to them and observing their purchasing behaviour.

Purchasing decisions are usually based on the following factors:

- ✔ Convenience
- ✔ Safety
- ✔ Price or value for money
- ✔ Quality
- ✔ Features and benefits
- ✔ Reliability
- ✔ Expertise
- ✔ Ongoing service and support
- ✔ Relationships
- ✔ Recognition of loyalty

Take some time to do a stocktake. How many of these do you offer? If you can't tick at least five, you've probably got a bit of work to do!

Customer research

Whether launching a new product, refreshing an old one or looking at ways to improve your customer service, the best way to find out what customers really want is to do some research. It doesn't need to be rigorous, expensive or time-consuming.

Imagine you're a physiotherapist and you're considering adding some other specialists to your team — masseur, podiatrist, nutritionist, counsellor, personal trainer and so on. You want to find out if your customers would use these services before you make any decisions, so you develop a list of things you want to ask your customers:

- ✔ What other health practitioners do you use to help with your physio condition, and your physical and mental wellbeing generally?
- ✔ Who do you currently see for these services and are you happy with them?

- ✔ If I brought in specialists in these areas would you consider using them?

- ✔ What days and times would you like to be able to see these specialists?

- ✔ How much would you be prepared to pay for their services?

- ✔ How often would you use their services?

- ✔ What are the most important qualities to you of these people? (They're on time, they're qualified, they follow up and so on.)

- ✔ If there is one thing I could do to improve my service or offering to you, what would it be? Any other comments or ideas?

Now you have your questions, you can do the research in four simple ways (or in combination):

- ✔ **Telephone interviews:** You ring your top 20 customers and 10 customers who haven't been in for a while. (A great way to get in touch again and remind them you're still around!)

- ✔ **Customer discussion group:** In return for a free physio treatment, you invite your customers in for a sandwich lunch to discuss your ideas as a group.

- ✔ **Online survey:** You use one of the many free online research tools available to develop a simple questionnaire and email it out to all your customers.

- ✔ **On-the-spot interviews:** Over a period of a few weeks you ask every customer who comes in for an appointment if you can ask them a few simple questions.

I love www.surveymonkey.com and www.zoomerang.com for providing free (or very low cost) tools so you can do your own online customer research and analyse the results. The surveys are easy to set up and can be emailed to your customers.

If you've got the dough and don't feel you have the time or expertise to do the research yourself, consider using a professional researcher. It probably won't cost as much as you think and many reasonably priced research companies provide services especially for small businesses like yours.

Tribe Research is one company with an unconventional research philosophy for the business, non-profit and government sectors. Check out their website, shown in Figure 2-5, at www.knowyourtribe.com.au for a lot more info and free advice.

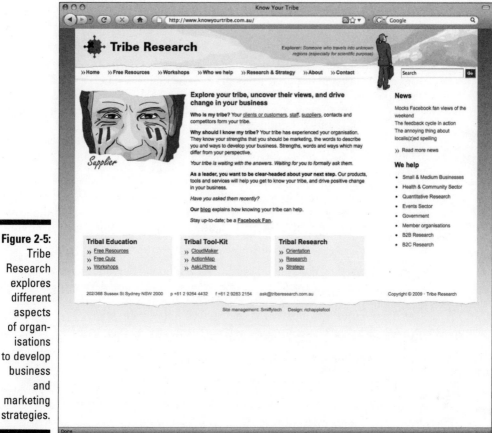

Figure 2-5:
Tribe Research explores different aspects of organisations to develop business and marketing strategies.

If you're doing research of any kind, be prepared for the honest truth and be willing to do something with what you discover. Many businesses spend lots of time (and money) on research, only to do nothing with it.

Testing your offering

One big problem with research is that people can say, 'Yes, yes, yes, we *love* your idea and *we want it*,' when you ask them for an opinion on your product but, when it comes to parting with their hard-earned cash to purchase it, you won't see them for dust. For me, the only true test of whether your product is wanted is if people open their wallets or hand over their credit cards. That's why it pays to test your offering before launching it to the world.

But, to be honest, some products and services are harder to test than others. Testing a new signature dish on your menu is much easier than testing a new ride-on toy. If the signature dish is a flop and no-one orders it you can simply remove it or replace it with something else. With the toy, you've got to do much more research and prototype testing.

Whatever you offer, testing is vital and can save you lots of time, money and pain.

Imagine you own a florist in the CBD of a big city. Your best customers are busy executives (mostly men) of the big companies in the surrounding office blocks. Through careful observation and simple questioning you discover the following:

✔ They often forget special occasions and make last-minute purchases.

✔ They buy flowers on average once per month.

✔ They buy them mostly for their wives and female staff.

✔ They spend on average $70 per floral arrangement.

✔ They prefer roses or mixed floral arrangements.

✔ They like to pay by corporate credit card.

✔ They like the convenience of being able to order by phone.

✔ They prefer them to be delivered to their offices.

Using this valuable information, you develop a new service concept called Flower Power: For Busy Executives. The idea is to collect all the customers' contact details, flower preferences, special dates and occasions such as wedding anniversaries and staff birthdays, and put all this information in your database. Then, a few days before the special occasion, you ring them to see if they'd like to place an order. You complete the order, charge their credit card, send them an electronic invoice by email and deliver the flowers straight to their desk or the recipient. Voilà!

You're pretty sure your new concept is going to work but you want to trial it before promoting it all over town. You select 20 of your best executive customers and ask if they'd be willing take part in the Flower Power trial over the next six months. In return for their willingness to be involved you give them a complimentary potplant for their desk (which, of course, has your logo and phone number on the side). Through their regular feedback you refine your processes and get your database working really well.

Fast-forward six months ... Flower Power is flying. You've created a unique new service that makes your customers' lives a whole lot easier while endearing them to their loved ones and staff. And you've probably got them telling everyone else about you too. Ready, aim ... fire! You're now ready to launch yourself at every executive in every office block in the CBD.

Launching and refining your offering

You've done your research, tested your product and given it a tweak here and there to make sure it's really appealing. How you launch and promote it, however, determines whether it sits on the shelf collecting dust or walks out the door like hot cakes.

To launch your product you need to go back to the basics and put in place a simple marketing plan. You need to be clear on your customer value proposition (what they get for what they pay) and your points of difference (in case they go shopping around for a better deal). And you need some clever copy and good design for your marketing materials and website to get people excited. See Chapters 9 to 13 for more on marketing through the media and Chapters 16 to 18 for information on online marketing.

 Start at the end. Visualise yourself selling or delivering your new product to your very first customer. When I hit writer's block with my first book, *Small Business Big Brand*, I would visualise myself greeting a small-business owner, selling them a copy and then autographing it.

Being in business is a case of continual refinement. We launch new products, refine old ones or get rid of ones that don't work anymore. One of the best ways to keep fresh and inspired in your business is to continually review and refine by cleverly combining what you know you can deliver with what you know the customer wants. Now that's a powerful combination.

Keeping Customers Versus Acquiring New Ones

I'm sure you've heard the statistics that it costs three times as much to get a new customer as it does to keep one. So why do so many business owners ignore their existing customers in the hot pursuit of new ones?

A mortgage-broking firm I know had over 5,000 customers on the books — all with only one home loan. The only time they kept in touch with their customers was to inform them of interest rate and repayment changes. Their marketing efforts were all focused on getting new homeowners to borrow, not keeping in touch with their existing customers, and some went elsewhere to renew their loans, as many borrowers do every five years or so. Imagine what results they might have achieved if they'd given a little more love and attention to their existing customers.

Existing customers are your best source of new business because they already know, like and trust you — providing they've had good experiences with you in the first place, of course. They're also your best source of referrals. So it makes sense to love them and keep in touch.

The secret to keeping in touch and showing you care is your database. If you have thousands of customers and no system to keep in touch, you'll almost certainly let your best customers slip through the cracks. Whatever you do and no matter how many customers you have, develop a system to keep in touch regularly. It keeps you top-of-mind when they need more of what you've got. You can find more on how to get a good database at the end of this chapter.

Creating customer loyalty

Creating customer loyalty in today's increasingly commoditised and homogenised world is a difficult task for any business owner. Remember the good old days when the bank manager was the most trusted and respected guy in town? If you were about to go broke or your wife was leaving you, he'd be the first guy you'd break the news to. You'd never even consider changing banks.

Fast-forward to the 21st century. You're lucky if you even know the name of your bank manager!

The easy part is getting new customers. The toughest bit is keeping them as customers and getting them to come back and buy more, and tell everyone else about you. A customer loyalty program should be included in every marketing plan for every business, regardless of its size and number of customers.

In writing this book, I'm assuming you have great products and good service. Without these two fundamentals, creating loyalty is impossible.

Creating loyalty is about going that extra mile — the mile that most of your competitors don't go! It's not all about giving away discounts and freebies. Your ability to build relationships and get to know your customers and really care for them is the biggest factor in creating loyalty. Here's a formula to get you thinking:

> Deep relationships + powerful incentives + exceptional customer service = customer loyalty

Everyone likes to deal with people they know, like and trust, and who they believe are experts in their field.

To give you an idea of how you can create loyalty, here are some very simple examples:

- A drycleaner builds relationships by remembering all his customers' names and by giving them a free suit dryclean on their birthday.
- A leadership coach exceeds her customers' expectations by emailing them every week with a personal and powerful motivational quote.
- An artist creates loyalty by personally installing and christening his masterpiece in the purchaser's home.
- A software business creates loyalty by offering a 12-month free trouble-shooting service.
- A fresh juice business creates loyalty by offering a 50 per cent discount on your juice when you bring in a friend who also buys a juice.
- A mechanic creates loyalty by giving your car a clean (inside and out) every time you get it serviced.
- A bookstore creates loyalty by giving you a $5 discount voucher on future purchases for every $50 you spend.

Getting old customers to come back and buy more

The best way to get old customers to come back and buy more is to give them a reason to come back. *Pareto's Law* says that 20 per cent of your customers will bring you 80 per cent of your business (and profit). So work on a strike rate to get 20 per cent of your customers coming back — but find a reason for them to come back.

You can get your customers to come back in three main ways:

- **New products:** Introducing new products or services to complement your current product range gives you a reason to go back to old customers. If you're a lawyer mainly focusing on wills and estates, you could introduce divorce and child custody services.

- **Loyalty programs:** The airlines have frequent-flyer programs to create loyalty. I'm not sure if they work and can only imagine how expensive they are to run! I love the Kidstuff stores because every time I go there and buy something, a percentage of my purchase is donated to my son's school. Their website is shown in Figure 2-6.

- **Communication and keeping in touch:** Every business should have a contact program that puts you in front of your customers every month or two. It could include an e-newsletter, personal phone calls, birthday cards, invitations to events — whatever is valued by your customers. Find out how often your customers like to be contacted, how they like to be contacted and for what reason. If you have thousands of customers, focus on the top 20 per cent.

Getting new customers from your old ones

I recently needed repairs on my roof (massive leaking in one corner of the house). I decided to get quotes from three different sources. The first source I got from an internet search in my local area, the second I got from the classified ads in the local newspaper, and the third from a referral from a neighbour who'd recently had his roof repaired.

Which one do you think got my business? The guy referred to me. Why? He was prompt, professional, less expensive and recommended — and he did a great job. This guy doesn't even advertise and he has heaps of work. His secret to success is keeping his customers really, really happy by doing a good job at a good price. He tells me that he gets over 60 per cent of his work from customers or tradies who recommend him to others.

My point? The best way to get new customers from old customers is to keep your old customers happy and to get them referring you. This guy lets the referrals happen by chance. Imagine if he actually asked for referrals and thanked people for them? Maybe that 60 per cent could become 80 per cent. For more on how to build a referral program into your business see Chapter 15.

Collecting Customer Information with a Database

The big companies spend millions of dollars on building database systems to manage their millions of customers. If you asked many of those companies if they were happy with their database systems, the vast majority (over 60 per cent) would say *no!* Many feel they don't get a return on their huge investment in these systems.

Just so you know, another term for a database is a *customer relationship management (CRM) system*. Sorry, another bit of jargon.

Basically your CRM system is the central database you use to capture the contact details and relevant information of all your customers and contacts. It's the platform upon which you manage your customer relationships. Investing in a CRM system is not about investing in technology; it's about investing in clients and business retention.

A CRM system — one that works for you and is simple and easy to manage — is the single biggest and most important investment you can make. Your CRM system becomes the backbone of your business. And it's the secret to creating freedom from your business, because all the customer knowledge happens to be kept in your database (not your head). And, if you ever decide to sell your business, your CRM system could add lots to the sale price.

A good database (or CRM system) allows you to:

- ✔ Identify and segment your customers.

- ✔ Profile your customers based on their personal and company information, and their profitability.

- ✔ Keep detailed contact reports so everyone in your business is up-to-date with all historical customer contact.

- ✔ Offer different levels of service to different customer segments, depending on their value to you.

- ✔ Run efficient and highly targeted marketing and communications campaigns to different segments.

Here's an example of how a smart database can help in the marketing and sales effort. A financial planner has a database of over 3,000 customers. She analyses the data to identify all those customers who have insurance and a small amount of superannuation, are between 50 and 60 years old and live in certain postcodes close by. This task nets the planner around 100 customers, most of whom she has had no contact with in the past year. Over a period of two months she contacts them all via letter, phone and email. The response — 13 interviews, four financial plans and over $2 million in new super funds.

Selecting a database and supplier

Thanks to the internet and great software advancements, you don't have to spend big bucks to put in place a CRM system. On the other hand, selecting the right one for your business can be daunting.

Sticking to the KISS principle (keep it simple, stupid — not that you're stupid, of course!) should be kept in mind at all times.

Questions you could ask yourself in considering the best option include:

- ✔ What is the maximum number of customers I'm likely to use the database for?

- ✔ Is my business more about one-to-one or one-to-many communications with my customers?

- ✔ Who will be required to use it? How many staff? Who will be responsible?

- ✔ What information and data do I want to collect on my customers? How simple or sophisticated does the database need to be?

- ✔ How many and what different segments or groups of customers do I need to classify on the database?

- ✔ Do I need to access the customer information remotely or just in my office?

- ✔ Do I prefer software solutions or web-based solutions? What are the pros and cons of each for my business? (I suggest you thoroughly investigate both options, by the way.)

I'm a big fan of web-based databases because I can access my customer information from anywhere in the world, anytime and on any computer. But that's just me — I see it as one of my tickets to freedom to be a global citizen.

Many of the off-the-shelf website solutions give you a package that includes a database system that you're able to customise. These packages also offer content management, shopping carts, an emailing facility, and all the other bells and whistles you'd expect from a self-managed website solution.

Choosing a web-based database is difficult, simply because so many are on offer. Some CRM solutions are even designed for specific industries like accounting and financial planning. Here are a few to check out to see if they suit your business:

- ✔ Business Catalyst (www.businesscatalyst.com)
- ✔ eknowhow (www.eknowhow.com)
- ✔ Joomla (www.joomla.com)
- ✔ Salesforce (www.salesforce.com)
- ✔ SugarCRM (www.sugarcrm.com)

If you're confused about where to start, write down a full list of what you want in a system and then go online and check out the options, get three quotes, and ask your friends what and who they use. A number of good CRM consultants are available to help you find the right system and then set it up for you.

Don't rush into making a decision. Take your time, do your homework and get it right. Getting it right up-front can save huge headaches down the track.

Customising your database

When working out what information about customers you want to collect, ask yourself what information you need and *how* you'll use it. For example, collecting your customers' birth dates has no point if you're not planning to send them birthday cards.

You obviously want to collect their first and last name, and gender, but do you require their salutation? I personally think the whole Mr, Ms, Mrs, Miss, Dr thing is a bit antiquated. I'm just Carolyn thanks! You also probably want to collect their email address, phone numbers, postal address, the company they work for, their position at the company and so on. And what about a field that allows you to record where they heard about you?

The real gold comes when you start to record personal details such as their interests and family members' names or even their pets' names. On the functional side, you can record details on products they've bought from you and their value to your business. You can add notes on discussions you've had with them, and store copies of emails between you or contracts you've sent.

One function I particularly love about my database is that I can add a note to a customer's file and then tag it to send a reminder to my inbox for me to call them — on the exact day and time that I want it.

You need to consider lots of things in customising your database. Again, the KISS principle applies. Too many fields and too much information and it becomes complicated and unruly to manage. Not enough information means it won't be effective enough to manage your customer relationships.

Be aware of privacy laws. Some data you may want to collect on customers *cannot* be collected. Get advice in this regard.

For more on the Australian Privacy Act, check out the government website at www.privacy.gov.au/law/act. In New Zealand, go to the Privacy Commissioner's website at www.privacy.org.nz.

Managing your database

If finding the best database is the most important task, the second most important task is making sure it's looked after with tender loving care. One in ten businesses end up finding themselves with two or three databases — and a real headache. They have some customer info on Outlook, some on an Excel spreadsheet and some on another database software program they got years ago. If you're in this boat, find the single best solution and amalgamate all your customer information — pronto.

Procedures are also important — for who is responsible for the database, who updates it, what fields are mandatory and how it is to be used for marketing and communication purposes. If you have staff, get them all engaged in using it. Invest in training on a regular basis — a great CRM system is only as good as the people who use it and enter data into it.

Be practical. Make sure you and your staff actually enjoy using the system and that it's easy to understand; otherwise it will be dropped like a hot potato!

Just as doctors recommend daily exercise, I recommend daily database updating. Make time for it and do a little every day (it may only be 15 minutes) so your database doesn't get unruly and unmanageable.

Growing your database

You've got a great database and have uploaded all your customer information, but now you want to add a few prospects to it. You can grow your database in many ways. Here are some examples of how different businesses could use their databases:

- An IT consultant offers a free research paper on his website for people who subscribe, who he then adds to his database.

- A graphic designer develops a list of all the local print shops via a web search and adds them to her database to post them a special offer for design work for their clients.

- A video and DVD shop collects the names and email addresses of everyone who comes into the shop to email them each month's new releases.

- The manufacturer of a revolutionary new baby pouch buys a list of the contact details of all the baby stores in the country to add them to the database and mail them an invitation to attend the launch of the product with a celebrity mum.

Just make sure the way you grow your database is legal and ethical, and that you get permission from the people you're entering into it. I hate opening my inbox every morning to find 20 unsolicited spam emails in it. And I dare not unsubscribe to many of them because then they know they actually did reach me!

How to use your database for marketing

A database is there to help you retain customers and communicate with them. It's also there to help you market to them. And maintaining a database is not just about sending out emails and letters to sell them stuff. It's about adding value to their lives and reinforcing in their minds that they've made a good decision to buy from you. And, if they haven't yet bought from you and are on your mailing list, your marketing task is to 'earn the right' to ask for their business down the track through value-added communications.

A real estate agent could add value to his database by sending his customers

- The monthly property sales results in the local area.

- The latest news in relation to homebuying, such as interest rate changes and new government incentives on offer to first-time buyers or property investors.

✔ A link to an online tool for people to work out how much they might realistically sell their home for.

✔ The opportunity to enter a competition to win the services of a free interior design consultant for a day.

Allowing your customers to buy from you rather than taking a hard-core sales approach produces a much more pleasant exchange. A good database facilitates that process very well.

It is not the employer who pays the wages. Employers only handle the money. It is the customer who pays the wages.

—*Henry Ford (1863–1947), founder of the Ford Motor Company*

Chapter 3

Being Mindful of Market Forces

*N*o matter how special your product or service is, outside forces will always affect your customers' decisions to buy and keep buying from you. Whether those forces are economic factors, the political environment or an aggressive unexpected competitor, keeping an eye on what's happening outside your business pays off. You need to be aware of how those external factors impact on your business, and therefore the way you position and market your business.

At various times, governments offer subsidies to householders or homeowners to improve energy efficiency or encourage water-saving practices, for example. If you happen to own a business in an industry that supplies these services, these initiatives could keep you busy for the life of the subsidy program — if you're smart enough to focus your marketing plan and messages on the program. Keeping an eye on the media and following what's happening in the political landscape has been the make or break of many a business.

In this chapter, discover why keeping an eye on the market you operate in is critical to staying ahead of the game and keeping your business afloat during the tough times as well as the good times.

History shows that peaks and troughs, up and downs, stormy weather and beautiful clear days are inevitable for every business. The key to success is determining what's worth taking on board and doing something about, and what's not. Being willing to adapt and change your business offering and the way you market yourself is crucial.

Taking into Account Economic Factors

Economic cycles are a fact of life. They're fairly predictable recurring patterns of periodic fluctuations most often measured by gross domestic product (GDP). All market economies go through a period of expansion, peak, recession and recovery, with no set timeframe for the cycle. Commonly, no theory or universally accepted reason for this is apparent. It just is.

If you're old enough, you may remember the stock market crash of 1987. At the time of writing, the global financial crisis (GFC) is still taking its toll, especially outside Australia and New Zealand, after stock markets worldwide crashed, with a considerable number of banks, mortgage lenders and insurance companies failing. Consumer sentiment is down, unemployment rates are up and people are spending less, selling up their holiday homes and battening down the hatches.

Think about what's happening in the economy as you read this. How is it affecting your business and will it affect it in the future? If so, how long will you need to weather the storm? At these times you need to remain optimistic and ensure you have contingency plans (and funding) to get you through. Don't just hope for the best and sit it out. Be smart and be proactive.

When economic factors are affecting your customers' willingness to buy, here are a few things you can do:

- ✔ Talk to your customers to find out why they're not buying and what you can do to help.

- ✔ Consider offering a new and more cost-effective product or service.

- ✔ Run special promotions and deals to attract more customers.

- ✔ Look at ways to bundle, unbundle and refresh your products to make them more appealing.

- ✔ Review your finances, sharpen the axe and slash unnecessary expenses.

✔ Make your payment and contract terms more appealing.

✔ Review your marketing activities and expenses and seek out more cost-effective tactics.

One of my favourite and most expensive restaurants had become very quiet because people were eating out less. The owners then started running a special 'in by 6 pm and out by 8 pm' deal that gives customers a choice of either an entrée and main or main and dessert with a glass of wine at $29 per head. It's now packed almost every night.

Surveying the Political Environment

I must admit politics wasn't one of my favourite subjects at school, and I'm not an avid follower of the political landscape now either. Shame on me. Although I do keep a friendly eye on what's happening at a local level.

But, undoubtedly, politics and government policy can have an impact on your business and marketing efforts, and affect people's willingness to buy. Consider the threats and opportunities for your business in these areas:

✔ **Taxes:** Income tax, import and export duties, goods and services tax (GST), capital gains tax (CGT) and all the rest of it can seriously impact on your pricing strategies and payment terms, and, of course, your margins and profit. Look out for new taxes being introduced or tax breaks being announced. As painful as it may be, getting a bit of a handle on what's what at the Australian Taxation Office (ATO) is worthwhile.

Periodically check out the small-business pages of the ATO website (www.ato.gov.au) — sometimes not even your accountant is aware of the tax breaks you may be eligible for. In New Zealand, tax is handled by the Inland Revenue Department (www.ird.govt.nz).

✔ **Government grants:** Grants are available for almost any kind of business, if you know where to look for them and how to access them. Depending on the kind of business you're in, you can use these grants to fund an aspect of your business, or help your customers access grants for spending on your services.

For government grant information in Australia, check out www.grantslink.gov.au. In New Zealand, go to www.business.govt.nz, click on Finances and Cash Flow in the Tell Me About menu and then choose Grants and Other Financial Assistance.

✔ **Area-specific funding:** Local, state and federal governments often hand out one-off funding to improve education, health and the environment. That represents big opportunities for your business if you happen to offer a service that targets these areas.

✔ **Departmental assistance:** Getting a handle on who's who at the zoo in government departments that might affect your business is also a good idea. If you happen to own a travel consultancy, for example, knowing what's happening in the department of tourism is worthwhile.

If you're an Australian operator thinking about launching into global markets, check out AusTrade (www.austrade.gov.au). For New Zealanders wanting to send their business global, go to the New Zealand Trade and Enterprise website at www.nzte.govt.nz.

Keeping Up with Technology

If you've been reading this chapter from the beginning, hopefully I haven't scared you off all together with talk of the GFC, GDP, politics, taxes and the whole shooting match. If you're still reading, read on!

I reckon technology is one environmental factor that's having far more impact on how you do business and how you market yourself than everything else put together. The internet and technological advances in general have had a huge impact on the way people communicate with each other, search for information and sift through available products and services — and eventually buy.

That's why including a technology and internet strategy in your marketing plan is critical. If you're really not abreast of how technological advances could be affecting your business, spend some time online and check out Part V for lots more on online marketing. If you think it won't affect your business because your target market is retirees, think again — they're embracing technology too.

Check out these ideas:

✔ Look at how your competitors are promoting themselves online and if they're selling online.

✔ Use search engines, such as Google, every day.

✔ Have a go at one of the online social media like Facebook or Twitter.

✔ Start a blog.

   ✔ Get your kids (or borrow some if you have to) to show you how to use Skype and YouTube.

   ✔ Subscribe to e-newsletters and media websites that interest you.

Whatever you do, get e-savvy and embrace technology.

My 12-year-old son, Billy, has been the best technology teacher I could hope for. The other night he cooked a delicious meal after being inspired by the *Master Chef* program, took a picture of it with the PhotoBooth application on his Apple Mac and had it loaded up on Facebook before we even sat down to eat!

Looking at Global Markets Versus Local Markets

Australia's population is over 21 million people and New Zealand has more than 4 million. In July 2009, the two countries were ranked as number 55 and 125 respectively out of 238 countries when it comes to size of population. The number-one country in the world is China, with a staggering population of over 1.3 billion, closely followed by India with a mere 1.1 billion people.

The Central Intelligence Agency of the United States doesn't just organise a spy network. Its World Factbook is a veritable fountain of information on world statistics, including population data. Check out the website (www.cia. gov) for some interesting population statistics. Select World Factbook from the Quick Links, click on Country Comparisons and then People, and select Population.

Realistically, Australia is pretty small on the 'potential to consume' scale compared with other countries. Technology, significant advancements in air travel, enhanced trade relations, and the vast array of government grants and incentives are all making it easier for any business to do business in or with another country. If you're finding that you're operating in a highly competitive market and are ready for a change, global opportunities are worth investigating.

David Thomas of Think Global Consulting considers the *BRIC countries* (Brazil, Russia, India and China) as the four countries to investigate. Loads of good articles and information are included on his website (www.thinkglobal.com.au).

Whether you operate locally, nationally or globally, going back to the basics and redefining your target markets pays off. Ask yourself these questions:

- Who are my target markets, where are they and how do I get to them?
- What other competitors are operating in these markets? What are they offering?
- Where is the real market opportunity for my business?
- What would I need to invest to get into this market (time, money, energy, expertise)?

You don't need to live in a particular country to market to potential customers there. You can choose from many ways to do business, from setting up shop or opening an office to working with agents on the ground or selling your products online and shipping them from home.

I don't recommend tackling any global market without help, advice, connections and someone on the ground in that country.

Sizing Up the Competition

Every business has competition. It's one of the great things about operating in the free economy. Competition is healthy, and it prevents people from being beholden to a monopoly. Competition can be direct or indirect and real or perceived — in your eyes and in the customer's eyes.

A butcher may perceive that his direct competition is other butchers within a one-kilometre radius of his shop who happen to sell exactly the same cuts of meat. The reality may be that his competition indirectly is any other shop within a five-minute walk that sells meat or any alternative to meat, such as the chicken shop, the Thai takeaway or the local supermarket.

A stockbroker may perceive his direct competition as all other stockbrokers, whereas the reality may be that he has indirect competition from any other business looking for a share of the nest egg, such as financial planners and investment property advisers. Interestingly, the biggest competitor may even be his target market — potential customers themselves. Perhaps they're buying their own shares online or using a family member to do it for them.

In sizing up your competition, think about how much of the customers' *share-of-wallet* you can expect — that is, how much they spend in the category you operate in. This can be more important than your direct competition.

Competition is everywhere and coming at you from every corner. You can easily become paralysed and pay the competitor too much attention. Keep a friendly eye on what they're doing, make some tweaks where required and then just get on with business.

For inspiration on how to become a market leader, I suggest you read up on the stories of successful business owners who are doing really well outside of your competitor set or industry. Check out some of the small-business magazines, such as *My Business*, to see who's doing well.

Rather than thinking about copying the competition, focus on how you are different and what makes you the most attractive option to your customers. In this day and age, new products and services can be copied and seemingly launched overnight. The only thing that really can't be copied is the quality of the relationships you have with your customers. Focus on them and you'll stay ahead of the game.

Now here's something a bit left of field. Your perceived competitor could actually be a collaborator and a great new source of business. Imagine you're a freelance graphic designer with another graphic designer in the office suite next door. There's a big job with the local council up for tender, but you don't think you can do it on your own, so you join forces with the other designer and present a joint pitch — and win it of course!

How to do a competitor analysis

An assessment of your competition is required as part of any good business plan and in helping to determine your target markets and the four Ps (and more — refer to Chapter 1) of your marketing mix and, most importantly, how you will be different.

Competitor analysis sounds a little technical but, in fact, it's really about getting out there and checking out what other companies offer, and how the marketplace responds. Here are some examples to help you stake out your competition:

✔ If you own a bakery and your market is local, take a walk around your local shopping precinct and note down all the possible competitors. Note what they sell, how much they sell it for and the kinds of customers coming in. Then buy something to check out how good (or otherwise) their customer service is. And, of course, do a taste test.

✔ If you're an IT consultant working in a specific industry such as accounting, do a web search to see who else is out there and check out their websites. They often list who their customers are, what services they provide and what their area of specialty is. Ask your customers who else they know who does what you do. For any jobs you pitch for but don't win, be sure to ask who got the job and why they won the pitch.

✔ If you're a professional speaker and trainer specialising in time management, do a web search on your competition, check out their websites and those of all the speaking-circuit bureaus. Go along to see them speak at their next public appearance to see what they speak on, how they deliver and the audience reaction.

✔ If you own the patent for a board game you've developed and are trying to sell it to a big toy manufacturer and distributor, check out what other board games the company has developed and sold, and what other board games are available that hit your target market. Before you make contact, work out how you're different and better, and why your product will sell really well.

✔ If you sell skincare products, offer free sample packs to your customers and friends to do a simple online survey to find out what other skincare products they have bought and why. Use this to discover the top three reasons why they should buy from you rather than the competition.

One of the quickest and simplest ways to find out which competitors are doing well in online marketing is to do a web search using keywords you'd associate with your own business. *Keywords* are words that are likely to be recognised by *search engines*, such as Google, so your website ranks high on the list of options the search turns up. If your competitors are ranking well in the search area, they're probably pretty good at marketing themselves — although that doesn't mean they have a better offer than you, of course. For more on keywords and online marketing see Chapter 18.

Market share analysis

Calculating your *market share*, or how much of the customers' share-of-wallet you can expect, can be tricky and time-consuming, but it's a must-do. If you have many competitors — perceived, real, direct or indirect — and therefore a small potential share-of-wallet, you may need to reassess your strategy and consider new target markets and products or services.

Sea Tonic Boutique Hotel is an upmarket establishment in a small seaside town in South Australia. Its owners, Mr and Mrs Pumicestone, developed the hotel ten years ago, renovating an old travellers' inn built in the 1880s, but business has slowed recently. The Pumicestones wanted to work out the hotel's current market share, in order to set goals and benchmarks for future projections. Table 3-1 sets out the step-by-step approach the Pumicestones took to analyse their market share. Read on for more about Sea Tonic's market share and check the sections 'Capturing your share of the market' and 'Keeping your share of the market' for some further ideas for Sea Tonic's marketing campaign.

The average occupancy rate, used to estimate the total nights the competitors' rooms were occupied, is almost impossible to work out accurately. Many industry reports on accommodation occupancy rates could be used as a benchmark. For example, a report on www. realcommercial.com.au reveals the occupancy rate for Cairns at as low as 63 per cent, and as high as 83 per cent for Perth.

Table 3-1   Sea Tonic Boutique Hotel, Market Share Analysis, 1 July 2008 to 30 June 2009

Factor to Consider	Sea Tonic	Local Competitors (43)
Total number of rooms available	20	500
Total number of nights available for occupancy	7,300 (20 rooms × 365 nights)	182,500 (500 rooms × 365 nights)
Total number of nights actually occupied*	4,088, or 56%	133,225, or 73%
Total market share of actual occupancy	2.97%	97.02%

* For competitors, nights occupied is estimated only, based on an industry average of 73 per cent.

These results should be quite sobering for Mr and Mrs Pumicestone. I reckon they'll be seriously looking at how they can increase Sea Tonic's occupancy rates closer to industry standards, and setting targets to increase their total market share up to around 4 per cent over a period of a couple of years. Other market information to analyse for Sea Tonic includes:

✔ Occupancy rates by season and holiday period

✔ Room rates and length of stay compared with competitors

✔ Profitability and margins per room

Capturing your share of the market

You've worked out you need to increase your market share and are pretty sure plenty of opportunities exist, but how do you go about it? You really have two options — steal a share from the competition or increase awareness of your offer to a market that may not have previously considered buying a product in your category.

The big guys have the luxury of huge marketing and advertising budgets to dominate the market in an attempt to steal market share. They can also invest heavily in product innovation and technology to stay ahead of the game and get a bigger bite of the cherry.

The beauty of being in small business is that you're nimble, lean, creative and opportunistic and therefore have a much better chance of capturing more market share by flying underneath the radar.

Capturing market share for the big guys is all about domination. For the little guys, it's more about infiltration. And it's not always about dropping your prices to get market share either; it's about packaging and value-adding (refer to Chapter 1).

Continuing with the Sea Tonic Boutique Hotel example from the previous section, here's how Mr and Mrs Pumicestone, the hotel's owners, go about capturing more of the market:

- ✔ **Gather information:** The Pumicestones start pounding the pavement to gather competitor information from the local Tourist Information Centre, and by walking about town and picking up any brochures they can find on noticeboards and in cafés. They check out their competitors' websites and read the tourist magazines, papers and brochures they advertise in.

- ✔ **Analyse the data:** They then prepare an Excel spreadsheet with data about Sea Tonic and its top 20 competitors. The spreadsheet captures all details on their room rates, services, facilities, payment options, special packages, types of customers and so on.

- ✔ **Mystery shop:** They get their daughter, Urchin, and a business colleague from Adelaide (someone who doesn't live locally) to *mystery shop* their competitors to ask specific questions and assess their customer service and quality of facilities.

- ✔ **Review the information:** They gather all this knowledge and decide they really need to review and refresh their offering and packaging, and the way they promote Sea Tonic to make it more attractive to potential customers.

✔ **Prepare a marketing strategy:** They hire a consultant to develop a new website, and they pay for search engine advertising, such as through Google AdWords (see Chapter 18). The consultant also produces new brochures and an ad.

✔ **Build relationships:** The Pumicestones then build relationships with the people at the Tourist Information Centre by inviting them in for dinner. They get the local paper to run a story on Sea Tonic, focusing on the background of the historic building, and their selection of luxury rooms, which each boast a four-poster bed, an ensuite spa, and fluffy robes and towels in the bathroom. Oh, and did I mention the special romantic weekend package they're offering? Icy bubbly on arrival and a discount organised with one of the top local restaurants for dinner that evening.

✔ **Get the message out:** They advertise the special romantic weekend package via travel consultants in Adelaide, and brochures in the Tourist Information Centre and local cafés. They've built a database to capture customer information, and sought permission to email their customers with the special weekend offer and more.

To capture more market share you need to be different and stand out, so, when potential customers are comparing apples with apples and shopping around, they're actually comparing apples with your juicy peach!

Keeping your share of the market

You've done a competitor review, had a brilliant year of marketing, increased your market share and generated a healthy increase in profit. But how do you keep your fair share?

You can bet by now the competitors of Sea Tonic Boutique Hotel, the hypothetical business introduced in the previous sections, are starting to sit up and take notice. They're probably staking out the competition too and starting to run bigger ads and offer greater discounts (because they haven't read this book!). My advice to Sea Tonic is this. Be aware and observe your competitors with amusement, but keep your eyes focused straight ahead — on your customers! When you've achieved your target market share, the secret is to love your customers, keep connected, keep them coming back and get them telling everyone about you.

Factors outside your control can always impact your business success, like economics, politics and the competition. In business it pays to think and act like an Aussie Rules football star. He's aware of the opposition on the field, but more focused on grabbing the ball and booting it straight through the goalposts — and then letting the competition chase it.

Chapter 4

Failing to Plan is Planning to Fail

In the story of Alice in Wonderland, Alice reaches a juncture in the road and meets the Cheshire cat. She asks the cat, 'Which way ought I go?'

The cat responds, 'Well that depends a great deal on where you want to get to.'

'Oh, I really don't much care,' says Alice.

'Then it doesn't really matter which way you go,' replies the cat.

And look where Alice ended up — somewhere she never planned to go or wanted to be! And it's the same when you're in business. If you don't know where you want to get to, and don't have a business vision and a road map to get there, then you'll almost certainly end up somewhere you never thought you would.

When working with my customers, and before I even sit down to address their marketing plan, I ask them three questions:

▶ **What are your personal dreams and goals?** Travelling every year, playing golf once a week, giving to the less fortunate, becoming a world-class dancer, spending time with family?

▶ **Why are you in business?** What are the five most important things it must give you? Fun, freedom, wealth, flexibility?

▶ **Does your business allow you to fulfil your personal dreams?** If yes, how? If no, why not and are you prepared to change?

I'd say that 80 per cent of my customers admit their business isn't allowing them to lead the personal life they want. They're frustrated and feel like they're living to work, rather than working to live.

Your business is *not* you. It's a separate entity. It's a vehicle that you should love working in and be inspired by so you can live the life you really want.

Business and marketing planning starts with personal planning. Your business growth should be directly proportionate to your personal growth. Putting your non-negotiable personal needs first, like health, family, relationships, spirituality, wealth and continual learning, is the ticket to ensure your business plan and marketing plan are actually implemented.

Writing a Marketing Plan

A cookie-cutter approach to marketing never works, and no two marketing plans are ever the same. The plan of a big company selling computers bears no resemblance to that of a small business selling computers. And the plans of two small-business competitors both selling computers will also be entirely different. What is the same, however, is the process you should go through in writing your marketing plan.

What you need to do is start at the end. What will business success look like to you and when will it be achieved by? The four simple questions to be answered in the marketing plan are:

- **Why do you do this?** This gives you your vision, mission and purpose.

- **What do you want to achieve?** These are your goals.

- **How are you going to achieve the goals?** Now you have your objectives.

- **What actions will you take to achieve the objectives?** And voilà, you have your strategy and tactics.

I define the difference between goals, objectives and strategies in the section 'Setting Marketing Goals and Objectives' later in this chapter. For a quick review of each of the separate sections you need to include in the plan, flick back to the information about marketing a start-up business in Chapter 1.

No doubt you have hundreds of creative ideas and thoughts that simply must be put into your marketing plan. The danger in putting everything in the plan is that you end up with so much to do you become daunted by the sheer weight of it all — and do nothing.

Your marketing plan must be simple, single-minded and focused, or it simply won't be implemented.

If you don't have a plan, it's now time to develop one. At the back of the book, in Appendix A, you find a template you can copy to help create a great marketing plan. Arm yourself with every bit of information you need to write the plan, such as competitor information, market share projections, new product research and ideas, and the rest. Take some time out of the business and start to map out your thoughts on a whiteboard or flipchart, and enter these on the template. Set yourself a deadline to complete the plan by making a commitment to a third-party mentor or adviser who can refine it with you.

Getting help with your plan

Throughout the course of my life as a small-business owner, I've called on numerous experts, advisers and successful friends in business for help and advice, particularly in the areas that I'm not so good at and inclined to avoid — like the money stuff.

When it comes to developing a marketing plan that works, does this tendency for avoidance sound familiar? If so, here are some low-cost (or no-cost) ideas to get help:

- ✓ **Find a marketing consultant with expertise in your field.** A consultant can take you through the marketing planning process and write a marketing plan with you. For example, I know of marketers who are former owners of successful hairdressing salons who can help guide a salon owner through a targeted marketing program for their salon.

- ✓ **Look for a marketing mentor.** A retired small-business owner in your local area or in your field may be prepared to mentor you on a regular basis to give you advice and hold you accountable to achieving your action plan. There are also many formal mentoring programs you can join. Check for mentoring programs online.

- ✓ **Set up a marketing mastermind group.** Find a handful of other small-business owners in a complementary field who also need marketing help and creative input, and hold regular meetings to give each other advice and encouragement to keep on keeping on.

- ✓ **Join online forums or programs.** A lot of great information and many programs are available online for small-business owners in specific areas of marketing, particularly how to grow your business via the internet. Many of them are free but some cost to join. Do your homework though, because there are also many people online with no proven track record.

If you need help, set yourself a goal to get it. In the long run, it can save you time and money in trying marketing tactics that simply won't work and it keeps you focused on the tasks that give you the best return on your investment.

Knowing if your plan is right

No matter how good your marketing plan, you can still have sleepless nights wondering if it will work and if you'll get the results you're hoping for. To be honest, sometimes you just have to put it out there and see if it hits the mark. It doesn't need to be a wholly unscientific exercise though. If you build goals into your plan (see the section 'Setting Marketing Goals and Objectives' later in this chapter), you can then evaluate their success after they're put into action.

One of my own major marketing strategies was to host regular breakfasts for small-business owners each month in the CBD of Sydney. I brought in expert speakers, and participants sat down to a yummy breakfast and made valuable connections with other business owners. They were very successful and I got, on average, 30 people who each paid $55 to attend. Over the course of seven years, I held 70 breakfasts and got in front of 2,100 small-business owners — and made a small profit along the way.

This year, I sat back and took stock of my personal goals and business vision, and reviewed my marketing plan — as everyone should do every year. I decided there was more than enough business in my local area in suburban Sydney, where I live, work and know a lot of people. So I decided to make a bold move. I changed my breakfasts into an evening 'Business Booster' event hosted at the local hotel and dropped the price to $35. At the first two events, 80 people attended and they travelled from all over New South Wales!

The reason for success? I had a marketing plan, of course. I knew who I wanted to be there, how I was going to get them to come and what kind of experience they would expect, to keep them coming back. I emailed everyone in my database, and enlisted the support of the local papers and local businesses to put out postcards — all printed and sponsored by Snap Printing — thank you. But did I know if it would be a guaranteed success? Not really. Nothing in life is certain. I had a hunch, though, and a track record for running good events.

Sometimes you have absolutely no way of knowing whether your plan will be a runaway success or a flop. Doing nothing, though, is not an option.

Keeping on track with your plan

The end goals of your marketing plan should rarely change. The path you take to achieve those goals, however, will twist and turn and take you in unexpected directions, until finally you reach your target.

The definition of insanity is doing the same thing over and over again, and expecting a different result. So, if you're doggedly sticking to marketing tactics that aren't achieving results, it's time to give them the toss or fix them up.

You need to keep a close eye on your marketing plan and efforts to make sure it's always working for you. Here are some tips to keep you focused:

- ✔ Put your marketing actions into a simple 12-month calendar or a spreadsheet and pin it up above your desk.

- ✔ Every Monday morning write a to-do list of the top ten marketing tasks for the week.

- ✔ Make one day (or two half-days) a week Marketing Day. Block it out of your diary and make it non-negotiable.

- ✔ Hold a weekly marketing meeting with your staff. Report on last week's results, successes and failures, and set marketing tasks for the week.

The only way your marketing plan will work is if you dedicate time and attention to it. Never stop marketing!

Setting Marketing Goals and Objectives

So what's the difference between all these terms — purpose, goals, objectives, strategies, tactics? Isn't it just splitting hairs to differentiate them? No, not really. Here's a simple definition of each:

- ✔ **Purpose:** This is the reason your business exists.

- ✔ **Goals:** These are the overall targets your business aims to achieve within a certain timeframe, most often expressed in terms of revenue, sales or profit. You can have one major goal or a few goals, but remember not to have too many or you risk losing focus and not achieving any of them!

- ✔ **Objectives:** These are the measurable results required to achieve the goals. You normally have several objectives all working in harmony to achieve your goals.

✔ **Strategies:** These are the plans required to achieve each of the measurable objectives; they focus on each of the four Ps of marketing — product, price, place and promotion (refer to Chapter 1 for more on the four Ps).

✔ **Tactics:** These are the actions you take to enact your strategy.

You should, in fact, be able to summarise all of these aspects of your plan in a single page. They're almost like the executive summary of the marketing plan and would be the stuff you'd present to the board if you were given 30 minutes to give them the heads-up.

Go Organic is a business based in Christchurch, in the South Island of New Zealand, that sells organic products from a range of local producers, packaging them with the Go Organic brand and retailing them through one shopfront outlet. Figure 4-1 shows Go Organic's annual marketing plan, for the first four categories. I look at some of the tactics Go Organic plans to employ in 'Setting simple action plans' later in this section.

The numbers game

Marketing is a numbers game. It's about generating a consistent flow of quality leads, month in and month out, and then converting enough of those leads to get the sales you need to make your business profitable. You need to ask yourself six critical numerical questions to help you set your annual goal (following the list of questions is a worked example of goal setting):

✔ **What are the total costs to run my business, including my salary?** A cash flow projection is essential here. If you don't have a cash flow projection yet, talk to your accountant, and refer back to Chapter 1 for other things you need in your business plan.

✔ **How much revenue do I therefore need to generate, including the profit I want to make?** Again, part of your cash flow projection.

✔ **What is my average revenue per service or product sale?** This gives you the number of services or products you need to sell to reach your revenue target.

✔ **What is my conversion rate from enquiry to sale?** The *conversion rate* is the percentage of your customers who actually make a purchase after their initial enquiry. It may only be 10 per cent; I suggest being very conservative in estimating this number.

Go Organic

Annual Marketing Plan

Purpose

To improve the lives and health of our customers by giving them the ultimate organic food experience.

Goal

To increase revenue by 20 per cent.

Objectives

- To improve local brand awareness of Go Organic.
- To serve 5,200 customers (100 per week).
- To attract 520 new customers into the store (10 per week).
- To increase the average spend of every customer by 10 per cent.
- To increase sales by 10 per cent by expanding into other organic products.

Strategies

Product strategy

- Increase product range by 15 per cent — organic cosmetics, baby foods, homewares.
- Bundle and package the five most popular product ranges.
- Improve range and quality of fruit and vegetables.
- Launch one new service, either Go Organic fruit and veg box delivery service or Go Organic Catering.

Price strategy

- Increase all prices by between 10 and 15 per cent, depending on competitor price review.
- Offer loyalty discount and incentive program.
- Develop Go Organic pricing menu for packages.

Place (distribution) strategy

- Increase brand awareness among local businesses and homes within five postcodes of store.
- Develop cross-referral program with 20 other local businesses.
- Develop website for online ordering and delivery.

Promotion strategy

- Build website and implement search engine optimisation and e-newsletter service.
- Develop database to collect customer email addresses and contact details.
- Host monthly Go Organic cooking nights in-store.
- Run advertising campaign and editorial content in two local papers.
- Run Go Organic stalls at six local markets and school fetes.
- Promote loyalty card program to all customers.
- Give staff communication and sales training and develop incentive program to increase sales.

Figure 4-1:
You should
be able to
summarise
your
marketing
plan in a
single page.

✔ **To achieve these sales, how many leads do I need to generate?**
You also need to consider how many different promotional strategies
(and what strategies) you need in order to generate these leads.
I recommend a multi-pronged approach of at least four, preferably
six, marketing strategies to my clients.

✔ **How much am I prepared to invest in marketing in order to achieve
this**? I recommend between 5 and 10 per cent of your estimated
turnover.

Here's how the answers to the preceding questions work to set your goal.
Let's say you've worked out your expenses are $415,000 (including salaries).
You estimate you need another $85,000 to cover marketing expenses and
leave you with a profit. Therefore you need to generate $500,000 in revenue
this year. Your average price per sale is $5,000, so that means you need
to make 100 sales. However, your conversion rate is only 20 per cent due
to the high cost of your offering. Therefore you need to generate 500 new
leads per year, or 42 new leads per month, not taking into account possible
repeat business. How much are you going to invest in marketing? You decide
on 7 per cent of your turnover, or $35,000 (read the next section for more
on marketing budgets). That leaves a neat $50,000 profit, or 10 per cent of
turnover. Now you just need to put those marketing strategies to work to
generate the business.

Setting a realistic budget

It never ceases to amaze me that, when times get tough, in most companies
— large or small — the first thing that gets slashed is the marketing budget.
Yet this budget is the very thing that has the potential to help you generate
more quality leads, which is what gets you more sales, right?

Although I don't believe in wasting money, I do believe that marketing
is the last thing companies should be cutting back on. If anything, your
marketing budget should be increasing, particularly at times when your
competitors are slashing theirs, because this puts you in an even better
position to stand out.

How much you allocate, however, depends on whether you're a start-up or
well-known established business, the type of business and industry you're in
(for example, lawyers probably spend far less than a retailer), how big and
wide your market is, and whether you're selling to other businesses or to
consumers.

You can set a marketing budget by:

- Looking at past years' actual expenditure on marketing
- Taking a stab at what your competitors may be spending
- Looking at the end revenue goal and allocating a percentage for marketing expense, as was done for the hypothetical in the previous section

I've found that the business owners who thrive year after year allocate at least 5 to 10 per cent of their gross desired revenue as their marketing budget. It's the general rule I tend to work with. This amount should also increase each year, at least keeping up with the consumer price index (CPI).

Whichever method you decide on, you need to check it against the estimated costs of the marketing strategies you intend to employ. At the back of the book, in Appendix B, is a budget template to help you allocate the costs. Be as realistic as you can in your estimates. You may find you need to either increase your budget or cut back on the strategies (try not to cut back to less than 5 per cent of your projected revenue though), or find more cost-effective ways to market your business.

Marketing success isn't just about how much you invest, but how you invest it. A property investment adviser I worked with was about to spend $40,000 of his $50,000 marketing budget on a one-month print advertising campaign. After spending a day with me creating his marketing plan (this cost $3,000 of his $50,000 budget), he slashed his advertising spend to zero. He was able to cleverly redirect his funds into a six-pronged marketing program that included strategies such as raising his profile and promoting his expertise to the local-area market through a speaking and media campaign; hosting a 'lunch and learn' series with clients and friends; establishing an active and targeted networking and alliance-building program; sponsorship of his local golf club (his biggest passion); and a whole new focus on the internet and e-marketing. His total marketing spend? $40,000. Projected revenue? $520,000.

To make money you need to spend money. Many business owners don't set a marketing budget because they've had their fingers burned and wasted money on marketing that didn't work in the past. Don't let that be you. Allocate a budget — even if it's not as much as you want.

Setting simple action plans

You've done your plan, set your goal, objectives and strategies, and figured out your budget. Now it's time to get tactical and practical, and roll up your sleeves. The next step is to take a look at your strategies and list your tactics — the actions you're going to take to make it happen.

Go Organic, the hypothetical business examined at the beginning of 'Setting Marketing Objectives and Goals', decided to establish a customer loyalty program as part of its marketing plan (refer to the price and promotion strategies in Figure 4-1). Table 4-1 shows how the business might develop an action plan to implement that particular strategy.

Action plans, the tactics part of your marketing plan, need to be straightforward, practical and realistically achievable in the timeframe and budget you set.

Table 4-1 Go Organic Action Plan for Loyalty Card Program		
What Needs to Be Done	*By Who*	*By When*
Research loyalty card programs of other businesses.	John	1 June
Hold team meeting to come up with three options for Go Organic Loyalty Card Program.	All staff	8 June
Work out costs, budgets and processes to manage each option and set sales targets.	Linda	17 June
Do research with 50 customers to determine best option.	Sales team	30 June
Gather findings, analyse results and present at team meeting. Get final input and agreement on program.	All staff	7 July
Produce loyalty card and promotional flyer, and add to website.	John	8 August
Train staff on how to promote Go Organic Loyalty Card Program.	Linda	19 Aug
Distribute flyer to local businesses and homes.	John	31 Aug

Measuring and evaluating success

You've got your marketing program under way and it's going gangbusters — or is it? The true test of success is if you're achieving sales targets, growing revenue and making a profit. It's necessary to set milestones, and to stop, take a breather, analyse the numbers and ask yourself if the effort and expense is reaping the return you expected — and, importantly, if your customers are happy.

Go Organic (flick back to the beginning of this section to check its marketing plan) decided to establish a customer loyalty program. Now that the company has implemented the strategy through the action plan shown in Table 4-1, it needs to put in place a simple recording system to check quarterly. This record needs to assess both quantitative and qualitative factors, detailing:

- ✔ The number of new loyalty customers signed up

- ✔ The amount customers are spending (average per customer) and how often they use their loyalty cards

- ✔ How much the program is actually costing per customer — in terms of time to manage and promotional costs

- ✔ What the overall increase in revenue for the business is — and what proportion is attributable to the program

- ✔ What the customers value most about the program (a simple feedback form or online survey would be useful here)

- ✔ How the customers feel it could be improved

Building relationships builds business

I was speaking to a real estate agent once, who'd been in the business many years. Her target market was the elderly selling up their homes to move into retirement villages. She'd been sponsoring the local bowling club for years, but hadn't been getting any business from it. She had signage all around the perimeter fences and regularly put out brochures in the clubhouse. I asked her if she was a member and a regular bowler.

'No, I'm not really into bowling and I don't have time,' she said.

And this is the very reason it wasn't working for her. She wasn't devoting the time to get to know the members and build relationships.

Fast-forward 12 months. She decided to have a go at bowls, found she loved it, became a member and joined the committee. And she's finding it's her best source of new business.

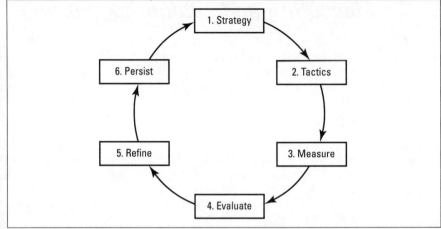

Figure 4-2:
For each
strategy
of your
marketing
plan you
need a
process to
evaluate
and refine it.

These aspects are the sorts you need to check for any marketing strategy. After you've made an assessment, you can work out what needs to change to streamline the effort and make it even more profitable. Figure 4-2 shows how the process works to continually review your strategy.

I caution against throwing out strategies too quickly if they don't seem to be working straightaway — say in the first six months. Often the best practice is to keep the strategy but change your tactics. And you might need to accept a break-even situation for the first 12 months, while the program is getting traction. I've seen many businesses throw out what I feel are really strong marketing strategies, when a little tweak in the tactics would've given them an entirely different result.

Resourcing Your Marketing

Dropping the ball on marketing is easy to do when business is good, but, when things slow down (and they usually do), you'll kick yourself that you didn't keep the marketing wheel turning. And the wheel can only keep turning if you devote time, money or people, or any combination of the three, to keep the plan in motion.

If business is really good, you may be able to afford to get some help and spend some money on things like a new website or sales materials. If business is not so good, then you can't afford not to make the time or find the money to get marketing.

Two heads are better …

Monique Field owns House About, a beautiful Asian furniture warehouse in regional New South Wales. For four years she had relied on full-page ads in the local newspaper to attract more customers. She recognised that she had a strong following of loyal customers but wasn't doing anything to reward them or keep them coming back more often.

Then, for the first time, she decided to really put some time, effort and focus into a marketing plan. She employed a freelance marketing manager for two days a week to help make it happen. Together, in just six weeks, they rebranded the business, developed new signage and stationery, built and launched their first-ever website (www.houseabout. com.au) and newsletter, gathered testimonials from clients, attended weekly networking events, developed a 'refer a friend' program and collected over 500 email addresses from customers. They also launched a Scholarship Education Program for the children of the Indonesian factory workers that supply their furniture. After all this was done, they had the best February and March sales months in four years of being open.

Monique says, 'The single biggest reason we achieved so much and got great results was getting my marketing manager on board. I just couldn't have done it by myself. It was definitely a case of two heads (and four hands) being better than one!'

Great plans are nothing without the desire, faith and will to execute them relentlessly. Every plan should outline:

- How much you will spend on marketing
- How you will spend it
- Who will execute the marketing plan
- When it will be executed by
- What results it will achieve

Getting the right help

Earlier in this chapter are some ideas on getting help to develop a marketing plan. This bit's about finding someone to help make it happen. You have a number of options:

- Advertise for a part-time marketing student at your local uni. Many students look for work (paid and unpaid) to practise what they're learning.
- Employ a new mum or a switched-on retiree with marketing skills who is looking for part-time work.

✔ Find a freelance marketing coordinator (one with a proven track record) for one or two days a week.

✔ Get a friend who knows marketing to help you out in return for something you can help them with (or pay them or give them a percentage of sales).

✔ If you have a staff member with a flair and interest in marketing, give him some training and the responsibility for marketing.

✔ If you're lucky enough to have a partner or close relative with a flair for marketing, ask her to help out.

Engaging employees in marketing

Make everyone in your business the head of marketing. Your staff (if you have them), apart from you, are your biggest marketing asset. If you treat your staff well, train them and engage them in what you want to achieve on the marketing front, they'll almost certainly rise to the occasion and become your best marketing weapon.

Here are some ideas on how to motivate your team to get marketing:

✔ **Engage your team in a marketing planning day.** Hold it in a fun location out of the office and let everyone get creative and provide input.

✔ **Hold weekly marketing meetings.** Get everyone to report on results achieved and new ideas.

✔ **Award incentives for new customers they bring in.** It doesn't have to always be about money either. What about a day off or a dinner voucher for their family?

✔ **Have a daily huddle for five minutes.** Ask everyone to share their one marketing task for the day.

✔ **Keep them learning.** Give them marketing, customer service and sales training on a regular basis.

✔ **Celebrate your marketing wins.** Have drinks and nibbles, a celebratory long lunch or dinner out.

Your staff are a walking billboard for your business. What message are they sending out to your customers and prospective customers? What can they do to help market your business?

Making time for marketing

Making time for marketing is non-negotiable. It needs to become a habit that is built into your daily work ritual. Allocate at least half an hour a day and four to six hours per week to work on marketing.

Daily marketing habits might include:

- ✔ Calling three prospective customers
- ✔ Sending three emails to existing customers who haven't bought for a while
- ✔ Sending out three thank-you cards to your best customers
- ✔ Adding people to your mailing list and database

Weekly marketing habits might include:

- ✔ Working on a particular marketing strategy
- ✔ Holding a team meeting
- ✔ Attending a networking event
- ✔ Meeting a potential alliance partner for coffee
- ✔ Sending out an email newsletter

Allocate time, break down your tasks and do them in the comfort of knowing they're all working together in perfect harmony to help achieve your end objective.

There's no time like the present to get on with putting in place a marketing plan, setting goals and objectives, and making it happen. Don't procrastinate. Put the wheels in motion to put marketing at the heart of your business and never, ever give up!

> *Patience is a key element of success.*
>
> *—Bill Gates, international entrepreneur and philanthropist*

Part II
Investing In Your Brand

Glenn Lumsden

'Originally I was aiming my food bars at the health-conscious, but now I'd like to rebrand them to include all the people who don't give a damn.'

In this part ...

I love branding. Getting your brand right is a big part of business success. It's one area of small business that's undervalued and misunderstood. A healthy brand has the potential to add thousands to the balance sheet of your business — invaluable if you ever plan to sell up — and it helps attract more business.

In this part of the book, you discover what a brand really is and how to get a professional brand — name, logo, marketing materials, websites and more. You also discover that branding is much more than how you look. Get the drum on how to create a grand brand experience and how to use your own personal brand to promote your business.

No matter how small your business, developing a big well-known brand that's respected in the marketplace you operate in is possible. Read on to discover the brand secrets of the big guys and the little guys, and get a fresh perspective on how to revitalise your brand.

Chapter 5

Brand Basics

- -

In This Chapter

▶ Understanding what a brand can do for your business

▶ Working out your brand personality and growing your image

▶ Choosing great brand names

- -

The concept of branding goes back eons, when farmers first used branding irons to mark their cattle as a sign of ownership. In those days, branding was nothing more than a way to tell everyone, 'This cow is mine!'

Then, somewhere along the way, big companies, heads of marketing, and branding and advertising agencies got hold of branding and turned it on its head.

Society is now dominated by brands. I once asked a group of people what their favourite brand was. One smart person said, 'I do everything to avoid brands, so I buy home brand.' Was he serious or just being smart? I don't know. But, of course, home brands are brands just like all the other well-known competitor brands sitting on the shelf at the supermarket.

In this chapter, you find out just how important branding is to your business. I look at how to develop and manage your brand image, as well as how to go about choosing a name for both your business and your products or services.

A branding program should be designed to differentiate your cow from all the other cattle on the range. Even if all the cattle on the range look pretty much alike.

—Al Ries, legendary American marketing strategist and author

Understanding the Value of a Brand

Before I go any further, it's probably a good idea to define what a brand actually is. I define a *brand* as all the tangible and intangible attributes of a business or product that impact on a person's perception of you, and that person's willingness to buy from you and to recommend you to others. A brand is also about how people perceive you to be different from and better than the competition.

An internet search to see if I could find a 'brand value' model that would be vaguely suitable for (and of interest to) small business proved fruitless. Disappointing, to say the least. I found lots of different big-business models and theories, but nothing I'd care to put in this book for you. So, here's my interpretation of brand value:

Brand value equals all the tangible and intangible parts of your business that add up to a single amount that can be added to your balance sheet as an asset.

Over time, as you increase sales and awareness and profit, and steadily grow your business, brand value also increases, just as your home increases steadily in value over the years. The true test of brand value, though, is when someone actually buys your business and that brand value is realised as money in your pocket. Table 5-1 outlines some of the tangible and intangible things you should consider in valuing your brand.

Table 5-1	Tangible and Intangible Brand Assets
Tangible Assets	*Intangible Assets*
Stock on hand	Customer service experience
Financials — profit or loss, sales, revenue	Brand awareness, penetration and perception
Databases	Patents
Systems and processes	Trademarks
Staff	Intellectual property
Website	Culture
Brand name, logos	Leadership
Office premises, equipment, furniture	Customer loyalty

Think about the assets listed in Table 5-1 in the context of the web search engine Google, which is estimated to be a $100 billion brand. How much of their brand is tangible versus intangible?

Use Table 5-1 to go through your own business and list everything you can think of that is tangible and intangible, and put some value on it — even if it's only small.

Brands that live in the minds of customers

Interbrand, one of the world's leading brand consultancies, each year rates brands globally and country by country according to brand value, which is calculated using a complicated model that takes into account both tangible and intangible aspects of the brand. Its top 20 brands in Australia for 2009 are shown in Table 5-2. The high dollar value attributed to these companies makes them also some of the most prominent brands.

These big brands might live in the minds of customers, but how many of them live in people's hearts? Making the heart connection is what marketers and brand experts constantly strive for in big business.

However, you know that the heart connection is made at the coalface. It comes from the way you look, the way you serve, and the way you reward and build relationships with staff and customers. That's why small businesses are better at building brand value and creating loyalty. You live and breathe your business every day, and you're really close to the people who matter — your staff and customers.

Big brands that live in my heart and mind are Apple Macintosh, ABC TV, Vegemite, Lindt, Google, Virgin and *For Dummies* books, of course, just to name a few. Another big brand I love is Harley-Davidson. According to legend, after the word 'Mum', the Harley-Davidson famous bar-and-shield logo is the second most tattooed design in the world. Talk about brand loyalty!

Small brands that live in my heart are too numerous to name and most of them are local businesses, like my coffee shop and hairdresser. Which brands do you love? Why do you love them? How can you take a leaf out of their book and insert it into yours?

Products are made in the factory, but brands are created in the mind.

—*Walter Landor (1913–1995), brand design legend and founder of Landor Associates*

Table 5-2		Interbrand's Best Australian Brands 2009	
Rank	**Brand**	**Sector**	**Brand Value A$ Million**
1	Telstra	Telecommunications	9,700
2	Commonwealth Bank	Banking or financial services	7,300
3	NAB	Banking or financial services	5,100
4	Westpac	Banking or financial services	4,800
5	Woolworths	Retail	4,600
6	Macquarie	Banking or financial services	3,200
7	ANZ	Banking or financial services	3,100
8	Billabong	Apparel	2,200
9	St.George	Banking or financial services	1,900
10	Harvey Norman	Retail	1,300
11	Australia Post	Postal and logistics	900
12	David Jones	Retail	760
13	Myer	Retail	670
14	Flight Centre	Travel	630
15	Crown	Gaming	560
16	Ansell	Manufacturing	500
17	Computershare	Share registry services	380
18	Origin	Utilities	220
19	JB Hi-Fi	Retail	190
20	Bendigo Bank	Banking or financial services	150

Brand image management

Building a great brand image can take years — and to destroy it, just seconds. You can most likely think of big businesses that have been thrown into turmoil and almost destroyed because of unethical behaviour and negative media coverage.

The bigger you get and the more customers you serve, the greater the need to manage every aspect of your brand. Brand image management means ensuring at all times that you operate ethically when it comes to:

- ✔ **Customers:** Ensure your customers get what they pay for, that delivery times are met, and that you communicate openly and honestly with them.

- ✔ **Employees:** Ensure your management practices, salaries, working conditions and contracts are in order and legal.

- ✔ **Environment:** Ensure your business practices are environmentally friendly and ethical, and that you are charitable and supportive of the local community.

- ✔ **Finances:** Ensure your finances are always well managed, that taxes are paid up, creditors are paid, investors are looked after and the relationship with your bank is solid.

- ✔ **Promotions and advertising:** Ensure you never make false claims or use misleading headlines or copy, and that what you promise is what you can, and do, deliver.

- ✔ **Suppliers:** Ensure suppliers are paid on time, their contracts are honoured and they are treated as you would want to be treated.

If you operate ethically, you reduce the possibility of your brand being damaged in the eyes of the people who keep you in business. Of course, even if you are ethical, an individual, the media and even your competition could decide to try to damage your brand, for whatever reason.

Be prepared. If you're about to dismiss a staff member for poor performance, for example, and he's upset with you, think about what he could do to damage your brand (if anything) and put in place a contingency plan to manage it.

Would you like attitude with that?

One of my favourite brand stories is from Justin Herald, who owned the Attitude brand and titled one of his many books *Would You Like Attitude with That?*

Flash back to 1995. Justin was the son of a minister, and at church used to be told by parishioners that he had an 'attitude problem'. Little did these parishioners know they had sparked an idea in his mind — an idea to develop a brand called Attitude. To Justin, having an 'attitude' is what gives you the edge to get somewhere in life rather than taking a back seat and letting life just happen to you.

He promptly went out and got the Attitude logo designed, and applied it to some funky T-shirts with slogans like 'I don't have an attitude problem, you have a perception problem.' He shaved his head, talked with attitude and promoted himself alongside the brand. As a result, in the first year he turned over $980,000 by selling his T-shirts to stores and at markets.

'It was a case of being in the right place at the right time. It just took off and before I knew it the media were interviewing me and we had over 3,500 stores licensing and selling Attitude street wear.'

And the coup de gras? After seeing Justin appear on *A Current Affair*, the CEO of Phillips contacted him and licensed the brand for a series of TV and stereo products aimed at the youth market. He sold his brand years ago and

is now a sought-after speaker, has authored several books and is building his new tribal range of sunglasses called Intimate. Here are four tips he'd give any small-business owner in building a brand:

✔ **Trademark your brand:** Make sure it's protected. If you can't protect it, don't do it. (I tell you more about protecting your brand in the section 'Steps to choosing a name' later in this chapter.)

✔ ***Be* your brand:** Feel it, live it and put yourself out there to promote the brand.

✔ **Keep it simple and dumb it down:** Don't get caught up in stuff that isn't about building the brand and getting awareness.

✔ **Get brand penetration in your market:** When you have that, the big guys start to sit up and take notice, and that's when you have the power to negotiate.

Every big-brand business was once a small business and brand. If your goal is to build a big brand, be patient. It takes time, faith and persistence and, of course, a healthy dose of Attitude.

Lessons from brand gurus

Many businesses that started out tiny are now household names. Think Boost, Fernwood Fitness Centres, Nudie, Roses Only, Macro Wholefoods, Crazy John's and more. You can learn a lot from these businesses. And you can find out their tricks of the trade through various means. Many of them have been featured in small-business magazines and in the media, or have written their own books.

Do some research on your own favourite brands and discover their secrets to brand building. Even if you don't want to get big like these guys, that's okay; you'll still learn some valuable tips and ideas.

Determining Your Brand

By now I'm sure you're convinced of the importance of investing in your brand, but how do you go about it? Always start by checking out the competition. You want to be sure you're different and avoid the possibility of being seen as a copycat brand. Check out these brand attributes of your competitors:

- Names, logos and taglines
- Website URLs (addresses)
- Brand trademarks or registrations
- Shopfront designs (if they have one)
- Advertising messages, images and colours
- Values and personalities (what they stand for)
- Methods of projecting themselves
- Target markets (who they serve)
- Means of differentiating themselves from you and other competitors

No idea is really original. Many businesses end up in court because of copycat claims. Even unintentionally, you could find this happening to you. Do your homework before you build or refresh your brand by starting with the section 'Steps to choosing a name' later in this chapter.

When you've done your homework on the competition and you know what you *don't* want to be, then you need to focus on what you *do* want for your brand.

Table 5-3 shows an example of how a small business went about determining the attributes of its brand. The business is a pre-loved clothing store for larger women, located in an upmarket affluent suburb. As you work through it, think about how you see your own brand.

Table 5-3	Determining Brand Attributes	
Brand Attribute	*Think About ...*	*Hypothetical Answers*
Brand name	What is our brand name?	BANG!
Brand tagline	What benefit do we provide?	For women who want to make an impact
Brand values	What do we believe in?	Big is beautiful Being real Value for money Quality (latest fashions, laundered, good condition) Personal service (advice, styling) Giving to the community
Brand personality	How do we express ourselves?	Fun Stylish Caring Fashionable
Brand lines	What products or services do we offer?	Advisory service Personal styling Pre-loved designer clothes Pre-loved designer shoes Accessories to match

In going through this process, understanding that your customers actually do value what you're offering, and your brand attributes, is important. Observe their buying patterns, ask questions and be prepared to refine your brand positioning as you go along until you get it just right.

Brand values and personality

People in branding circles often talk a fair bit about brand values versus brand personality. To be honest, I think it's a case of splitting hairs — they're almost the same thing. A web search turned up these definitions:

> *Brand values are the core set of values and qualities that sum up a brand.*

> *Brand personality is an expression of the fundamental core values and characteristics of a brand, described and experienced as human personality traits, such as friendly, happy, fun.*

To keep it real, you could say that brand values are what's inside and brand personality is what's expressed on the outside. The brand values of Virgin (all of Virgin's offshoots, not just the airline) are quality services, innovation, fun and value for money. The brand personality might be irreverent, young, cheeky and caring. I'd say these things are actually an extension of Richard Branson's own values and personality.

Saying your business values and personality are most likely an extension of your own personal values and personality is probably a pretty safe bet. So, in defining your brand values and personality, I recommend starting with yourself.

I recall talking to a successful businessman a couple of years ago, who had built his business into a $60 million company and recently sold it. I asked him why he sold it. Here's his response:

> *I wasn't having fun anymore. When I first started the business on my own, I was operating according to my own values, and then we got big and employed lots of people and I found the values of the business had changed dramatically and I wasn't aligned with it anymore. That's when I knew I had to sell up.*

If your own personal brand values and personality are not aligned with your business, you'll find it very difficult to bounce out of bed in the morning. And, if you're considering buying an established business or going into a partnership, make sure there is a *values fit* (the alignment of your personal brand values and those of your business) or walk away.

Projecting the right image

Your business is making an impression every minute of the day. Someone somewhere is seeing your ad, checking out your website, dealing with your salesperson or talking about you with a friend.

In the case of BANG! — the hypothetical pre-loved clothing store for larger women noted in the introduction to this section — projecting an image in accordance with the company's values and personality is vital to attracting more customers. Therefore, the owner probably wouldn't employ waif-like 18-year-olds as her sales assistants or use images of young skinny models in her advertising or website. If the business held a fashion parade, she'd probably get some of her customers as models and a personality like Magda Szubanski to host it — not an Elle Macpherson type of model. In giving to the community, she'd probably support the local women's shelter by offering to fit out any women wanting a makeover.

Like attracts like. The image you project every day influences the kinds of customers you attract. That's why marketing yourself in line with your brand values and personality is critical. Be very clear on who your target markets are and what's important to them.

Growing your brand awareness and reputation

Where do you want your business to be in five or ten years' time? This is a hard question to answer for most businesses, as most people tend to live and think from week to week and month to month, rather than year to year. You may decide that you're happy to stay small and build a business that provides a healthy income for you and your family. Or you may decide to build a business that's scalable and saleable, and that'll get big or turn into a franchise or licensee-type business.

If you want to stay small, you still need to increase brand awareness and build your reputation, but your task will be much smaller than if you want to get big and build a franchise business, like Jim's Mowing, for example.

If you're planning on building a franchise business, one of the key things your franchisees will be buying from you is the brand. They are buying brand awareness, customer loyalty to the brand, your advertising and marketing promise to help them generate more business, and the established systems and processes to run the business.

On the other hand, if you're starting up in business, you may want to consider becoming a franchisee. There are more than 1,250 franchise groups already in Australia and New Zealand, and that number is growing at a rapid rate. Check out *Franchising For Dummies*, 2nd Edition, by Michael Seid and Dave Thomas (Wiley Publishing, Inc.).

The best way to learn how to build brand awareness, whether you want to stay small or get big, is to check out how the successful franchise groups have built their brand awareness in your industry (and outside too). Franchises like Gloria Jean's Coffees, Domino's Pizza, Price Attack, Red Rooster, The Coffee Club, 7-Eleven, 1800-GOT-JUNK? and more.

For a list of franchise groups to give you some inspiration, check out the official directories of the Franchise Council of Australia, at www.franchise business.com.au (shown in Figure 5-1), and the Franchise Association of New Zealand, at www.franchisebusiness.co.nz.

Figure 5-1:
The
Franchise
Council of
Australia
(FCA)
official
directory
lists more
than 1,250
franchise
systems on
its website.

Choosing a Name for Your Business

When my beautiful son was born many years ago, I remember the agonising decision of choosing a name for him. After months of reading baby name books and going through the process of elimination, we decided on William — commonly (or not so commonly, thank goodness) known as Billy.

Choosing a name for your business is not unlike choosing a name for a child. You have to do it with love and care. Sometimes a name can simply pop into your head as a sign from the universe (like Justin Herald's Attitude brand, whose story is noted in the sidebar 'Would you like attitude with that?'), and you just know it's meant to be. At other times you need to go through a process of brainstorming and narrowing down the name options until you get it just right.

A name carries a lot of meaning and it can have a huge impact on the future success of your business. I read recently that one of the name options for Virgin (in its infancy as a record company in the 1970s) was Slipped Disc. That might have been perfectly fine when Richard Branson owned only a record company, but would you fly on Slipped Disc Airlines?

A name can be powerful and attention-grabbing, like Sumo Salad, or it can be respectful and serious, like Smith and Associates. If you don't have much money to market yourself and you need people to sit up and take notice, I know I'd rather go for the power hit!

Steps to choosing a name

Choosing a name has no clear-cut process. It's a strategic and creative process. Many business owners make the mistake of choosing a name before even working out what their business actually is. I've seen many businesses forced to go through an expensive name change because the business had evolved so dramatically that the name didn't fit anymore.

Your ideal customer and the type of business you're in should be the two determining factors in choosing a name. If you're a legal firm serving the elderly, you probably want to use something sensible like your name. If you own a Spanish restaurant, you probably want to be far more adventurous and use a powerful word or made-up name. Table 5-4 lists some options to think about in helping you choose a name.

Before choosing a name, review your business vision and plan, check out what your competitors are named, decide on the best naming options (by reviewing the types listed in Table 5-4) and then brainstorm as many names as you can. If you can afford it, you might employ a professional to help. Or you could enlist the support of one or two trusted and creative friends to help come up with ideas. Once you have a huge list, narrow it down to your top five to ten favourites.

Now the process of elimination really starts. You need to ask yourself the following questions to narrow your business name down to the top picks:

✔ Do I love it? Will my customers love it?

✔ Is it original and memorable?

✔ Is the name easy to spell and pronounce?

✔ If I want to go global, will it work in other countries?

✔ Will it sound great when I answer the phone?

✔ How will it work with my product or service names?

✔ How does this name compare with the competition?

✔ Will I use this name with a tagline? If so, how will they work together and what will the tagline be? (A *tagline* is a short statement — no more than, say, six words — that appears with your logo as a business descriptor.)

✔ Will it allow me to grow into other services or products?

✔ Can I register it at the Office of Fair Trading?

✔ Is the name trademarked or registered already?

✔ Is an obvious website URL available?

Table 5-4	**Types of Business Names**
Name Type	*Examples*
Person's name — often the name of the person or people founding the business	David Jones, Coles, Myer, Grace Brothers, Price Waterhouse Coopers, Dick Smith, Harvey Norman, Cadbury, Gowings, McDonald's, Ray White Real Estate
Made-up names — sometimes a combination of two words to create a unique name	Microsoft, Westpac, Telstra, Quicken, Vegemite, Ansell, Intel, Optus, Vodafone, Coca-Cola, Samsung, Colgate, Omo, Breville, Yahoo!, Google, Oporto
Words — names that are common dictionary words alone or in combination	Apple, Virgin, Attitude, Freedom, Billabong, Sportsgirl, Country Road, Dairy Farmers, Sydney Swans, Wizard, News, Facebook, LinkedIn
Acronyms and abbreviations — first letter of each word making up the name, which often begin as a full name such as Kentucky Fried Chicken (now KFC)	Alcoa, Oxfam, UNICEF, MYOB, ABC, ANZ, NRL, AFL, CSR, CSL, CSIRO, KFC
Functional names — names that tell people what you do	Barbeques Galore, Jim's Mowing, Lollypot, Clark Rubber, Foot Locker, Bathroom Werx, The Coffee Club, Pizza Hut

Protecting your brand name and identity is critical in eliminating the chance that someone else could use your name and trademark it, making yours redundant. The last thing you want is to end up in a legal battle over who really owns the name. You can do this yourself quite easily and inexpensively now online or, if you're really serious about getting big and global, you might want to appoint a trademark lawyer. Do a web search to find a lawyer or ask a friend who's been through the process to give you some advice.

To find out how to trademark and register a brand name, patent or design in Australia, visit `www.ipaustralia.gov.au`. In New Zealand go to `www.companies.govt.nz/cms` (shown in Figure 5-2).

Figure 5-2:
The New Zealand Companies office website offers lots of online tools.

Names can be eliminated fairly quickly from your list if the obvious and most user-friendly domain names or URLs aren't available. Many companies can do this for you, such as www.webcentral.com and www.melbourneit.com.au, and www.domain.co.nz and www.nzregistry.co.nz in New Zealand. I often use www.netregistry.com.au. This site covers all markets, Australian, New Zealand and global. Check out Chapter 18 for more on registering domain names.

Where to get help choosing a name

If you need help choosing a name, a number of marketing and branding professionals who specialise in this service can assist. Again, do an online search to find one or ask around to find the best professional to help.

 You can even find online systems and services that help you generate business names at random, such as www.names-n-brands.com and www.cazazz.com (from the Resources dropdown menu at the top, choose Business Links and scroll down to Brand Name Generator).

When you should change your name

Changing your business name isn't a decision to be made lightly. My motto tends to be 'if it ain't broke, don't fix it'. If you're already well known and recognised, and have invested heavily in marketing and promoting your brand name, you really want to think twice about it. The expense of getting a new name and rebranding everything can be huge and take you away from the real task of finding more customers and getting more business.

Consider changing your name if

- ✔ You've had complicated and negative legal or media issues that have seriously damaged your brand, whether inside or outside your control.

- ✔ You need to move with market forces and add a range of new services or products, and your current name no longer works for you.

- ✔ You didn't invest wisely in getting the right name, logo and positioning in the first place, and you don't feel it projects the professionalism you'd like.

- ✔ The competition forces you to consider a name change for legal reasons or public perception issues.

Before making a decision to change, work out how much it's going to cost you (both in time and money) and what reasonable return on investment you can expect.

Choosing a name for your products and services

Your business name isn't the only thing that needs attention when choosing a name. You don't want a great name and then boring product names. If you have lots of products, consider how their names fit with the business name.

The car industry does the naming process quite well. For example, Holden has 12 different makes, including the Holden Commodore, Holden Rodeo, Holden Ute, Holden Cruz, Holden Epica, Holden Barina, Holden Caprice and the Holden Combo.

If you happen to manufacture a range of products in your business, I again suggest getting professional help.

Chapter 6

Creating Your Visual Brand Identity

In This Chapter

▶ Getting a knockout visual brand to start with

▶ Giving your brand a refresh

▶ Keeping branding consistent

▶ Designing a great logo

▶ Producing great marketing materials

You've got a great name, so now it's time to turn it into a great-looking design and logo. Now is not the time to cut corners and do it on the cheap. Getting someone to create your design and logo properly for you is definitely worthwhile.

I'm often asked by small-business owners for an opinion on their logo and marketing materials. Straightaway I can tell whether they've been done by a pro or they're a homegrown job. Once I was even asked for an opinion on a homespun logo drawn up on an Excel spreadsheet! Of course I was diplomatic but he went away with the business cards of two fantastic graphic designers I recommended.

Every time people see your logo, business card, letterhead, website, marketing materials and even your invoices, they're forming an impression of the professionalism of your business. If they see tired and overused images or misspelled words on your website it seriously affects their willingness to buy — and to recommend you to others.

In this chapter, you discover how to create a professional, eye-catching logo, sales brochures and other point-of-sale materials, and how to get them all fitting together nicely so you stand out from the crowd.

Visual Identity for a Start-Up Business

If your business is just getting started and you're reading this book, great! Here you discover how to avoid wasting money on bad designs or ending up with something you didn't plan on.

It all starts with knowing what you want and don't want when it comes to design, but also what you actually need to get your business off the ground. Go through this checklist to work out what you need:

- Advertising templates
- Business cards
- Document or proposal templates and folders
- E-newsletter templates
- Invoice
- Letterhead
- Logo design (with or without tagline)
- Office or shop fit-outs
- Point-of-sale stands
- Posters and poster holders
- Presentation templates
- Product packaging
- Promotional giveaways such as umbrellas, pens, notepads, fridge magnets
- Promotional postcards
- Sales brochures and brochure holders
- Signage
- Thank-you card
- Uniforms
- Vehicle decals
- Website
- With-compliments slip

If you've got limited funds, as most start-ups do, you can just get the essentials to begin with and then add a few new items as you require them. However, it may end up cheaper in the long run to acquire as many items as possible up-front.

Once you know what materials you want, you need to find the right person to produce them for you. I cover this in the section 'Producing Great Marketing Material' later in this chapter.

Refreshing Your Brand for a Growth Business

If you've been in business a while, you can use the checklist from the previous section to have a think about what items you don't currently have that might help promote your business. If you're keeping your brand name and logo, but it's looking a bit tired, I recommend using a graphic designer to refresh it and to gradually integrate it into different items when you replenish old stock as it runs out. I don't believe in just ditching all the old stuff unless it's seriously sending out the wrong message about your business.

Many of the big businesses that have been around a while constantly refine their logos to ensure they remain current and fresh. Our much-loved and iconic ABC (Australian Broadcasting Corporation) has had many logo evolutions in its 75-plus years of operation. Shown in Figure 6-1 (left to right), are logos from 1965, 1985 and 2001.

Figure 6-1:
The ABC has refreshed its logo many times over the years.

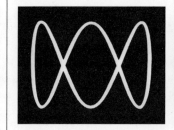

Creating Brand Consistency

I once did a brand audit for a department within a big investment bank. I asked them to lay out on the table every business card, letterhead, brochure, proposal document and promotional item they had been using in the last year. I'd estimate there were about 30 items lying on the table.

The result? We discovered three variations of the logo, all printed in five different shades of blue, ten different font types, 20 different colours and varying styles of imagery, charts and graphs. There was absolutely no consistency and anyone looking at these items would have been forgiven for assuming they came from 30 different companies. Subconsciously or even consciously, this inconsistency seriously had to affect their customers' willingness to buy.

Creating strong brand recognition — and, therefore, customer predisposition towards it — comes from ensuring all your promotional items, from your business cards to your website, and even the shape and design of your products, fit neatly together to form an overall impression of uniformity and consistency. In fact, your goal is to get so well recognised in all aspects of your visual identity that, if your logo was removed, the customer would still know that it belonged to your company. Ponder this. If the Coca-Cola logo was removed from a Coke bottle would you still know it was a Coke bottle? If the Boost logo was removed from a Boost juice store, would you still know it was Boost?

As you develop your brand identity, listen for subtle or even direct feedback on your brand or even ask for customer feedback. Every 12 months, take stock of the brand, do an audit (read on), get rid of old promotional materials that no longer fit and make sure everything is still fresh.

Doing a brand and image audit

Doing an audit is a good idea if you feel things are a bit out of hand and you know your look and image isn't as slick as it could be. Start by gathering everything you can find and then get everyone in your business to complete the audit with you. If you don't have staff, a critical third-party eye is a good idea. Ask yourself the questions in Table 6-1 and then note down things to improve.

Table 6-1				Conducting a Brand Audit
Brand or Image Question	*Yes*	*N/A*	*No*	*How Can We Improve?*
Is our brand look and image as good as it could be?				
Is our brand and logo appropriate for our business?				
Does our brand reflect our business vision and target client?				
Is our signage appropriate?				
Is our stationery (letterhead, invoicing, business cards) appropriate?				
Does our office presentation (reception, offices) reflect the appropriate brand image?				
Do our people (presentation and service or phone standards) reflect the appropriate image?				
Is our website branded appropriately? Do we need a refresh?				
Are our newsletters well branded with well-written content?				
Are our seminar presentations and proposals professional, clean and well branded?				

(continued)

Table 6-1 *(continued)*

Brand or Image Question	Yes	N/A	No	How Can We Improve?
Are our sales materials and brochures professional, well written and well branded?				
Do we have an audio logo (what you and your team say when people ask what you do)?				
Do we apply our brand (colours, fonts, logos, layouts) consistently across all our communications?				
Are all our letters and other correspondence professional and do they reflect the brand and image we want to portray?				
Is our clients' brand experience (through service, follow-up and communications) always a consistent and positive one?				

Developing a style guide

One thing that really helps you keep your business looking sharp is a simple style guide. A *style guide* outlines how all current and future promotional pieces will look to ensure consistency. When you get your logo and items designed, your graphic designer should put this style guide together for you. It will outline your preferred:

✔ **Colour palette:** A range of colours to use that complement each other. I recommend two or three colours to be used consistently in your brand and logo, and then a range of five or six further colours or shades to use on your website and brochures. Invoices and other workaday stationery might use a monocolour version (usually black) of your logo.

✔ **Imagery:** Types and styles of images to use, whether people, photos, contemporary or abstract images or even cartoons.

✔ **Logo:** Size, colours (including exact PMS colour identifiers) and layout of your logo for your business cards, letterhead and stationery. This is important so printers get it right every time.

✔ **Stock:** Paper type, weight and colour for letterhead and business cards.

✔ **Typefaces and sizes:** The style of the type to use for letterhead, your website, business cards and brochures. You might also hear a *typeface* described as a *font*.

Your style guide should be used by everyone in your business and given to suppliers such as designers, manufacturers and printers. Be sure to give your style guide to your website developer to ensure the web design is coordinated with the rest of your printed materials. Every time you complete a new promotional piece make sure it's checked against your style guide before it hits the printers or gets put up online.

Uniformity and brand extension

If your business offers a range of products or services that require their own unique identity, thinking about how they fit with the range and how to maintain uniformity alongside that unique image is important. Again, find a graphic designer who really knows his stuff and can extract the right information from you so that you end up with exactly what you're looking for (I give you more on this in the section 'Getting a Great Logo' next in this chapter).

The Australian Broadcasting Corporation, for example, has a number of services targeted at various markets, like Triple J, Dig Music, ABC1, ABC2, ABC for Kids and ABC Local Radio sports program Grandstand. Each of these has its own brand and unique identity. Figure 6-2 shows a few of these logos, Grandstand being the most like the standard ABC logo and ABC for Kids illustrating a fitting adaptation. The Triple J logo has pretty much nothing in common with that of its parent organisation because it represents the ABC's youth radio network and caters to a strongly alternative market — marching to a different drum.

Extending your brand and image to different divisions of your business is where your style guide is critical. Without it you may end up with a mishmash affair that just confuses your customers.

Figure 6-2:
The ABC has logos for each division of its business, such as ABC for Kids, the Triple J youth radio network and ABC Grandstand.

Getting a Great Logo

The two essential ingredients for getting a great logo are knowing what you want and finding a great graphic designer. I've had a number of business owners tell me they've been disappointed with what their graphic designer has 'come up with' for their logo. My question? Were you clear on what you wanted in the first place? Most often the answer is no. If you don't know what you want, how is your designer supposed to know? Sure, you want a graphic designer who'll push your boundaries and give you options you'd never thought of, but she still needs some clear guidelines on what you expect to see.

Here's how I suggest you do your homework to work out what you like and what you want:

✔ Pull out your collection of business cards from other companies (if you actually still keep them and haven't ditched them after putting them in your database) and select the ones with great logos that you like.

✔ Check out your favourite small-business (and big-business) websites, taking a critical look at their logos and design work to show your designer.

✔ Collect brochures, flyers, postcards and packaging that you like. If you need shopfront signage or car decals, for example, take photos.

✔ Identify in priority order the items you need and determine how much you're realistically able to spend.

✔ Think about the colours, fonts, styles and images you like, and why.

✔ Prepare yourself with a one-page summary of your business plan that highlights your target market, goals, objectives, strategies and vision for the business.

The nudie juice story

Tall Tim Pethick is the entrepreneur behind the much-loved Australian juice and smoothie brand, nudie. In late 2002, after many years working across three continents as CEO for LookSmart and in roles at Encyclopedia Britannica and Microsoft Network, Tim decided to jump ship and do something entirely different — to use his skills to build his own enterprise and create a product that would bring a smile to people's faces every day!

Tim went through a process to discover where the market opportunity was and how he would position the product. He was a big fan of fruit and fruit juice and was inspired many years ago by a US juice brand, US Fantasia. He wanted to shake up the Australian bottled juice market that he knew was dominated by the big players: Berri, Spring Valley and Coca-Cola. He knew his juice brand had to be *fun* and, at the same time, be universally acceptable across all ages and cultures. It also had to be a product that people would buy every day and even multiple times a day, and a brand that could be built without the use of expensive mainstream advertising, through customer advocacy and loyalty.

Within two and half years, and despite a devastating arson attack, nudie was selling 130,000 bottles a week across 4,500 stores and turning over $18 million per year. After all this, nudie was named as one of the top ten most influential Asia–Pacific brands!

Tim kindly shares these tips with you on how to go about building a brand:

✔ If you're starting from scratch, you want to be big and are up against big competitors, invest in getting a clever creative agency on board straightaway — not just a graphic designer. An agency can help with everything from naming to logo to packaging, messaging and more. My company came up with 280 names, which was narrowed down to about 15, one of which was 'nude'. Then the creative director suggested 'nudie' — and that was it!

✔ In choosing a name, make sure that it says something about the product, you can own the name and there are no other names like it. It must be able to be trademarked and the domain names must be available.

✔ Always look for the emotional hook in your branding and positioning of the product. It's about the experience you provide, not about the product attributes. My company really wanted to be humorous and irreverent, almost like the Virgin brand.

In 2006, just three years after launching nudie, Tim sold the business, which is still going strong with nudie juice, nudie smoothies and nudie crushies being sold across the country by the likes of McDonald's and Gloria Jean's. Check out www.nudie.com.au and you'll see what a really fun brand nudie still is.

Tall Tim is now an entrepreneur at large, a brand guru and a sought-after speaker and consultant with a string of new brands under way. For more information on Tim check out www.talltim.com.au.

What you get out of the process of designing a logo comes from what you put in. Don't just rock up to a graphic designer unprepared.

Choosing the best graphic designer

Finding the right graphic designer for your logo isn't always easy. Some designers tend to have their own view or perspective on design and may be great at designing logos and printed materials, but not so good at understanding how it might work online or on packaging. Here are some ideas to stake out the best graphic designer:

- ✔ Talk to your friends in business with great brands and logos, and ask if they would recommend their graphic designer.

- ✔ Contact the owners of logos and brands of other small businesses that you like from cards or websites you've seen or collected along the way.

- ✔ Search online for graphic designers in your local area and check out their own logos and brands. If you don't like what they have for themselves, then they're probably not for you. They should also have a portfolio of work you can preview online.

- ✔ Read marketing, advertising and graphic design magazines such as *Marketing* and *B&T* (also available online) and find a designer from their directories and ads.

- ✔ Check out the Australian Graphic Design Association (read on for the web address) for a list of designers and find one from there.

- ✔ Another option for design is to outsource globally to designers in other countries through online sites (which are listed next). Knowing what you want and expect is particularly important if you do this.

For a list of registered professional graphic designers visit www.agda.com.au. To outsource your design and all other marketing services at low competitive prices check out www.elance.com.

If you're building a business with a big online presence or are, in fact, going to *be* an online business, I suggest you take a whole different approach and start by looking for a website developer first. They usually work with great designers who understand online design really well.

Creating a clear brand brief

When you've identified a handful of graphic designers you think can do the job for you, meet up with at least three and get quotes before selecting the best one. This may seem tedious but it gives you peace of mind that you're getting the best person on board. Your graphic designer is someone you want to build a long-term relationship with, as you'll always have little jobs (or big jobs) that will no doubt need quick turnaround.

When you first meet the graphic designer, make sure that you like the person, and are confident of his expertise and ability to deliver. He'll show you his portfolio of work and then should take a good brief from you and ask many questions — and, most importantly, listen. He'll most likely ask questions like:

- How did you find out about us? What do you like about what we do?
- What is your business vision, goals and objectives?
- What are your brand values and personality?
- Who is your target market?
- What other logos, brands and designs do you like?
- What items do you need designed?
- For each item, what are the specifics you require?
- How many of each item do you need?
- What colours do you love?
- What images and typefaces do you love?
- What is your budget?
- When do you want this by?
- Are you getting competitive quotes?
- What's most important to you to appoint us for this job?

Getting what you pay for

After your meetings with potential designers, they'll come back to you with what they understand you want, in a proposal outlining costs, deliverables and timelines. When you get the proposals back, don't just choose the cheapest option. Ask them for some references and check them out before making a decision.

No general rule exists for what you should pay for graphic designers. Usually their experience and quality of work dictates their hourly rate. Try to negotiate a fixed fee for a certain number of items as a package. That way you know what you're up for.

Producing Great Marketing Material

A great logo is just the start. To get the message out far and wide, you need some knockout promotional items like sales brochures and a website to ensure you make an impact. Apart from a graphic designer, some other essential service providers are definitely required in producing great marketing materials, including:

- **Copywriters:** The headline and images attract attention, but outstanding copy is what gets action. I don't recommend writing your own copy unless you have the skills. A good copywriter can make a world of difference to your marketing materials.

- **Creative advertising services:** If you need advertisements with compelling headlines, powerful imagery and great copy that will get the phones ringing, you may need the services of a small ad agency. Many publications and radio stations offer creative services for free if you advertise with them.

- **Printers:** Building a relationship with a good printer is important. Over time the printer will get to know your business and start to give you preferred pricing and service.

- **Product and package designers:** Designing actual products and packaging requires a different set of skills to, say, logo design. If you've got serious work to do in this regard, look for experienced package designers.

- **Promotional item producers:** If you plan on giving away pens, notepads, fridge magnets, umbrellas or even branded wine, you need to find someone to do this for you too.

- **Signwriting and car decal specialists:** You may want a shopfront sign or billboard, or have vans or cars that need branding work. Check out those you like and find out who did their work.

- **Website developer:** Your graphic designer may or may not have the website development skills to build you a great website and get you found well online. Check out Chapter 17 for information on developing a website.

The process of selecting these services is no different from that for selecting a graphic designer. Or you may find your designer can manage everything for you, from logo design to printing and delivery right to your door. You could also outsource all of this to a freelance marketing coordinator or employ someone in the business who has a mix of all these skills. And lucky you if you happen to have these skills yourself!

I can hear you saying, 'Ouch — I just don't have the money for all this stuff.' And I completely understand. I suggest you go through the proper process to work out what it would cost to get all these services done professionally. Then decide how important each one really is, how you might be able to stagger delivery and payments, and how you might fund the work.

You never get a second chance to make a good first impression!

Setting up your promotions toolkit

Every business should have what I call a *promotions toolkit*. It's the range of items you have on hand at all times to promote your business. My own toolkit includes my last book, business cards, postcards, referral cards, website and e-reports.

What goes in your toolkit depends entirely on what type of business you're in, who your target market is, where and how you serve them (such as your place or theirs) and, most importantly, how your customers look for information on products or services like yours.

An accountant's marketing priorities will most likely include a professional range of business stationery, presentation and proposal templates, and an informative website. A mechanic's priority may be workshop signage, business cards and a flyer listing his services and pricing. A plumber's priorities may include van decals, fridge magnets and a classified ad in the local paper. A restaurant's priorities may be fit-out and furniture, menus, business cards and stylish aprons.

The Tap Doctor is a good example of how to use a vehicle as a great promotional tool. Check out its website (in colour) at www.tapdoctor.com.au (shown in monotone in Figure 6-3).

Go back to the list in the section 'Visual Identity for a Start-Up Business' earlier in this chapter and make your own list of the marketing and promotional items you may need.

One thing most businesses can't afford not to have is a website and online presence. I devote the whole of Part V to online marketing. If you can't wait to find out why you need a website and how to go about getting one, leap ahead now.

Figure 6-3:
The Tap
Doctor's
website
includes lots
of features
of good
marketing.

Business stationery

Your business card is not merely a piece of cardboard to tell people your company name and where they can find you. It can be a powerful marketing tool to get people saying, 'Wow, I want to find out more about these guys and take a look at their website.' Or it can be so bland that people just throw it in the bin and forget all about you. Here are some ideas to make your business card stand out:

✔ Include your photo on the front or use a visual image of some kind.

✔ Make it bright, bold and friendly.

✔ Use the back of the card — you can list your services, include an inspirational quote, or use it to record appointment times or referrals to others.

✔ Make sure your name and contact details stand out and are easily read.

✔ Give yourself a creative title like Chief Cook and Bottle Washer or The Boss to make people smile, rather than using, say, Company Director.

✔ Consider using a fridge magnet as an alternative to your business card.

 Keep your business card standard size, as people may find it frustrating if it doesn't fit in their business card holder or wallet (if they still use those things).

Of course, the business card is just one item in the stationery suite to consider. Letterhead, a fax cover sheet, with-compliments slip, thank-you card and invoice in print and/or electronic format are necessary too. You have a lot of scope to use all of these items creatively to brand and promote your business. In fact, I always joke that your invoice is the best marketing tool you have, because it's the one thing you can guarantee will be read from front to back!

 Consider how Max Macey, a public relations consultant, might use his invoices for marketing purposes. Max has a well-branded invoice that lists his full services. On it he offers a 5 per cent discount for invoices paid seven days before the due date. He has a statement that says: 'Thank you very much for your patronage. If you've enjoyed working with us, your referral would be our biggest compliment.' Max never emails his invoice and always mails it in a brightly coloured envelope. In the envelope he also includes another business card and a friendly handwritten thank-you card. Max finds it's a fantastic way to get invoices paid on time and to remind his customers that he is always keen for new business. If you don't ask, you don't get! And it really is how you ask that counts.

Sales brochures

Sales brochures and flyers are not merely pieces of paper telling people all about who you are and what you do. The best sales brochures include the following:

✔ **A powerful headline that is thought-provoking or funny, and benefit-driven:** If you run a kids' tennis-coaching clinic you could use something like, 'Need the kids out of your hair these school holidays?'

✔ **Simple, direct and well-written copy that lists the features and benefits of your services and packages:** The tennis-coaching clinic would include details of the clinics and benefits such as lunch provided, fun activities the kids will do, skills they will learn, free T-shirt and sunscreen, and even a money-back guarantee if your kids don't have fun.

✔ **Great, fun and professional images:** The tennis-coaching clinic might include photos of kids from previous clinics, with their coach playing tennis or everyone eating lunch together.

✔ **Testimonials, which are statements from customers recommending you:** The tennis-coaching clinic brochure could include statements from parents and kids about how much fun they had and how much their tennis skills improved.

✔ **Case studies or real-life stories of how your product or service helped someone:** The tennis-coaching clinic might profile a kid who has been to the annual tennis camp for years and has gone on to become an A-grade player and medal winner.

✔ **A call to action that will get people ringing up to find out more:** You could include a discounted early-bird booking price or a free gift for the first 20 customers, or the opportunity to win something in a competition. The tennis clinic might have a well-known tennis player come to give a talk one day and sign T-shirts or they might award a tennis racquet to the most improved player of the clinic.

✔ **Your contact details and how to purchase:** You could include a tear-off slip to mail in for more information, a 1300 or 1800 freecall number to call, a reference to your website and even a form to fill out to provide credit card details. The tennis-coaching clinic includes the 1300 number printed boldly across the flyer in a number of places.

Whether you decide to use a 1800 or a 1300 number is up to you and how much you can afford. Check out this website for details on the difference between the two and how they can be used to generate more enquiries. www.1300-1800-numbers.com.au.

In determining if you need a sales brochure at all, work out how your customers best like to find out about the kind of services you provide. A family divorce lawyer, for example, probably won't want a sales brochure. She'd be better to get a great business card that clearly directs people to her website, which lists her services and provides valuable articles, information and links for people to help them through the divorce process.

Other businesses may need to invest in something far meatier than a simple sales brochure. If you happen to own a business that sells promotional T-shirts you'd probably need to produce a printed catalogue.

If possible, however, don't go overboard on printing — save trees by directing people to a website. A website can quickly and easily be updated and prevents the possibility of you having outdated printed material taking up valuable shelf space.

Promotional items and giveaways

Everyone loves something for free.

I was at a fete recently and a local real estate business had sponsored a jumping castle where kids could jump for free. While they were 'jumping for free' the staff were talking to parents and handing out free caps and drink bottles (branded of course), and collecting their names and email addresses to send them a free property report. I like this kind of marketing. The kids get to have fun, the adults get some free stuff (most likely for the kids) and then get sent some valuable information on what the local real estate market is doing. It's fun for everyone and it allows the real estate agent the opportunity to have a chat and get to know people without going into hard-sell mode.

> *There's no such thing as a free lunch.*
>
> —*Milton Friedman (1912–2006), American economist and public intellectual*

Promotional items and giveaways are great methods of keeping your brand in front of people — hats, pens, T-shirts, chocolates, calendars, umbrellas, mugs, mouse pads, notepads, sticky notes, stubby holders — the list goes on. Literally thousands of ideas and options are out there.

The important thing is to find something that is the right fit for your business and to be creative. If you own a lingerie shop, a stubby holder probably wouldn't work but a lovely branded washing bag for the lingerie would.

And you can choose from literally thousands of companies that can source and brand just about any promotional item you can think of. Check out the range via a web search on the phrase 'promotional items', set yourself a budget and find something that is different and would really appeal to your customers.

Sales support kits

If you're a solo operator, you're most likely also the salesperson for your business. Another fancy term for this person is the business development manager. No matter what the title, whether you're the one that needs to bring in the bacon or whether you have salespeople on board, having the sales tools on hand to help guide you through the sales process when you're speaking to customers is important.

When I needed new gutters and a rainwater tank, I got three quotes. The company that won the job was the one that had a professional salesperson on board with a sales toolkit. He started the process by asking me lots of questions about my current guttering. He then showed me samples of the three different gutters and a palette of colour options, and then he whipped out a mini DVD player to show me a five-minute presentation on how guttering works and how to know if it really needs replacing. He handed me a simple well-designed brochure that included customer testimonials, and then measured up and completed the quote on the spot on a professional order pad. The other two guttering providers rocked up with not even a business card in their hands! Which one would you have chosen?

In a competitive marketplace where consumers are becoming more and more discerning, they want to deal with businesses that have a professional sales approach and sales tools to help guide them through the decision-making process.

Dressing up the sales kit

My local costume hire shop, Christina's Costumes, has a great sales tool. You've got a fancy dress party to go to, the theme is disco. You're lucky to remember that era, let alone have any clothes that might work.

Enter Christina's. You tell her the theme and she guides you through her catalogue with photos of literally hundreds of outfits, and their hire costs and sizes. You narrow down your disco outfit selection to five possibilities, try them all on, select one and happily walk out

knowing you'll feel fabulous burning up the dance floor.

Christina's catalogue is also on her website (www.christinascostumes.com.au) so you can browse through and enquire about costume availability before you drop into. Christina's sales toolkit (the costume catalogue) and her personal service are the keys to helping her customers make a buying decision and keeping them coming back.

Sales tools are there to help you communicate the most important messages to your customers and to help guide them to make a sound decision. What do you need in your sales support kit?

Office and shop fit-outs, uniforms and signage

If you're a business owner with an office, retail store or showroom that customers regularly visit, it's important to put some effort into your fit-out, signage and layout.

Your ideal target market and brand positioning should again be at the heart of how you look. For example, visit any Two Dollar Shop or some small local hardware stores and you'd be forgiven if you feel things seem a bit unruly. That's all part of their brand and their charm. They're designed for people who like to drop in and potter around, seeking out the best bargains. A professional slick image would deter the bargain hunters who are their ideal customers.

On the other hand, the dentist with old-fashioned premises, peeling paint, and antiquated computer and dental equipment might give people the impression he's also not that up-to-date on the latest dental practices. I wouldn't let a dentist like that go anywhere near my mouth, no matter how much expertise he has!

Some or all of these items will need to work together to give an overall impression of professionalism:

- Equipment — cash registers, computers, printers
- Furniture — desks, chairs, coffee tables, meeting tables, work stations
- Merchandise layout — shelves and racks
- Paintings and art
- Reception desk and reception area
- Service counters
- Signage
- Storage — filing cabinets, fridges, storerooms
- Uniforms
- Wall colours and lighting
- Water cooler or coffee machine
- Window displays

Plenty of companies specialise in office and store fit-outs. If you're just starting up or need a refresh, check out other premises you like that appear to be talking to the same target market as yours and find out who did theirs. Also do an online search to find a local company and review its portfolio. Of course, if money is limited and you need to do it yourself, it would be worth paying for a few hours of consulting time with an interior designer or specialist to get her to map out a simple plan and list what you need and where to get it before ploughing ahead.

Point-of-sale displays

Point-of-sale display items are promotional pieces used to enhance the way your product stands out among the competition. Here are some examples:

- A manufacturer of a beautiful skincare range distributed through pharmacies might provide a branded stand for the products to sit on.

- A portrait photographer who promotes himself at local shopping centres needs a stand and boards to showcase his work.

- A professional speaker and author needs roll-up banners, product order forms and a stand for her books.

- A manufacturer of olive oils and dips who sells at the local markets needs tasting tools, signage and a menu board with prices.

- A distributor of baby foods to organic stores might need shelf-talkers (little cards that sit out from the shelf under the product).

- A business that sells caravans at motor shows and expos needs an exhibition stand, signage, a computer, brochures and much more.

Your marketing plan might call upon you to take your business to the people rather than waiting for the people to come to you. If that's the case, then you'll definitely need point-of-sale displays to attract your audience.

Other marketing material

A myriad of marketing materials are available that might go into your marketing toolkit, such as direct mail letters, letterbox flyers, postcards and banners. Some marketing materials work forever and only require refreshing from time to time. For example, I know of a pest controller who says his very best marketing weapon is his fridge magnets, and he's been using them for ten years. Some marketing materials work for a period of time and then for some reason just don't work anymore. I know a real estate agent who has stopped letterbox drops after doing them for eight years because she's found much more effective marketing tactics.

Chapter 7

Brand You

*Y*ou are the face of your business and the buck stops and starts with you. A powerful, cheap (yay!) way to market your business is to market yourself. Just think of yourself as a brand, Brand You. Richard Branson (Virgin), Dick Smith (Electronics, Foods), John McGrath (Real Estate), Janine Allis (Boost), Naomi Simson (RedBalloon Days) are all incredibly successful entrepreneurs who have used their own names and personalities to promote themselves and their companies. You can do the same.

Before you come up with excuses like 'but I'm not Richard Branson' or 'I don't have enough time', remember, if you choose not to build Brand You, you're potentially throwing away a relatively inexpensive and fun (yes, please believe me) way to get more business and bring in more bucks. If you don't promote Brand You, you can bet one of your competitors will promote herself and corner the market.

In this chapter, I talk about what Brand You really is, how to overcome any misgivings you may, quite understandably, have about self-promotion and how to get started. Although working on Brand You is guaranteed to take you outside your comfort zone at times, it is personally rewarding and fulfilling.

You Are a Brand

People buy you first and what you have to sell second, whether you're an accountant or happen to sell widgets. They make an immediate assessment of you, whether you like it or not. And they continue to scrutinise your appearance and performance during the course of your dealings with them. If the truth be told, you're probably making an assessment of them too. Do they really look and sound like they're likely to buy (and keep buying) from you?

As the CEO of your business, your most important job is to be head marketer for Brand You.

Putting your best face forward

You are the face of your business. Everyone you meet will be checking out:

- What clothes, shoes and accessories you're wearing
- How well groomed you are
- How warmly you greet them and shake their hand
- Your posture and body language
- What you say and how you say it
- What's unique about you and if you stand out
- Your expertise, experience, knowledge and work history
- How interesting (and interested) you are
- How well you listen and respond to their needs

Having said all that, don't manufacture yourself into something that's not the real you. A girlfriend of mine recently had an image consultant give her a makeover and dress her in an expensive suit. She ended up looking and feeling like a matronly corporate executive. Needless to say, the suit was thrown away and she swore never to wear a suit again! People prefer to deal with someone who's the genuine article and doesn't try to be someone she's not.

Promoting your business

If you get Brand You in tip-top shape and feel really good about yourself, you'll have all the confidence you need to get out there and press the flesh (or your computer button) and make an impact. You can find lots of inexpensive ways to use Brand You to promote your business, and many, but not all, may take you out of your comfort zone and involve putting yourself in front of your target audience. Check out the ideas in Table 7-1.

Table 7-1   Ideas for Different Businesses to Promote Brand You

Business Type	Promotional Idea
Image consultant	Giving a presentation to girls and their mothers at local private schools
Mortgage broker	Publishing a mini e-book on how to find the best mortgage
Women's fashion store	Modelling your clothes at a school fundraiser fashion parade
Website developer	Writing a regular column for an online media company
Accountant	Running mini seminars for people on how to read a profit and loss (P&L) statement
Travel consultant	Hosting educational travel evenings
Café owner	Hosting a regular breakfast for other local business owners
Training company	Publishing a regular blog on how to get results from staff training programs
Property investment adviser	Getting a regular segment on an investment program on TV
Drycleaner	Networking by attending regular chamber of commerce events

Brand You, On the Inside

Perhaps the toughest part of getting Brand You humming along and working for you is getting it right on the inside. By that I mean understanding your deepest motivations, why you're special and how you can personally make a difference to your prospective customers. At the risk of repeating myself, people buy you first and what you have to sell second.

When promoting your business generally or a product or service you offer, it may be easy to promote the features, benefits and compelling reasons for your customers to buy. But can you sell yourself just as well? Know thyself and it's easy to sell thyself!

People need to know you, like you and trust you, and get a feeling for your personal motivations, expertise and experience before they're completely comfortable buying from you. So it pays to understand Brand You on the inside and get comfortable talking about yourself (not too much though).

Defining your passions, visions and goals

If you're clear about your personal passions, visions and goals, and are able to communicate them with enthusiasm, you'll win over the most sceptical prospective customer. I talk about this extensively in Chapters 1 and 4, so you may want to flick back and review some of the questions, such as:

✔ Why am I in business?

✔ What is the vision for my business?

✔ What am I passionate about and what are my strengths?

✔ What values do I hold?

Now find a trusted adviser (preferably no-one related to you and preferably another business owner who knows you well) and get that person to answer the same questions about you. By now you should feel pretty good about yourself and have a good idea about why you're such a special and unique individual!

Standing out from the crowd

Oscar Wilde once said, 'The only thing worse than being talked about, is not being talked about at all.' I'm guessing that he meant it pays to be real, to stand out and make a statement, regardless of what people think of you, because that's when people remember you (and talk about you).

When you're done soul searching to discover Brand You on the inside, it's time to find your own special uniqueness. Review the answers to the questions in the earlier section 'Defining your passions, visions and goals' and identify what makes you different from every other competitor in the marketplace. Choose the answers you think will have most appeal to your prospective customers. These *points of difference* — that is, those aspects of what you can offer prospective customers that differentiate you from the rest — now become your key talking points.

Overcoming any weak points

Identifying your strengths and uniqueness, and what your business has to offer that will appeal to your customers, is a great starting point. But what about your weaknesses? It pays to understand your weaknesses, too, and be ready to fill deficiencies with good people who complement your skills. In the process, you help to build Brand You.

You can't risk Brand You being damaged in the event that you can't deliver in an area that's critical to your relationship with customers and potential customers.

Putting the customer first

Mary, a mortgage broker I worked with once, started her broking business after many years working as a nurse. She wanted to work flexible hours from home so she could care for her two young children. After a very bad experience, when a mortgage broker had sold her the wrong home loan, which ended up costing her dearly, she realised a need existed for mortgage brokers who put the interests of the customer before making a quick sale.

Mary had a real passion to grow a successful business that would enable her to live comfortably. Her unique points of difference were her integrity, her sixth-sense ability to question, listen and analyse a client's needs, her client-for-life philosophy, her care for the environment and her support for the less fortunate. She brought all these personal qualities to her business.

As a result, Mary has won many new clients. She also gives 5 per cent of her commissions to environmental and local community charities.

For example, if you're not good at public speaking and you fear it more than death, don't do it unless you can acquire the skills beforehand. A bad public-speaking performance can do untold damage to Brand You and your business. So, if you get asked to do a speaking gig, tell them you'd love to be there and you'll bring along someone else from your team who is a knowledgeable and dynamic speaker on the topic. If you don't have someone suitable, find someone quickly and be there on the night to co-host the talk. Find a friend or employee who is an enigmatic speaker, knows the topic well and has a good knowledge of your business and what you offer. Or you may even pay someone to speak on your behalf.

 I'm a big believer in not focusing too hard on trying to constantly eliminate your weaknesses (unless it's in an area that is critical to your business success, such as financial management). If you spend too much time trying to sharpen up your weaknesses, your strengths could become diminished, and then you risk the possibility of becoming mediocre at everything! This is definitely not going to help you stand out in a cluttered marketplace.

Brand You, On the Outside

After you identify what makes you special on the inside, it's time to polish yourself up on the outside. A quick glance and three seconds flat is all it takes for people to pass judgement (wrongly or rightly) on you.

People who observe you check out what brand of watch you're wearing, how well groomed and manicured you are and whether your clothes were bought some time this century. These people assess your poise and posture, the way you smile and greet them, and whether you look them in the eye. They make a mental note of your diction and the language you use, and how positively and engagingly you express yourself. All these factors affect their willingness to engage with you and the likelihood of you making them your next customers.

As you gain confidence in yourself, you gain confidence in your image. You learn how to put your best foot forward while never compromising your own unique style.

By now you might be thinking you're long overdue for a bit of a makeover. Don't worry, you don't have to go out and spend thousands on the latest Armani suit. You may just need a fresh look. Every five to ten years a house needs painting and new appliances need to be installed because old ones wear out. Humans are no different.

If you feel you need a head-to-toe makeover and have some money to spend, you may like to consider paying an image consultant who has a proven track record to do it with you. A personal consultation helps you avoid making expensive mistakes and saves you heaps of time in the process.

I can do no better than to direct you to a terrific website that allows you to assess your appearance and grooming, courtesy of style queen and image consultant Elena Reed at www.evolutzia.com.au.

Image consultants are best found through word-of-mouth referral. Look out for the consultants that really make an impact on you — not just how they look but how they present and engage with you. Or do a web search to find a directory of image consultants in your area and visit at least three before making a decision. Ask them to show you their portfolios of other people they have 'made over' and ask for references.

Talking Up Brand You

Hands up if you've ever been to a networking event with other business owners and been asked the question, 'What do you do?' Put the other hand up if you've ever asked this question yourself. I bet there's not a business owner reading this book without both hands up.

Incidentally, 'What do you do?' is my favourite question. I just love hearing (and timing) people's answers. It's amazing how many people have such a boring response to this question and how quickly they launch into telling me about every service or product they offer in the vague hope that I'll be faintly interested. Half an hour later, I'm desperately trying to extract myself from this person's clutches; not once has he asked me one question about myself.

Too many business owners don't pay enough attention to their language or their responses to such a simple question. They miss the opportunity to really engage with the other person.

Another term I frequently use in talking up Brand You is *verbal branding*. By this I mean that what you say, even in seemingly casual conversation, is just as important as how you look. In fact, I believe it's even more critical and, for many business owners, is their biggest missed marketing opportunity.

Using positive can-do language

To demonstrate the power of positive language, here's a story about a real estate agent. I had turned up for an open inspection on a home that was for sale in my street. Of course, I had no intention of buying the home or even selling my own home; I was just curious to know how much the owners were asking for it so I could gauge what my own home might be worth.

The following day I received a call from the agent to see what I thought of the property and if I might be interested in purchasing it. When I said that I wasn't buying, he moved on to ask me if I owned my own home and if I had considered selling it? I told him I was actually going to be renovating and that I wasn't interested in either buying or selling.

By now, of course, I was expecting him to launch into his sales pitch to tempt me to get the home valued so that at least I would know what it was worth. But his response could have knocked me over with a feather. 'That's great. I really think now is a good time to hold on to such a home in your area. If you're looking for some great tradespeople to look after your renovations, I have a list of trustworthy local people I can recommend.'

Instead of trying to sell me something I didn't want, he listened to me, put my needs first and then used positive can-do, helpful language. Needless to say, when I do want to sell my home, he'll be the first agent I contact.

Next time you speak to someone, whether a customer, a family member or even the girl serving you at the bank, think of ways that you can help them, connect them to others or add value to their lives through positive language. You never know who is listening, who is watching and who remembers. And, believe me, your thoughtful actions will be repaid tenfold.

Answering simple questions

You're at that dreaded networking event. The first person you met when you walked in is still talking at you and hasn't asked you one question. She's looking over your shoulder for the next victim to bore, spots someone she knows and rushes off after pressing her (unasked for) business card into your hand.

Phew, you are thinking. Time to fill up my glass and get ready for the next attack. Then you meet Bruce, and this time the conversation is quite different. He asks you a whole bunch of questions:

- ✔ How are you tonight?
- ✔ What brings you here?
- ✔ What do you do?
- ✔ What services do you offer?
- ✔ Who is your ideal client?
- ✔ What do you love and hate about being in business?
- ✔ Is there anyone you would like to meet here?
- ✔ How's business at the moment?
- ✔ How can I help you in your business?
- ✔ What did you think of the speaker, the networking, today's media headlines, the story about ... ?

The most common question is, of course, 'What do you do?' And the most common response (and biggest mistake) people make is to answer it literally. 'I'm an accountant,' or 'I'm a mechanic.' But with some thought, a hint of fun and a bit of cheekiness, you could answer, 'I help business owners pay the tax man less money,' or 'I keep your car in tip-top shape.' You get the picture. Turn the answer to this simple question into something that shows them what you can do for them. And then turn the conversation back to them. 'Are you paying the tax man too much?' or 'Is your car in as good a condition as you would like?'

The second most common question is 'How's business?' Whether you're really busy and have lots of new business or whether you're desperate for more, think about how you answer this question. Don't lie, but don't go into negative mode and say you're too busy or that business is dead; tell the person that you've always got room for more clients. Open up the conversation and let him know what you need to help you grow your business. And then, of course, ask him how you can help him.

Be prepared. Write down and practise your answers to the questions I set out in this section. Next time you're networking, you'll have productive conversations. You'll make great new friends and may even find yourself a prospective new client in the process.

Perfecting the 30-second elevator pitch

Imagine you're going down in a lift with the CEO of the company you've been trying for ages to win over as a new client. You introduce yourself and the CEO asks you to tell her about your business. You've got just 30 seconds before you reach the ground floor to tell her who you are, what you do, who you do it for and how you can help her business. Oh, and get her to agree to a meeting with you.

What do you say? How do you say it? How do you get the CEO's business card? And, most importantly, how do you get her to agree to make time for a meeting in her very busy schedule?

Many business owners would have difficulty in clearly and passionately delivering a 30-second elevator pitch. They'd chat aimlessly about themselves and so risk losing the attention of the person they want to impress. The most important thing is to leave a positive impression, be different and be bold.

Again, just like you practise the answers to the various questions you might be asked, it's important to write down and practise your 30-second elevator pitch. You never know when you'll be asked to deliver it.

Stating clearly what you're about

In Chapters 2 and 19, I go into detail about the importance of having a powerful customer value proposition (CVP), great points of difference and clearly communicated benefits. A CVP is a clear and succinct statement of the value you offer your customers and, in my unique model, it answers ten clear questions. Be sure to visit the model in Chapter 2 and the hypothetical answers in Chapter 19, and have your answers prepared for when you are asked the questions or receive an invitation to give your 30-second elevator pitch.

Getting all your staff on board

As the CEO of Brand You, it's important you ensure your staff are just as effective in marketing your business as you are. They need to give off the same vibe as you and tell people the same things about your business and what they do. When your PA is asked what she does, you don't want her to simply answer, 'I'm a PA for John Smith.' You want her to say, 'I work with John Smith, the best PR agent in Australia, with a track record for getting consistently strong media coverage for our clients.'

Get all your staff around the lunchroom table and ask them to write down what they currently say when asked questions about your business. Then, as a team, work out the answers and get everyone comfortable with what you want them to say. Take them to some networking events and be a good role model for them. Give them feedback on how they talk up your business.

A business with five team members, each of whom gets asked five times a week what they do, could net you 260 new leads a year!

Ideas to Build Brand You

You look good, sound good and present like a pro. Along the way you've collected a whole lot of expertise and had some real wins with your clients. Now's the time to take Brand You out to the marketplace in a big way.

But how do you do it in a low-cost (preferably no-cost) way that gets you noticed and generates quality new business opportunities? Draw up a simple plan of attack that allows you to express your opinions and demonstrate your capabilities. In this section, I describe three of the most simple and effective ways to build Brand You.

Harnessing the power of the written word

Writing informative articles and publishing them in as many ways as you possibly can is a good start. See the 'Driving the message home' sidebar for an example of how publishing in different types of media has helped a driving instructor expand his client base.

Writing good-quality stories, articles, reports, advice columns (and even books) and then publishing them on the World Wide Web or in printed format is a powerful way to establish your expertise and get your message out to a broad audience.

If you're not good at writing text of this nature, find a professional writer who can help. People get to know you, like you and trust you if you regularly distribute well-written, informative publications.

Making a presentation

One way to get your message out is to make public presentations on your topic of expertise. It's a great way to give some valuable information to your target audience, make valuable connections with a large group at once and demonstrate that you know what you're talking about. I cover how to become a master presenter and how to get speaking gigs in detail in Chapter 15.

Your presentation must give your audience some valuable information and a clear direction on what to do, and get them asking questions. A good test of the impact you've made is the number of people who line up afterwards to have a one-on-one conversation with you.

Putting yourself in the media spotlight

Getting in the media and creating publicity for yourself, whether it's in the local paper, on TV or online media websites, is another great way to get Brand You out there to promote your business. I discuss how to get publicity in much more detail in Chapter 12.

Getting Brand You in the media spotlight is not easy but, once you get some traction, it's a mighty powerful way to prove your expertise in front of a massive audience and, best of all, it's free.

The main thing to consider is the image you want the media to convey about you, and the area of expertise you want to position yourself in.

Passion and a healthy dose of confidence helps when it comes to promoting yourself. It does take time and is personally very challenging, but the skills you develop will hold you in good stead for life, no matter what business or career you might find yourself in.

Driving the message home

John Harrow owns a driving school, No Crash Track, and teaches young people how to drive with confidence, skill and safety. He has a proven track record and none of his past students have ever failed their driving tests or had an accident in the two years after gaining their driver's licence. He prides himself on his follow-up and the ongoing training and support he gives his students. The parents of these students are equally as important; John knows it's vital to give them peace of mind and encouragement in how to handle their children during this important period in their lives.

To demonstrate his expertise and track record, John does the following:

- He's written an e-book entitled *Top Ten Ways to Ensure You Sleep at Night Once Your Children Get Their Driver's Licence*, which he offers for free to parents who subscribe to his website.

- John writes a monthly article that he sends out to people on his database. The articles include facts and figures on road safety and some tips on how to be a better driver.

- The same article is sent to other businesses that cater to the youth market and parents, which often publish it on their websites or send it out in their newsletters.

- John has his own Drive Safe opinion blog aimed at high school students that is linked to his website and other youth sites.

- He has produced a series of live mini video clips that show students driving under his tuition. He publishes them on his website and on YouTube and other websites.

- John gives a simple ten-page printed handbook with checklists and driving do's and don'ts to students, their parents and local community groups.

John has found that by writing, producing and distributing good-quality articles he has been able to win the confidence of parents and students alike.

Chapter 8

Creating a Grand Brand Experience

....

In This Chapter

▶ Being comfortable with selling

▶ Making first contact

▶ Landing the sale

▶ Getting your customer service program in place

▶ Assessing the customer experience

....

*W*hen it comes to your brand, first impressions do count and can win you business, but, if the experience doesn't back up the first impression or the promise you make to your customers, then you pretty soon find yourself out of business.

Looking good and presenting well is just the beginning. In this chapter, you find out how to give your customers a great experience from the time of first contact to making the sale and then delivering on what you promise. You also discover how to put in place a customer service program and how to go the extra mile for your customers so you keep them coming back and generating positive word-of-mouth business for you.

Everyone lives by selling something.

—*Robert Louis Stevenson (1850–1894), Scottish poet, novelist and essayist*

Understanding the sales process

I was once at an event where the speaker asked a room full of 80 small-business owners who was a salesperson. Surprisingly only 20 or so people put up their hands. Of course, if you're a business owner, you *are* a salesperson and, if you're not being a salesperson, then you're in trouble.

You've most likely bought a car at some stage. Think back to the experience you had with the salesman and what he did or didn't do to make the sale. Did he tell you about fuel economy and colour options and extras like sunroofs? Did he take you for a spin so you could really experience how fantastic the car was? Did he discount? Did he throw in any warranties, free rego or a first service free? I'm sure he did. Car salesmen, as much as you may dislike them (sorry to those car dealerships who may be reading this), know how to make a sale. They know how to get people interested, ask questions and explain their products well, even if some don't have the personal touch you may like.

All small-business owners can learn a thing or two from car salesmen. If you had their skills and added a big dose of your own unique, warm and authentic approach to the mix, just imagine what your strike rate might increase to!

The sales process is different for every business, depending on what you sell and how big the buying decision is for the customer. A decision to buy a $50 piece of costume jewellery is relatively simple for most people. Whereas the decision to buy a $10,000 engagement ring is probably a whole lot harder to make.

Another factor to consider in the sales process is the timeframe. I know of a consultant who had been having discussions with a big company for nigh on 12 months before the deal was actually signed. That's why it pays to have lots of qualified prospects and lots of irons in the fire, so you can end up saying no because you're too busy, instead of having to say yes (at any price) because you're dead quiet.

Generally, the sales process follows the model shown in Figure 8-1.

The prospecting part is what this book is really all about — marketing — or generating enough leads and interested prospects to generate enough enquiries to convert a significant percentage into sales.

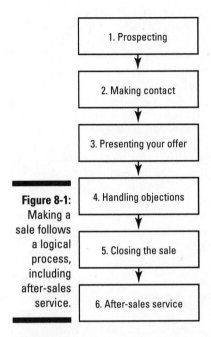

Figure 8-1:
Making a
sale follows
a logical
process,
including
after-sales
service.

Successful small-business owners train, empower, encourage and reward their staff for taking on the job of marketing and selling, even when it may be way out of the scope of their job description.

Lots of sales training courses and programs are available online. Do a web search for local courses or to find an online course. Some of the international masters of sales who've been around a while are Tom Hopkins, Brian Tracy, Zig Ziglar and Jack Daly, and they all have online programs and tools you can access to help with your sales skills.

Making First Contact

Whether you own a shopfront business or a professional service firm, the impact you create on prospective customers at first contact can mean the difference between them walking out or hanging around.

Recently I went to a big department store knowing specifically what I wanted to purchase in the clothing department. I went up to the counter to ask for help. No-one there. I walked around the floor looking for a sales assistant. Eventually I found one buried in the clothing racks, putting out new stock, not even looking up to see if any customers might need help. I asked her about the item I was looking for, only to be told, 'That's not my department. You'll need to see the girls at the desk over there.' I told her there was no-one at the desk. Her response? A shrug, saying, 'I'm sure someone will be there soon, you'll just have to wait.' I left the store to go to the competitor.

Of course, *you* would never treat your prospective customers like this, but do you know how your staff are treating your prospective customers? Remember, this is where the brand experience begins, and could well end.

You could actually be losing customers before they even get to have a conversation with you, and you may not even know it. Get your staff on board to ensure your brand is held in a positive light.

Welcoming walk-in prospects

How your staff greet and talk to prospective customers could be the difference between people moving from a 'just looking' to a 'why not, let's seriously think about it'.

Take the example of a pet store, Pampered Pets. You have an enticing window display (with cute little puppies and kittens) and a great offer (free puppy and kitten accessories and food). Lots of people walk in for a play, but very few people make serious enquiries. Buying a puppy or kitten is a decision not to be made lightly. Here are the things you and your staff need to make a responsible sale and a lasting brand experience:

- **To be well groomed and in uniform:** Pampered Pets aprons and caps, clean and neat.

- **A warm friendly smile and greeting:** 'Hi welcome to Pampered Pets. My name is Amy. How can I help you today?'

- **Good eye contact and questioning skills:** 'Have you owned a pet before? Do you have a suitable place for a puppy or kitten? Which breeds do you like?'

- **Expert knowledge:** A love of animals and a good knowledge of each pet, what they should eat, how to look after them, how much they cost, where to get booster vaccinations and so on.

✔ **Great product knowledge:** The ability to explain in a simple and engaging way the features and benefits of each pet, and your pricing and special offers.

✔ **Sales skills:** The skills to take customers from 'just looking' to interested and then to sale. Six-monthly sales training helps Pampered Pets staff stay on top of their game.

Check out Chapter 2 for information on the process of how customers move from awareness to purchase and *post-purchase analysis* (whether they've made the right decision in buying from you).

Calling prospects

If you happen to own a business such as a financial-planning practice, mortgage-broking business, consultancy or creative services firm, you're far less likely to rely on walk-by traffic to get more business. You most likely need to do some warm or *cold calling*, phoning prospective customers who you don't know. (I talk more about warm calling a little later on.)

Nothing is more annoying than getting a phone call from some unidentified person who doesn't even know your name just as you're about to sit down to dinner. No doubt, telemarketing, or cold calling, has a bad reputation. That's the reason the Do Not Call register has been established in Australia and New Zealand. But think about it; there must be some reason cold calling has become so prolific. Maybe it's working.

Most people break out in a cold sweat at the thought of having to do cold calls. Me too. Probably because of a fear of rejection or that you won't know what to say. Yet it's far more humiliating to be rejected by someone you know than by someone you don't. Why do we take it so personally?

Fear of rejection is a major reason why many businesses take the safe marketing option of advertising and letterbox drops, rather than cold calling or networking and other more personal approaches.

Here are some tips to get over the cold-calling hurdle:

✔ **Do your research:** Know who you're calling, what their company does and the person you need to speak to, and check out the company's website before calling.

✔ **Get past the gatekeeper:** Getting past the PA or receptionist to the prospect can be a tough one. Treat the PA with the same care and respect you would treat the prospect. Be pleasant, engage the person, ask questions and thank the person when you're done.

- ✔ **Write a script:** A script with the key points and benefits you need to get across helps keep you on track. Your opening sentence needs to establish who you are, what you're calling about and how long the call will take. Always ask if your prospect has time to speak now or if you should make a time to speak later.

- ✔ **Practise:** You only get one chance, so don't practise your script on the prospect. Practise it on a professional who will give you feedback and help you refine it. You could even go to a course on telemarketing or cold calling to refine your approach.

- ✔ **Make time for it:** Set yourself a goal to do 5 calls a day or 20 a week, whatever works for you. You'll only get good at it by doing it consistently.

- ✔ **Follow up:** You've made a call and got someone's interest, so don't let the opportunity slip through the cracks by not following up and delivering what you promised.

Check out the Telesales website for articles and information on its training techniques at www.telesalestraining.com.au.

Another option to cold calling is *warm calling*, which is when you make contact with a person you've connected with previously or someone who has been introduced to you by a third party. It's about re-establishing a relationship or using third-party relationships to get in front of your prospect.

Let's say you own a catering business and you really want to connect with the person who organises events at a big company down the road. The event organiser doesn't know you exist, but you happen to have a friend who works there in the accounts department. You ask her if she would be kind enough to make a call or send an email to introduce you to the event organiser. She does and, of course, you make contact the same day. Because you're creative, you follow up the call to the person with some of your world-famous muffins all packed up in a lovely box!

If someone is not interested in talking to you or buying from you, she's not rejecting *you*, she's rejecting your offer. Don't take it personally.

Writing to prospects

Writing a letter is another way to introduce your business to a prospective customer. The experience someone has when opening the letter, from the envelope to the quality of the paper, to the layout and tone of the letter, determines whether it gets tossed in the bin, kept in the filing tray or acted upon immediately.

When writing letters:

- ✔ Use professional letterhead on good paper stock.

- ✔ Use a subject headline to grab attention so they'll read on.

- ✔ Ensure the first sentence sums up your offer and the second and third paragraphs cover the who, what, why, where, when and how.

- ✔ Write in a tone and style that shows you care and understand their needs.

- ✔ Make your offer enticing by explaining its benefits and a special deal if they buy by a certain date.

- ✔ Keep the letter short (to one page) and make it clear and to the point.

- ✔ Be clear about what you actually want the customer to do.

- ✔ Make sure your contact details are bold and clear.

- ✔ Finish the letter by indicating that you will call them if they don't call you.

- ✔ Post the letter in a professionally and personally addressed envelope with your brochure and a business card (and, if budget permits, a gift).

Direct-mailing prospects

Direct mail is a form of one-to-one marketing that is the exact opposite of mass advertising and publicity. It involves sending addressed or unaddressed mail that includes letters, brochures, newsletters or offers directly to a targeted list of people.

Although direct mail can no doubt play a very important part in your marketing effort, it can be expensive, and to make it work you probably require the services of your creative agency or a direct mail specialist.

Many of the rules of developing good ads (see Chapter 10) also apply to direct mail. Here are a few other ingredients for a successful direct mail campaign:

- ✔ **Put together a target list of prospects.** This list can come from your own database of past customers or prospects, or you can buy lists by demography, geography or industry type, or even a combination. You could even create your own list of people by developing a list from online directory searches.

✔ **Develop a great offer.** You need to spend some time working on your offer and fine-tuning what you think will be attractive to your prospects. Test the offer with a few people first before you send it to everyone on your list.

✔ **Use a great concept and design.** You need good imagery, well laid-out content, an interesting and attention-getting envelope and a personalised letter or card. A few specialist companies offer personalised direct mail where the image used is overprinted with the recipient's name. In fact, many years ago, I signed up for a season membership to the Sydney Swans just because the brochure I received had a picture of Tony Lockett (the then club captain) on the front with a voice bubble on it saying, 'Hey you, Carolyn Tate, that's your seat over there!'

✔ **Write brilliant copy.** The importance of getting the words right in your direct mail cannot be overemphasised. Paying someone who is a direct mail specialist copywriter pays off.

✔ **Make it a call to action.** Direct mail is the most direct form of advertising one to one and is only done if you really want the prospect to do something *now*. Make sure you have coupons, toll-free numbers and credit card payment options available. Tell people it's a limited and exclusive offer that closes by a certain date to incite action.

✔ **Use a reputable mailing house.** Unless you're confident of doing it yourself and have less than around 1,000 envelopes to mail out, using a professional mailing house is advisable. A mailing house can do everything from sourcing lists to merging, updating and maintaining a mailing list database for you, as well as the actual folding, inserting, packing and distribution. Do your research, ask around for a reputable company and get three proposals and quotes before proceeding.

Lots of marketers (mostly online ones) are out there talking about the power of what they call *long-copy* sales letters and email letters. These letters can be anywhere from four to ten pages long. Personally I am not a big fan of them, but I do acknowledge they can work for some kinds of businesses. If you think a long-copy letter might work for your business, do a web search to find out more about composing one.

Whether you have 10 prospects or 2,000 to send a letter to, the same personalised approach should apply. Sadly, less than 4 per cent of direct mail letters actually get acted on. So direct mail really is a numbers game that needs to be accompanied by a personal follow-up call. If you do have 2,000 prospects to send a letter to, I suggest staggering the mailouts so you can take the time to call and follow up.

Every business is different when it comes to direct mail. If you're going to get serious about it and it's going to be one of your major marketing tactics, I suggest you get some help to make sure it works for you.

For more detailed articles and ideas on direct mail and other forms of direct marketing, visit www.malcolmaulddirect.com. You can also check out www.centrica.com.au and www.futuresources.com.au. Australia Post and New Zealand Post provide some great free direct mail resources and advice, and, of course, help with distribution. Check out their websites at www.auspost.com.au and www.nzpost.co.nz.

Converting Customers from Prospect to Sale

Making the call can be tough, but getting the big meeting is even tougher, even if you're just asking for half an hour over a coffee. When you've landed the meeting, don't blow it. You need to make a big impact and get your prospective customer excited enough to want to keep communicating with you and eventually to buy from you, of course, overcoming any obstacles to the deal being clinched.

Making the presentation

Often, depending on the type of product or service you're offering, a deal relies on a personal meeting with someone in the organisation who carries enough weight to make a sales decision or at least a recommendation. That can be a scary thought. But you can do a few things that will help you put your brand forward through the presentation.

Imagine you own a customer service training company and you've got the attention of the CEO of a medium-sized software company. You've got one hour to present and make an impact and you know you're up against two other competitors. Here are some tips for making a presentation that hits the mark:

- ✔ **Do your homework:** Present what you know about the company, their competitors and what their customers think of their service. You should also present what you know about world-class customer service practice.

- ✔ **Know your competition:** Find out who you're up against if you can. Work out how you're different and better so you know what to focus on in your pitch. Never bag the competition, though; just demonstrate you're aware of them and their services.

✔ **Get them talking:** Be prepared to ask questions, and then listen. Have a list of open-ended questions prepared, like: What customer service training have you undertaken in the past? What were the results? What do you think the winning company needs to do to get your business? At least 50 per cent of your meeting time should be taken up with questions and listening.

✔ **Prepare a professional presentation:** Cover the questions in the customer value proposition model I set out in Chapter 2 and the hypothetical answers in Chapter 19, and tell them about your experience and services. Use testimonials and case studies to demonstrate your expertise. Tell them about your guarantees and your own customer service standards.

✔ **Ask for the job:** Be sure to show your eagerness to take on the job and tell them you will do what it takes (within reason) to get it. (Don't act too desperate though!) Ask what you need to do next and when the next meeting will be.

Shrinking violets need not apply. To win the job, you've got to show confidence, professionalism and a passionate desire to work with the organisation to make a difference to its operations.

Most big firms and government departments ask businesses to put in a tender for a job. Depending on the size of the job and how much it's worth to you, you may like to consider taking on a communications professional to help with the tender process.

Overcoming objections to buying

You've got your prospective customer really interested and he's now weighing up the pros and cons of your product or service, and whether to put his hand in his pocket and fork out the cash.

He might be 'umming and ahhing' over the decision for lots of reasons. Your job is to discover what aspect of your offering may be causing the hesitation. You may need to employ some skilful questioning to find out, and then, if possible, you may be able to modify the offer to eliminate the barriers to buying.

Here are some reasons prospective customers may be reluctant to buy:

- They might need to get someone else's approval or opinion to purchase, such as the head of their department, or their wife or husband.

- They may not be convinced that your product or service is better than the competition and might still be weighing up their options.

- They may not believe or trust in your product or business.

- The product or service simply doesn't meet their needs.

- They think your product is too expensive.

- And the obvious one, they don't have the bucks or budget to buy!

Whatever the reason people are not buying, be a good questioner — and even better listener — acknowledge their objections and ask if there's anything you can do to help in that regard.

Never lie. Plenty of times I've tried on clothes and been told how lovely I look by the shop assistant when I know the outfit looks completely wrong on me.

Customers buy — they don't get sold to. Don't oversell or you'll turn customers off completely and they'll leave without buying, and never come back.

Building a Customer Service Program

A customer is the most important visitor on our premises, he is not dependent on us. We are dependent on him. He is not an interruption in our work. He is the purpose of it. He is not an outsider in our business. He is part of it. We are not doing him a favor by serving him. He is doing us a favor by giving us an opportunity to do so.

—Mahatma Gandhi (1864–1948), Indian political and spiritual leader

Remember the distinction between services and service. The *services* you provide may be consulting or business coaching, but the *service* you provide in your delivery is what really distinguishes you from the competition.

Wet and wild

In Chapter 6, in the section on sales support kits, I tell a story about how I found the business to install my guttering. I was really impressed with the professionalism and approach of the salesperson, who gave me an on-the-spot quote. I chose his company because its approach really stood out from the competition.

Fast-forward 12 months. Would I choose this company again, if I had my time over? My response? An absolute resounding *no!* The first impressions were powerful, but the delivery, timeframe and approach to getting the job done were frankly quite shocking.

During the course of getting the gutters installed (which, by the way, took three months), I dealt with no less than seven different people: the salesman; the office girl; the gutter delivery person; the two installers (contractors — one of whom installed the gutters with a brace on his leg and no harness!); the manager; and some other guy from the office who came around to inspect the finished job. Over three months I had reason to call them no less than six times to find out what was happening and what the progress was, and then finally to complain because the gutters hadn't been sealed properly and water appeared to be leaking into my walls.

As hard as you try to be different from your competitors, there's no guarantee that they won't catch up with you and copy the products or services you deliver. What's much harder to copy, however, is the service you provide. It's your service that builds the relationships and gets the customer coming back time and again. And it's the service that gets people talking about you to generate more word-of-mouth business.

Going beyond the call of duty when it comes to customer service is a powerful way to generate more word-of-mouth business. If you can place your business firmly in the hearts and minds of the customer, and maintain a great customer service program, you'll always have a business you are proud of, and a business that will grow and prosper.

The customer service process

The wise business owner, if asked, 'What business are you in?' responds, 'The business of customer service.' That same wise business owner knows who they serve best, how to attract these people to their business, how to get them to become customers and how to keep them as customers.

Too many businesses, however, make the sale, get the cash, deliver the service and then let the customer get lost somewhere between their desk and the database. They don't follow up, ensure 100 per cent satisfaction, ask how else they can help or keep in touch. When they haven't heard from a customer for a while they assume the customer no longer needs their services or has moved elsewhere, never questioning that they might instead be going to their competitor up the road.

That's why every business needs to understand that customer service is king and that the customer service process is central to your operations.

My favourite local grocer is Maloney's. I go there at least three or four times a week. When I asked Tony, the owner, one day how business was doing, he replied with an unequivocal, 'It's brilliant, and we've just opened another store.' Then I asked him his secret to success. 'That's simple,' he said. 'Our customer service process. We take it very seriously and have appointed one of our staff as our training manager. We also go out of our way to offer that extra service that others don't, like home delivery.'

To ensure a consistent customer service experience, you need to follow a simple process and ensure all staff are well trained. Check out Figure 8-2 to see how a simple customer service process works.

Actions speak louder than words. If you expect your staff to give brilliant customer service, you need to demonstrate it in front of their very eyes!

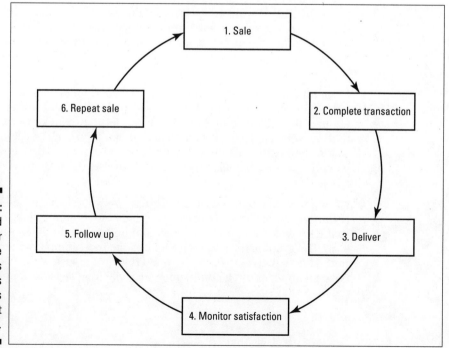

Figure 8-2:
Good customer service involves a process that ensures repeat sales.

Providing a WOW service experience

If you own a retail store or sell a specific product, the focus on creating a WOW experience is right then and there, at the point of purchase. Other service businesses that have long, ongoing and deep relationships with customers, such as lawyers or accountants, need to provide a WOW experience before, during and long after each transaction.

Here are some WOW factors you could add to your service process to help your business stand out. Most of them are pretty obvious, but I estimate 80 per cent of businesses don't do these things at all and, if they do, they don't do them very well:

- ✔ **Follow up:** You've made the sale and delivered the service or product, but have you followed up to ensure 100 per cent satisfaction? This is one of the most under-utilised opportunities to ensure you've delivered on your promise and that the customer is happy, and to ask if there is anything else you can do to help. A simple phone call is all it takes. If you'd just had a baby, how nice would it be to get a phone call from the gynaecologist who delivered your precious bundle to find out how you were doing?

- ✔ **Over-promising and under-delivering:** Ever ordered something and been told it would be delivered within three days, and five days later it still hasn't turned up? Never promise something you can't deliver. If you know that it will take at least five days to deliver something, tell the customer it will be delivered within seven days and then delight them by delivering it in five days. The consultant who promises to deliver me a report in ten days but delivers it in seven is the one I want to work with.

- ✔ **Communications:** Keeping in touch with customers even when they're not buying anything is the key to creating loyalty. And it's not just about selling them something; it's about letting them know about things that are relevant to what you offer that can improve their lives. The hot water installation business that lets me know about a new government incentive to install solar-powered hot water is the business I'd call for a quote.

- ✔ **Giving people something for nothing:** Everyone loves a free gift or reward for being a loyal customer. What can you give your customers that they will value, to keep them coming back and telling others about you? The graphic designer who invites me to accompany them to the hottest new play in town is the one I'd want to work with. The business coach who gives me a complementary coaching session is one I'd value.

✔ **Stimulating the five senses:** In the business world it's not uncommon to only tap into two of the five senses, sight and sound, unless you happen to own a bakery or a restaurant or a kids' play gym that is. Most businesses can either improve the way they use the senses they currently tap into or add a couple more into the mix. How can you maximise the use of taste, touch, sound, sight and smell in your business to create a lasting memory? The home for sale at open inspection with the smell of fresh-brewed coffee or baking bread, mood lighting, beautiful music playing and the sound of tinkling water would pique my interest.

✔ **Following a customer charter:** Sometimes referred to as the *customer promise*, a *customer charter* is a written statement of the service you provide to customers, covering things such as service standards, hours of operation, delivery times, how to handle a complaint, guarantees and the like. The tyre repair company that offers me quick 30-minute turnaround on a small tyre puncture would get my business.

✔ **Loyalty programs:** A program to reward loyal customers is well worth considering, especially if you happen to own a retail store or food outlet. However, it can work just as well for service providers with a bit of creativity. The travel consultant who rewards my loyalty with free travel insurance every time I travel would be worth talking to.

✔ **Guarantees:** A guarantee that you will deliver goods as and when promised is worth a lot these days. A money-back guarantee or a 30-day free trial is also very attractive to many people. If you were an accounting software company, offering a 30-day trial would be well worth considering.

Just adding one or two simple WOW factors to your customer service program could make the difference between creating customers for life or alienating customers for ever.

Handling complaints

Unhappy customers who bother to complain should be considered a blessing, not a curse. It's far better they complain and give you the opportunity to fix the problem than for them not to complain and tell everybody else about their bad experience. Remember, making a purchase is a brand experience and your brand is there for the long haul.

When you get a complaint, you can either go on the defensive or you can politely acknowledge your customer's complaint, ask questions, listen to the answers and fix it.

Granted, some customers will complain about something that was not your fault and some complaints, after investigation, can appear to be invalid. And some customers would whinge or complain about anything! That's when it's most difficult to smile, handle the complaint and make sure your customer leaves happy.

Here's a simple step-by-step process to handle complaints:

1. Take the customer into an area where other customers won't hear.

2. Listen to the complaint, let them rant and don't argue.

3. Empathise and tell them you're there to help.

4. Make notes to show you're taking their complaint seriously.

5. Ask questions to investigate further.

6. If you're at fault, apologise. If not, give the customer the benefit of the doubt.

7. Tell them what action you're going to take and by when.

8. Offer a refund or replacement if appropriate.

9. Fix the complaint and ensure they're satisfied.

10. Follow up to make sure they're happy and ask what else you can do for them.

11. Turn the complaint into an opportunity to get more business or ask for a referral.

12. If you've identified any flaws in your products or business that have caused the complaint, or others similar, fix them.

Your most unhappy customers are your greatest source of learning.

—*Bill Gates, American business magnate and philanthropist*

Evaluating the Customer Experience

You think you're giving your customers a grand service experience, but do they agree with you? The proof is in how many times they come back and how many people they refer to you.

What you think customers value may not actually *be* what they value, so evaluating the customer experience regularly is important. Seek feedback from both the customer and the staff at the coalface serving customers every day. Then, when you get the feedback — good, bad or indifferent — you need to do something with it to make a change.

Seeking and assessing valuable feedback

Customer research is a vital part of developing a great product or service, and creating customer loyalty (refer to Chapter 2 for more on research). And the same research methods I outline there can be used to get feedback on how your customers feel about your service delivery.

Here are a few ways you can seek feedback, formally and informally:

- Ask simple informal questions each time you see your customer.
- Ask customers to fill out a survey form when they visit your store or by mailing them one to return in a reply-paid envelope.
- Put together an online survey using services such as www.survey monkey.com and emailing the link to the survey for your customer to complete.
- Conduct telephone surveys.
- Hold group get-togethers for staff and valued customers, say over lunch.

When seeking feedback, go with the online survey or mail questionnaire first and then, if you need to explore some of the findings further, conduct some face-to-face group sessions to discuss and explore ideas.

In evaluating your customer service experience, you may first want to look at how you and your staff think you're doing in the customer service arena. Use the questions in Table 8-1, scoring yourself from 1 to 10 (with 1 being extremely poor and 10 being excellent) and then write down some ideas on what you need to do to improve. Get your staff to do it too and then ten of your best customers. Then, if you dare, compare the results!

Table 8-1	Evaluating the Customer Service Experience	
Question	*Score*	*Areas for Improvement*
How committed are our staff to providing excellent service?		
How well trained are our staff in all areas of customer service?		
How good are they at making customers feel really special?		

(continued)

Table 8-1 *(continued)*

Question	Score	Areas for Improvement
How does our customer service compare with our competitors?		
How well do our staff know customers' names and orders?		
How proactive are our staff in seeking feedback from customers and offering suggestions?		
How well do we deliver on time and on budget?		
How good are we at exceeding customers' expectations?		
How good are we at communicating with our customers on a regular basis about new offers, products and services?		
How well are we handling customer complaints or concerns?		
How well do we understand what our customers value most about our business?		
How well do we understand who our target market is and work towards attracting these customers?		
How strong is our customer loyalty and frequency of repeat business?		
How well do we know the average spend for our good customers and go that extra mile to thank them?		
If there was one major thing we could do to improve our customer service, what would it be?		

I once used a catering company that sent me a lovely personalised thank-you email the next day with five simple questions to answer:

- Out of 1 to 10, how would you rank the quality of our service?

- Out of 1 to 10, how would you rank the quality of our food?

- Out of 1 to 10, how would you rank us with regards to value for money?

- If there was one thing we could do to improve our service, what would it be?

- Would you be willing to refer us to your friends?

- Would you be willing to provide a testimonial for our website?

- Any general comments?

Whatever you do, never be afraid to ask. It could be the difference between staying in business for the long term or going broke in no time!

Too many businesses believe that 'no news, is good news'. In other words, if they're not getting negative feedback or complaints, then everything is okay. If customers aren't complaining but aren't coming back either, it probably means they're not happy and can't be bothered giving feedback. They're just going somewhere else.

If you're not receiving repeat business, be proactive and find out why. Get to know your regular customers and make sure you have their contact information on a database. If they stop buying from you, make sure you call them and try to subtly find out why.

Acting on the feedback

Nothing is more annoying to staff or customers than if you ask for feedback but don't act on it. Your brand identity needs to be trustworthy and reliable. You need to be sure you're prepared to make changes as a result of the feedback and manage their expectations of what can reasonably be done to affect change. Be sure to:

- Summarise and analyse the feedback to identify consistent findings.

- Make an assessment of the most common and important areas to address.

- Hold a staff meeting to report on the results, and to discuss what you need to change and how you might go about it.

✔ Communicate back to your customers the results of the findings and let them know what you're intending to change.

✔ Thank everyone involved for their input with a gift or thank-you card.

✔ Contact the customer again after the improvements have been made to invite them back to witness the results.

✔ Let all your customers know about the positive new customer service enhancements you've made, either directly or through advertising, publicity, letters or flyers.

Part III
Getting Your Business in the Media

Glenn Lumsden

'Business has been a bit slow, so I've been working on some new marketing strategies.'

In this part ...

The media today is bigger and broader than ever before. You have the choice to broadcast your message through newspapers, niche magazines, pay TV, bus backs, radio, outdoor billboards and even takeaway coffee cups! Not to mention the whole internet arena. No wonder many people go into a head-spin when it comes to working out the best media to choose to get their message out.

Take heart. With a little knowledge, a clever creative approach and a big dose of persistence, you can make the media work really well for you.

This part covers the two main areas of the media — how to advertise your business and how to get publicity for your business. I take a look at the difference between the two, the role each plays and how they can work together or independently. Find out how to select the most appropriate medium for your message.

I also show you how to avoid the scattergun approach and build an affordable advertising and publicity plan that helps you generate a consistent flow of new leads and business. And, importantly, I show you how to get creative to ensure your headlines really hit the mark.

Chapter 9

Mastering the Basics of Advertising

*W*hat is advertising? Advertising is a form of communication that attempts to persuade potential customers to purchase a particular brand of product or service.

If you need to get your message out to a broad market pretty quickly, smart advertising no doubt helps you do it. Advertising takes your message to places you personally can't get to — like letterboxes, television screens, computers, car radios and even your child's school via the school newsletter.

Powerful advertising is creative, entertaining, easy to understand and has a compelling offer. It's also aimed fair and square at the target market you want to hit. It gets people through the door or ringing up to enquire about your service and, if you're smart, purchasing your product online.

In many cases, advertising does not sell directly. It creates attention and paves the way for you to make the sale happen. That's why it's important to have a knockout offer and great sales skills.

Bad advertising is a waste of money. And, sadly, this is an all-too-common problem for many businesses (both big and small).

In this chapter, you find out if advertising is for you and how to go about getting it right.

Understanding Small-Business Advertising

I'm betting you're already thinking advertising equals big bickies, but that's not always so.

Big business has the bucks to spend up big and advertise on TV and in national newspapers and glossy magazines. Most small businesses don't have the big bucks, so you need to get clever to make your advertising dollars stretch and work for you.

Thinking about how to advertise

As a small business, you can advertise effectively and cheaply through many different media outlets, such as local papers and online directories. For example, one of the most successful Australian publications for small businesses is the monthly *Beast* magazine, which is distributed across Sydney's eastern beachside suburbs. It's irreverent, fun, gossipy and informative, and a great community publication that goes to more than 60,000 homes and cafés. Check out its website at www.thebeast.com.au.

An important thing to remember, though, is that it's not just where you advertise but how you advertise that counts. Here are a few questions to determine what type of advertising will work for you:

✔ How many customers do you actually need to attract?

✔ Who is your target market and where are they located?

✔ Is your market mass or niche, consumers or other businesses?

✔ What is your target market reading, watching and listening to?

✔ How much will it cost to advertise? What is your budget?

✔ What return on investment do you expect?

✔ Where in the paper, website or magazine, for example, would you want to be positioned?

✔ What do you want to advertise — the whole business or a product or service?

✔ What will your message be? What special offer will you make?

✔ What do you want people to think, feel and, importantly, *do* after reading your ad?

✔ How big will the ad be and how often will you run it?

✔ Who will do the creative work, design the ad and write the copy? (I don't recommend doing this yourself, by the way. In my experience this is one of the biggest reasons ads fail.)

✔ How will you measure the number of people responding to the ad?

✔ How will you respond to ad enquiries to make sure you get the sale?

✔ How will you follow up on enquiries and leads?

Say you own an Indian restaurant. It would make sense to be listed on dining websites like www.eatability.com.au or www.menufeast.com.au, and advertise in the local paper and in the *Yellow Pages* locality directory or by food category. You could even ask to pay for an advertisement in your child's school newsletter with a special offer for families. If you want to attract people from outside your local area, you might consider advertising on radio to reach more than just the surrounding suburbs. You could support the ad campaign by having one of your staff hand out flyers at a nearby shopping centre, offering a lunch deal or giving a discount coupon to shoppers, and by doing a letterbox drop to homes in the area.

Avoid the spray-and-pray approach at all costs (that is, don't simply advertise to the masses). Never spray your message as far and wide as you can, then pray that some of it will stick. Effective advertising is about sharpening your arrow before you pick up your bow. This means being really clear on who are the people most likely to buy your products or services — your target market — and then clearly aiming your message at them using the medium they are most likely to be reading or consuming.

Brand advertising versus product or service advertising

You can advertise to raise general brand awareness of your business or to market a specific product or service that you offer.

The kind of advertising you do is determined by your type of business, who you serve, how long you've been in business and the current exposure of your business in the marketplace. For example, if you're a tax agent doing low-cost tax returns, consider advertising heavily on radio around tax time with a special offer to mums and dads (service advertising). If you're a tax specialist serving the country's wealthy, you can do some upmarket advertising in a niche wealth magazine to tell people about your business (brand advertising).

For most small businesses, pure brand advertising may seem like an indulgence, as it won't necessarily bring in immediate enquiries and sales like a special product or service offer.

Whatever your budget, develop an overarching creative strategy that helps build brand awareness and ultimately sells the product. The creative strategy should work together across all your communications, from your website to your brand advertising and flyers. Finding a good creative advertising agency to build the strategy can be a worthwhile investment.

Giving Your Advertising a Winning Edge

Great ads are memorable and fun, and they stimulate all the senses. Bad ads are, well, forgettable or, in fact, so bad you never forget them! Even bad ads can work in some way. It's the ones in between that are bland and neither great nor terrible that are the worst because they leave no impact at all.

Not withstanding all that, your ads need to be nothing short of brilliant to stand out and make people pick up the phone.

> *Advertising says to people — Here's what we've got. Here's what it will do for you. And here's how to get it.*
>
> *—Leo Burnett (1891–1971), American advertising executive*

Defining your unique selling proposition

I know the phrase *unique selling proposition (USP)* sounds like a bit of jargon. Sorry. However, getting a handle on what it means is important. You also need to understand why it's so critical to creating successful ads that drive traffic.

The unique selling proposition (also called a *unique selling point*) is a marketing theory that suggests every advertisement must make a single unique proposition to the consumer that the competition either cannot or does not offer or promote. It must be compelling and single-minded. Each ad must say to the reader, 'Buy this product and you'll get this specific benefit.' And an advertisement often hits the pain-or-pleasure button that I talk about in Chapter 2.

Many advertisers try to squeeze too many messages and ideas into an ad, and end up confusing and turning off the potential customer. A powerful single-minded benefit is the key to creating interest and action. The USP is *not* the headline. It is the single idea or benefit customers believe you offer after reading your ad.

A flick through today's ads in the paper turned up the ads outlined in Table 9-1, offering a unique selling proposition that gives the reader a specific benefit.

Table 9-1	Ads with Unique Selling Propositions
Company	*USP*
Domayne	50 per cent off, no deposit, no interest for 24 months
Harvey Norman	Massive government rebates available for solar hot water
Coles Express	Save 10c per litre on fuel when you shop with us
IGA	Working together to make our community a winner
Save the Children	Making child soldiers a thing of the past
Westpac	Get cash flow relief with our Business Foundations service
Subaru	Create your own adventure
Clinique	Guaranteed great skin or your money back
ING Direct	Your savings just keep growing
Hairstop	Remove hair permanently

Defining the USP for your ads is not always easy. Here are some ideas to help you work it out:

- Collect copies of your competitors' ads and flyers, and decipher their USPs (if they have one!). Which ones are compelling to you?

- Collect copies of any other ads that really talk to you, and figure out their USPs and why they work for you.

- Take a look at your customer value proposition and points of difference (refer to Chapter 2), and pick out three different USPs to explore for advertising.

- Test these USPs with your staff, good customers and other small-business owners. Which ones do they like? What would get them interested?

- Find a creative agency that understands what you're looking for and can fine-tune your USP with you. In Chapter 10 I cover how to go about refining your USP. Read on for some tips on what makes a good creative agency.

Finding a good agency

A good agency that won't cost you the Earth and has a strong track record can be hard to find. A good ad agency must be able to

✔ Demonstrate the measurable results of previous ad campaigns they've produced (not just show you a whole reel of pretty, award-winning ads).

✔ Show you a healthy list of long-term customers who are prepared to offer a reference.

✔ Respond well to your brief, suggesting improvements where appropriate, but understanding what you want.

✔ Offer strategic thinking and planning skills that ultimately result in brilliant creative ads and media placement options.

✔ Provide flexible payment options, such as payment on results, instead of the ad industry standard of hefty monthly retainers.

✔ Take a holistic approach to your advertising and consider it in light of your overall marketing plan and how it will work across all media from print to outdoor ads, online advertising and more.

Deciding what you want your audience to think, feel and do

You've got your USP. Now you need to ask yourself two questions: Who is my audience? And what do I want them to *think*, *feel* and *do* as a result of seeing my ad?

Imagine you've started up a business selling babies' clothing online. Your USP is that you offer a whole coordinated wardrobe of clothes for babies so that it all works together and mums don't need to shop anywhere else. Your prime audience is pregnant women and mums with babies up to the age of 12 months. They are most likely reading online magazines like www.motherinc.com.au, or baby and family magazines like *Mother and Baby*, also with an online presence at www.motherandbaby.com.au. You want people to *think* about your offer of unique, affordable, beautiful and coordinated wardrobes for their bundles of joy. You want them to *feel* like they'll have the best-dressed babies at the best prices. And what you want them to *do* is browse through your online catalogue to purchase a wardrobe starter kit or call the 1300 sales number (refer to Chapter 6) to order by phone.

By clearly articulating the USP and what you want people to think, feel and do, you can then get to work on producing creative, emotive and compelling ads that really work and drive enquiries and sales.

Creating Ads That Work

Take a pen and a few minutes to write down a list of all the TV ads you can remember. What were they selling? Which companies were they for? Why did you like them? What did you do about it (if anything)?

Memorable and powerful ads are funny, emotional, bold, irreverent and in-your-face. They stop traffic, fuel interest and engage people. They also direct customers to do what you want them to do.

Defining your call to action

When it comes to getting my son to go to bed, a vague muttering about going to bed from me while I'm in the kitchen cleaning up after dinner doesn't cut it. I need to go up to him, look him in the eye, ask him to stop whatever he is doing, tell him specifically what he has to do — put on his pyjamas, clean his teeth, get a drink of water, choose a book and hop into bed — by 9 pm. Is it just me, or does this happen for every parent?

The same goes for advertising. If you don't tell people what you want them to do, then how are they to know? Your ad needs to arrest their attention, speak directly to them, and tell them what you want them to do and by when.

So, if you want them to visit your website, download a catalogue and order $500 worth of product, tell them that and tell them what you're prepared to offer them if they do it by a certain date. Make your offer limited and exclusive if they act now. Be sure to include your website or 1300 phone number or even include an order form in your ad.

When developing advertising, as with other aspects of marketing, 'starting at the end' pays off. Work out what you want your audience to do specifically and then design your ad to make sure it tells them a compelling enough story to guide them to the best decision — to buy your service or product.

Writing knockout ads

Writing a fantastic ad is not easy and it's best to get your agency or a professional ad copywriter to do it. Whether you do it yourself or get someone else to do it, go through this checklist to make sure your ads will be winners on all counts:

- ✔ **Hit your audience between the eyes.** Know what they're really thinking and what they really, really want.

- ✔ **Get your offer right.** The best ad in the world will fall flat every time if not backed up by a great offer.

- ✔ **Write a knockout headline.** Around 70 per cent of your effort should be spent on this alone. If you don't grab your audience's attention with the headline, they won't keep listening, watching or reading.

- ✔ **Use powerful imagery and photos.** A picture (whether still or moving) tells a thousand words, so they say. Use imagery that talks directly to people and that makes them laugh, cry, and sit up and take notice.

- ✔ **Write fantastic copy.** Although the headline grabs attention and the image gets them emotionally engaged, it's the words that sell. Good copy (whether written or spoken) is worth its weight in gold.

- ✔ **Test your ad.** Try a few smaller ads with different headlines and check the response. Then run the more successful ones and make them a bit bigger.

- ✔ **Add some other promotional tactics to the mix.** Try some direct mail (refer to Chapter 8), still linked to the ad concept, or see if you can get the media to write up a story on you and your business (see Chapters 12 and 13).

- ✔ **Include a story.** Testimonials from happy customers and stories of how you helped can really add impact.

- ✔ **Use stats and facts.** Dig around for facts and stats to support your claim or to highlight a problem that your product or service fixes. For example, if you were a dietician, you might use: 'Did you know that one in two Australians are overweight?'

The Pros and Cons of Advertising

How much money and effort you put into advertising (if any), depends on the kind of business you're in and how many customers you want. In most cases, businesses needing to sell many products to many consumers need to put a fair amount of investment and attention into advertising; whereas businesses selling services to a select group of consumers probably don't.

It pays to understand the pros and cons of advertising in different media before jumping in headfirst and deciding if any one medium is for you.

> *Half the money I spend on advertising is wasted. The trouble is I don't know which half.*
>
> —*William Hesketh Lever (1851–1925), English industrialist*

In years gone by, this statement may have had a ring of truth to it. But now, thanks to the internet and smarter advertising techniques, business owners have become much smarter at tracking where their leads and sales come from and therefore the effectiveness of their advertising.

Television advertising

In the 1950s and 1960s, brands were built on television. The whole family would gather around to watch their favourite programs and sit right through every ad. Television was the focal point and entertainment centre of every household. And big companies with big dollars to spend on advertising created household names for themselves.

More than half a century later, TV-viewing habits have changed dramatically. People now watch free-to-air and pay TV on the big screen and online, recording their favourite shows and screening out the ads. Many people spend as much time (if not more) on their personal computers, playing on the internet, than watching TV. For most families, TV is no longer the centre of the household. However, TV advertising still has its advantages, and some drawbacks, as shown in Table 9-2.

Table 9-2	The Pros and Cons of TV Advertising		
Advantage	*Why*	*Disadvantage*	*Why*
Targeted reach	TV stations generally have a lot of intelligence around who their audience is, so you can target your message to them with the right offer on the right program and in the best geographic area.	Long lead times	You can't dream up an ad and have it on TV overnight. It can take months of creative development, planning and scheduling before your ads go to air.

(continued)

Table 9-2 (continued)

Advantage	Why	Disadvantage	Why
Brand building	TV is great for brand building because you can reach a large audience very quickly and with almost instant appeal. That is, of course, if your ad is really good and you have lots of money!	Costly	Significant amounts of money need to be invested to make advertising work, both in developing the ad as well as the cost to place the ads on TV. Buying airtime can be expensive and most often requires the expert services of a media planner and buyer. However, in regional areas TV advertising is often much more viable and affordable than in city or national areas.
Emotional appeal	Unlike many static media, like print, you can use TV ads to stimulate emotions with music and jingles, words and powerful imagery.	Cluttered	You'll find your ad not only competing with your competitors but with every other advertiser competing for the attention of viewers. This makes it difficult to stand out.
Memorable	Really good TV ads can live in the hearts and minds of people for years and can subconsciously affect their loyalty to buy from you for just as long — even a lifetime.	Wastage	Many of your ads will go sight unseen, as people either screen the ads out or use the break to make a cuppa or use the toilet.

Radio advertising

Before TV, there was radio. So when TV came along, advertisers had to spread their ad budget across yet another medium. Now there is the internet, iTunes and iPods, and people listen to music in a whole host of ways, so radio has become a relatively small piece of the media pie.

I once worked with a real estate agent who had wasted $30,000 on radio advertising. They'd been sold the dream by the radio station salesperson that the ad would bring them lots of new business. Never mind that it was the wrong medium, wrong audience and wrong geography! Buyers beware.

Radio advertising can be a relatively inexpensive medium and can work well if done consistently. It can work particularly well in country areas with local stations, where the audience is geographically defined and the cost to advertise is much lower. Check out Table 9-3 for more of the pros and cons of radio advertising.

Table 9-3	The Pros and Cons of Radio Advertising		
Advantage	*Why*	*Disadvantage*	*Why*
Flexible rates	Radio stations are usually willing to negotiate rates and offer bonus spots to advertisers. Be prepared to bargain to get what you want.	Repetition required	For your ads to really stick in people's minds, you need to vary them and repeat them regularly. You need to buy a certain number of spots per day, per week and per month to make it work.
Targeted audience	Radio is a great medium if you want to hit a targeted audience with your message. You can pick the time and programs to place your ad depending on listener age groups, interests and listening times.	Over before you know it	Unlike print ads, you can't flick back and listen to a radio ad. Ads can vary from 15 to 60 seconds and be lost in the clutter of other radio ads.

(continued)

Table 9-3 (continued)

Advantage	Why	Disadvantage	Why
Immediate	Unlike TV and print, radio is very quick. You can have an ad written and recorded to go to air almost overnight if you need. You can also produce ads for the radio announcer to present live to air.	Distracted audience	Like TV, people can turn off or flick stations when the ads are on. That's why it's important to get professional creative people to produce a really great ad for you that keeps people listening.

Newspaper advertising

Since the advent of the internet, there's been a lot of talk about the future of printed newspapers. Why would people buy a paper, when they can get all the news they'll ever need, hot off the press on the internet — for free? No doubt the internet has caused traditional print media to suffer and will continue to do so. You only have to check out the way the big media companies such as News Limited have embraced the internet to keep their readers engaged.

Whether national newspapers such as the *Australian* or the *New Zealand Herald*, metropolitan or state-based newspapers such as the *West Australian* or local newspapers such as the *Waikato Times* or the *Townsville Bulletin*, most small businesses consider advertising in papers at some stage. Table 9-4 sets out the advantages and disadvantages.

The advertisements are the most truthful part of a newspaper.

—*Thomas Jefferson (1743–1826), Third President of the United States*

When considering newspaper advertising, make sure you check out the opportunities to advertise in their online versions as well. Some national newspaper examples include www.theaustralian.com.au and www.nzherald.co.nz.

Table 9-4	The Pros and Cons of Newspaper Advertising		
Advantage	*Why*	*Disadvantage*	*Why*
Coverage options	Depending on your business and target markets, you can choose broad national coverage or very targeted local coverage.	Limited lifespan	Unlike magazines, newspapers are usually read and discarded as they are replaced by the next edition, which means, if people don't see your ad when first reading the paper, they're unlikely to return.
Accepting readers	Generally, people reading newspapers expect ads and may even look for them. If they're in the market for what you're offering, they'll use the paper to do their research and compare your offer with the competition.	Cluttered environment	Take a look at your daily paper and you'll see that it's full of ads. Remember your ad is not only competing against your competition, it's competing for the readers' attention against other advertisers, news stories and more.
Good detail	Unlike TV and radio, papers are a great medium to give people more detail on what you're offering and how to get it. And if they're interested they can go back and read the ad again or cut out a coupon to send in, for example.	Limited audience	Newspaper readership among younger generations is quite weak compared with the baby-boomers and older generations, making it not suitable to attract some audiences.
Short lead times	Unlike TV, you can produce and place ads within a relatively short timeframe if you have the right creative services on board. Some papers offer creative services too.	Flat medium	Unlike TV, radio and the internet, it's harder for newspapers to stimulate the senses and leave a lasting impression on readers.

(continued)

Table 9-4 *(continued)*

Advantage	Why	Disadvantage	Why
Flexible options	You can be very specific about the size of the ad you want, where it is placed (in early general news or specific sections such as the real estate or motor vehicle sections) and whether it's produced in colour or black and white.	Wasted money	You'll pay full price for an ad based on total circulation and readership figures; however, only a small percentage of readers are actually your target audience.

Magazine advertising

Give me a good magazine over a newspaper any day!

Interestingly, most of the big papers have their own magazines to increase circulation and keep their readers loyal. The *Sydney Morning Herald* produces *Good Weekend* and the *Sydney Magazine*, and the *Australian Financial Review* produces *AFR Magazine* and *AFR Boss*.

For many small businesses, advertising in full-scale national mags like the *Australian Women's Weekly* may not be a financially viable option. However, many smaller local and niche magazines out there are well worth considering. Table 9-5 gives you some of the pros and cons of magazine advertising.

You can be creative with magazine advertising in lots of ways and really hit your target audience between the eyes. Most often it's not about how many people you reach but the quality of the prospects you reach.

If you own an investment company and are targeting the wealthy 50-plus market, you might consider advertising in *Golf Australia*. If you sell cool kids' backpacks online you might consider advertising in *K-Zone*. If you're a child psychologist based in Melbourne you might advertise in *Melbourne's Child*, which is read by parents all over the city.

Table 9-5	The Pros and Cons of Magazine Advertising		
Advantage	*Why*	*Disadvantage*	*Why*
Long lifespan	Unlike newspapers, magazines stick around for a long time and in many instances are kept for years. *National Geographic, Reader's Digest, The Australian Way* (Qantas inflight magazine) and many women's magazines are read more than once and often in a leisurely, relaxed manner, meaning your ad has a better chance of making an impact.	Long lead times	Magazines can be produced weekly but are more often monthly, and publishers work to very specific production schedules, often months ahead of the release date. So, if you want your ad in a good position, you need to book the space and get the creative work done way in advance.
Highly targeted	Niche, regional and trade magazines such as *Wheels, Beast* or *Dolly* can provide you with very specific readership data. They know the age, interests and exact locations of their purchasers, making it easy for you to produce a knockout ad relevant to your target market.	Expensive	A full-page, full-colour ad in a national magazine can run into tens of thousands of dollars. Smaller niche and regional magazines are less expensive of course, but you still need to invest heavily in quality creative copy, design and production. You also need to run your ad more than once to make an impact.
High quality	The high-gloss colour production of magazines means your ad has the best chance of looking good and standing out. Magazines also allow for the use of inserts, samples, special offers and competitions, and you can sometimes get the publisher to include a newsworthy story on you.	Reader apathy	Unlike other media, magazines often don't provoke an immediate response. Readers can be rather passive and, depending on the magazine, may not even pick it up for weeks or months after they receive it.

Outdoor advertising

The sky's the limit when it comes to outdoor advertising — quite literally! I recall one day at the beach last year, where ads were scrawled across the sky constantly and helicopters trawled up and down the coast trailing big banners for some telco company. Is nothing sacred?

Outdoor advertising is sometimes referred to as *out-of-home* advertising and refers to hundreds of different types of advertising, from skywriting to the posters placed on the wall at your local café.

Out-of-home advertising focuses on marketing to consumers when they're on the go in public places — in transit, waiting or at specific locations. It includes such things as:

- Advertising on street furniture in a park or at a bus shelter
- Posters on noticeboards at the local supermarket
- Billboards on buildings, highways, at airports and in train stations
- Neon-lit, sometimes moving billboards
- Ads on the backs of buses, taxis, trucks, water taxis and boats
- Posters wrapped around telephone poles (illegally, mind you)
- Banners and flags flying from city flagpoles
- Motorbikes and cars roaming around pulling trailers with billboards
- Outdoor sandwich boards
- Coffee cups, floor stickers and placemats at eateries
- Signwriting on vehicles

Love it, or hate it, outdoor advertising is here to stay. Selecting the best outdoor advertising tools for your business can be difficult, but be sure to include at least one or two outdoor tactics to assist in your promotional effort. Table 9-6 gives you the advantages and disadvantages to consider.

Table 9-6	The Pros and Cons of Outdoor Advertising		
Advantage	*Why*	*Disadvantage*	*Why*
Semi-permanent	Except in the case of skywriting and moving vehicles, of course, outdoor advertising generally stays in one spot for a long time, meaning that everyone who passes it is exposed to it.	Requires maintenance	Outdoor ads are susceptible to vandalism, bad weather and dirt, so you need to monitor them constantly to ensure they put out the image you want.
Message specific	You know exactly where your outdoor advertising is placed and who it reaches, meaning you can target the message directly. You often see on highways, for example, 'Next McDonald's 5 km'.	Moving audience	Unlike TV and newspapers, outdoor advertising tries to hit people while on the go and most likely distracted with other things, which means they could miss your ad altogether.
High impact	A great outdoor ad can have a lasting impact. If you've ever been to Times Square in New York, you know what I mean.	Expense	Billboard advertising in high-traffic areas like airports can be very expensive, and the cost to produce the artwork can be prohibitive.
Brand building	Outdoor can work very well for building a brand in a specific market or location, particularly where the same people pass by and see your ad every day.	Long lead times	Like magazine advertising, to get prime placement and produce the best artwork, you need to book way in advance to get your outdoor ads up and running.

Online advertising

Online advertising is a form of promotion that uses the World Wide Web for the purpose of delivering your marketing message direct to your target audience. Examples of online advertising include:

- Ads on search engines like Google and Yahoo!, which usually appear as sponsored links and are text-only
- Ads placed on specific websites that include graphics and words, and can be almost any size
- Interactive or rich-media ads, such as games, videos and quizzes that invite a two-way interaction
- Social networking ads on sites such as Facebook, YouTube, MySpace, Twitter and LinkedIn
- Online directory ads on websites like Yellow Pages, Hotfrog and True Local
- Email ads sent directly to targeted lists or your own database

In Chapter 18 I discuss how to advertise in each of these areas in much more detail. But Table 9-7 gives you some of the pros and cons to consider in the meantime.

Table 9-7	The Pros and Cons of Online Advertising		
Advantage	*Why*	*Disadvantage*	*Why*
Instantaneous	You can produce online ads very quickly and have them up on the web almost overnight and driving traffic to your site.	Cluttered environment	It can be difficult to get your ad to rank and stand out, not only from the competition but all the other companies advertising out there.
Testability	You can test different headlines, images and copy to gauge the response and then change them quickly and easily if they're not working.	High-speed viewing	Unlike many other media, the internet world is fast-moving and fast-paced. Users are very fickle and tend not to hang around too long on any one website, let alone take the time to click through to ads.

Advantage	Why	Disadvantage	Why
Measurability	Unlike most other media, you can measure the direct response of every ad. You can measure how many people have clicked through on your ad or visited your website, discover how long they've hung around and, of course, if they've bought anything.	Limited target market	Online advertising is good for the younger generation but might not be so good for the older generation. It pays to know what your audience internet habits are before considering advertising online.
Lower cost	Advertising online can be less expensive than other forms of advertising and in some cases it can be free. However, to make a big impact and drive serious sales you need to put some serious money behind it.	Time-consuming	Checking, managing, refining and rerunning ads to make sure they're continually hitting the mark is a big job. You need to seriously get the knowledge and devote considerable time to it if you decide to do it yourself.
Higher potential interest	Consumers who go online to research or shop specifically for the type of product or service you offer are more predisposed to your ad than consumers reading other media.	Limited knowledge	Most business owners find the world of internet advertising confusing and don't know where to start. If you're serious about it and aren't interested in mastering it, you need to be prepared to bring in the experts.

Directory advertising

Business directory advertising can be one of the least costly and most effective ways to get your business in front of your target market. A directory is a website or printed list of information on businesses that fit within a similar category. Businesses can be categorised by business type, location, activity or size. The details provided in a directory vary. They may include the business name, address, telephone numbers, location, type of service or products the business provides, number of employees, the service region and more. Some directories include a section for user reviews, comments and feedback.

Although they're not search engines, online business directories most often have a search facility. Some directories have better reputations than others, and they differ greatly in quality and content, so you need to do your homework.

Many businesses rely on directory advertising alone to get the message out about their business. If it works for you, great — but try to add a couple of other media to the mix.

Directory advertising is not for every business. For example, I personally wouldn't choose a GP or lawyer via a directory, but I would look for a plumber on a directory. On the other hand, if I was new to town and didn't know a soul, I'd probably use the local business directory to get whatever help I needed.

Taking a look at the full list of directories and what's on offer before jumping in is worthwhile. Find out what they offer and cost, who their audience is, what traffic and results they get, and what other advertisers have said about them. Make sure you can link your listing through to your website. If you don't have a website, some directories actually provide a mini website page for you.

Check out this list (which is by no means complete) of general business directories for a start:

- www.yellowpages.com.au and www.yellow.co.nz
- www.whitepages.com.au and www.yellow.co.nz/whitepages
- www.truelocal.com.au (Australia only)
- www.hotfrog.com.au and www.hotfrog.co.nz
- www.au.yahoo.com and http://.nz.yahoo.com
- www.thegreenpages.com.au and www.greenpages.co.nz

In addition to the more general directories, definitely check out if there are any specialist directories you should be listed on. For example, if you're a tradesperson, you may want to consider being listed on www.homeimprovementpages.com.au; if you're a masseur you may want to be listed on www.naturaltherapypages.com.au.

The list of directories you could be found in is endless. But be sure to do your homework before investing time and money on directory listings — check out Table 9-8 for starters.

Table 9-8	The Pros and Cons of Directory Advertising		
Advantage	*Why*	*Disadvantage*	*Why*
Readers are ready	Directories are used most often when people are ready to buy. They're actively looking for the services you offer and know they want what you have to offer (at the right price and value of course).	Too much choice	So many directories are out there it can be difficult to work out which one will work best for you and how much time and money you should spend on it.
Low cost	Relative to other types of advertising, directory advertising can be very good value. Some directories offer discounts, and bonus listings and placement to get your business.	Poor return on investment	Some businesses spend lots of money on directory advertising with very poor response. You need to be sure that the kinds of customers you want will look for your service or product on a directory.
24/7 listing	Your listing is up there for the long haul, so people searching for your product or service will be able to find you any day or time of the week.	Hard to be noticed	It can often be difficult to get good placement so that your ad comes up first and is the best and brightest (you need to pay a premium for this). Be sure to check out your competition and how they position themselves, and manage the listing on an ongoing basis.

Other types of advertising

Some types of advertising just can't be classified. Consider some of these ideas to add to the mix:

- ✔ Letterbox and post office box drops or direct mail (refer to Chapter 8)

- ✔ On-street handouts, where someone may dress in a costume (or not) and hands out flyers with special offers or product samples

- ✔ Viral advertising, where you post videos on YouTube to spread your message or you give your product or service to a cool person to use and recommend to their friends

- ✔ Giveaways such as hats, fridge magnets, pens or any other relevant promotional item with your brand on it

- ✔ Spruiking, where someone stands at the front door of your business to advertise your offer and encourage people to come in

I could go on forever, and you could probably add to the list with your own ideas. Every business is different and no one advertising plan looks the same as the next.

Chapter 10

Developing Your Advertising Plan

· ·

In This Chapter

▶ Getting started with your advertising plan

▶ Working out where to advertise

▶ Hitting on the great creative idea

▶ Producing terrific ads for print, TV, radio and outdoors

· ·

*T*he Carlton Draught Big Ad of 2005 is one of my favourite ads. Originally created for television, it was sent out virally over the internet and was allegedly downloaded more than 162,000 times within 24 hours, and one million times in 132 countries over the following two weeks. The online viral campaign was apparently so successful that Carlton's TV media budget was greatly reduced. The ad created a massive amount of commentary from journalists and media commentators, and a great debate around whether the ad really did get people buying more Carlton Draught.

The creative teams and media buying agencies working on the ad obviously had a plan and I'm betting they knew they were on a winner way before they even started filming.

Now, of course, you don't have the budget to produce that sort of stuff, but there are lessons to be learned from looking at what big business does to create successful advertising campaigns. They plan.

The mistake of many a small business is to panic when business slows down and hurriedly stick a one-off ad in the local paper in the desperate hope of pulling in more business. Don't let this happen to you!

If you're going to advertise and make it work, you need to do it consistently, and with reasonable reach and frequency. This chapter shows you how to plan for advertising success so you don't waste your valuable advertising dollar.

Getting Started

If you've been through the checklist of advertising considerations outlined in Chapter 9, you may have decided that advertising is an absolute must for your business. Before doing anything, you need to work out two critical things: how much money you need and how you're going to get help.

If you're serious about making your advertising program work, don't do it yourself. You'll only waste time and money. Be prepared to bring in the experts.

Working out a budget

You need to consider two difficult questions in working out an advertising budget. How much do you realistically need to spend to get the number of enquiries you need to convert into sales? And how much can you actually afford to spend? For most small-business owners, the answers to both of these questions will vary greatly.

For example, you may know you realistically need to spend $200,000 on your advertising plan, but you can only afford $50,000. If this is the case, you need to assess how critical advertising is to your success and find some creative ways to fund it. And, if there's no way to get the dough, you may be best to eliminate advertising altogether and look at other low-cost ways to attract more customers.

By having marketing objectives and goals (take a look at Chapter 4), you can set some numbers and targets around your expected return on your advertising investment.

In setting your budget, you need to consider what you need to spend on the following:

- A creative advertising agency to come up with the big idea and design the ad
- A copywriter to write the ad
- A legal company to approve the fine print
- A photographer or production company to film or record the ad
- A media planning agency to help develop the *media plan* (that is, where and when you'll advertise)
- The placement of the ad — this being the biggest expense of the lot

✔ Other expenses, like the cost of a launch party or development of a specific website to support your advertising campaign

✔ Costs to fulfil the ad campaign, such as extra staffing, production of product, mailing and so on

I recommend also adding a margin of 20 per cent to your estimated costs for unexpected expenses.

If you really have no idea where to start or what you should be spending, meet with a couple of creative and media agencies to get a realistic gauge of what you may need to spend.

Getting the best help

The process of finding a fabulous creative agency and a savvy media planning and buying agency can be tricky. To set things straight, the staff of the *creative agency* are the ones who come up with the big idea, the big headline and the great copy, and then design the ad. The folks at the *media planning and buying agency* work out where you're going to place your ad and how often it will appear. Many smaller creative agencies don't actually do media buying, and vice versa, so you probably need to form relationships with both parties.

Today, it's a tough decision as to which comes first — creative development or media buying. I personally favour going to a media buying agency first because this allows the creative agency to develop really unique ads for each specific medium, whether a magazine or online banner ad, for example.

To find the best agencies, write a *request for proposal (RFP)*, which asks the agencies to draw up an outline of what they'd propose, and make a time to meet with no more than six different agencies to hand over and explain your RFP. A business associate can recommend these agencies or you could find some ads you like and contact the advertiser to find out who did them.

For a good list of agencies, both big and small, check out the Advertising Federation of Australia website at www.afa.org.au or the Communication Agencies Association in New Zealand at www.caanz.co.nz, and B&T magazine at www.bandt.com.au.

Your request for proposal should include the following:

✔ Brief background information on your company

✔ An overview of your brand values, image and reputation

- ✔ A description of your target markets in priority order and, importantly, where they are located
- ✔ An overview of the features and benefits of the product or service you want to sell
- ✔ An idea of your points of difference from your competition
- ✔ A statement about what you believe to be your single biggest unique selling proposition (USP — refer to Chapter 8)
- ✔ A simple statement telling them what you want your audience to think and feel, and what action you want them to take as a result of your ad
- ✔ An idea of the kinds of media you'd like to appear in
- ✔ An indication of when and how often you want to advertise

I don't usually recommend including your budget in the RFP. I suggest you ask them to give you an optimal budget required in their response to your request.

At the time of meeting the agencies, be sure to give them a copy of the RFP and agree on the date you'd like a response. You can usually weed out a couple of the agencies during this process and be comfortable with selecting from a smaller group.

The agency should respond to your RFP with an overview of their process, an approximate budget, how they charge, a portfolio of their work to date, their terms and conditions, their guarantee to you, and some customer references and testimonials. They may even come up with some initial creative ideas or concepts to whet your appetite and prove to you they have what it takes.

Advertising responsibly

In many, many cases, advertisers have been taken to the cleaners over irresponsible, immoral and unethical advertising, and for making outrageous claims in their advertising. And lots of discussion surrounds issues such as the sexualisation of children in advertising and the media, and the responsibility of alcohol companies and fast-food chains in their advertising.

Never, ever produce an ad that you wouldn't be proud to show your mother or your child.

For more information on responsible advertising, visit the Advertising Standards Bureau website, shown in Figure 10-1, at www.advertising standardsbureau.com.au or the NZ Advertising Standards Association at www.asa.co.nz.

Figure 10-1:
Australian advertisers must adhere to codes administered by the Advertising Standards Bureau.

Developing a Media Plan

Now it's time to work out where you want to put your ad and how many times you want it seen. Take a look at the pros and cons of each kind of advertising media you have to choose from in Chapter 9, from TV to newspaper and online ads. You need a combination of your ads to appear in different media at different times. A media planning and buying agency will help you do this.

Imagine you own a luxury boat company selling and maintaining yachts for the rich and famous. Your prime target market is wealthy professional men aged 40-plus. In any typical week they might be reading *Modern Boating* magazine (both in print and online), *BRW* and the *Australian Financial Review*, and checking out the weather on www.seabreeze.com.au. They may also be doing their research to find a new boat to purchase on www.boatpoint.com.au. Your media plan would almost certainly feature these publications and websites (depending on your budget, of course).

The right media planning and buying agency can be worth its weight in gold because it

✔ Understands the whole media landscape and has detailed knowledge of each medium and each outlet, and which ones would be the most powerful for your business.

✔ Will come up with really creative media options that you may not have even thought of, like advertising on water taxis across Sydney harbour.

✔ Has access to detailed information on the number of people who read, watch or listen to each outlet (often referred to as circulation and readership).

✔ Can analyse the specific demographics and psychographics (refer to Chapter 2) of the audience for each outlet to make sure your ad hits the mark.

✔ Understands the actual cost of each outlet compared with the others and what you should be paying.

✔ Manages the relationships with each of the salespeople of the papers or radio stations, which frees you up to focus on delivering your advertising offer.

✔ Has bargaining power and can negotiate better rates because the agency may be buying space or airtime for other clients as well.

If you do decide to go it alone and not work with a media buying agency, do your homework thoroughly before committing to any media outlet.

A very useful tool to find out what outlets are available and the contacts for each one is the *Media Directory*, which covers Australia and New Zealand, and is put out by Media Monitors at www.mediamonitors.com.au and www.mediamonitors.co.nz. Click Services in the menu bar and choose Target the Media from the dropdown menu, and then select Media Directory, shown in Figure 10-2. In addition, many of the industry bodies associated with each medium have great information and tools to help you plan for their medium. For example, www.commercialradio.com.au has some excellent planning and briefing tools to help you make the most of your radio ads.

If you get a call from a radio station or local paper urging you to advertise and offering you a great deal to do it quickly, say thanks but no thanks. Rarely do one-off ad campaigns work. Like any business decision, your advertising needs to be approached with foresight and planning.

Figure 10-2:
Media
Monitors
produces
the compre-
hensive
*Media
Directory* for
the whole
Asia–Pacific
region.

Niche media versus mass media

I define *niche media* as publications (most often magazines and their equivalent websites) that target enthusiasts who share a common interest. *Mass media* such as national newspapers and TV, on the other hand, are produced to appeal to the masses.

I'm a big believer in niche media advertising if you have a very specific target and don't need mass appeal. Mainly because readers of niche media are a captive and engaged audience who are predisposed to receiving and reading your message. And, importantly, it can also be less costly to advertise.

Check out the website at www.magshop.com.au, which contains a complete list of magazines in hundreds of categories from food and travel to business and finance, motoring, gardening, sport, health and fitness, children and many more.

If you're lucky enough to have a business that targets a specific business type or industry, your advertising plan will be much simpler, as many niche publications are produced specifically for different industries. For example, mortgage brokers read *Mortgage Professional Australia*, doctors read *Australian Doctor*, marketers read *Marketing* magazine, vets read *The Veterinarian*, architects read *Architecture Australia* and so on.

Of course, many mass media publications have niche segments or magazines, as well. For example, the *Australian* has the 'Entrepreneur' section for business owners; however, the cost to advertise may be outside your budget.

Targeting your audience

Wastage can be a big problem in advertising. It refers to the number of people who read the publication your ad is in, or watch or listen to the program it appears in, but don't tune in to your ad. Determining wastage is almost impossible, as you purchase advertising based on circulation or ratings rather than the number of people who may respond to your ad.

So that's why there appears to be a recurring theme in this book. Have you noticed? *Know your audience.* This is also the biggest single piece of advice I can give to help you reduce wastage. Know your audience and target your advertising fairly and squarely at them. In developing a brief for your media agency or, if working directly with the publication or station to produce your ad, be sure to give an accurate and detailed description of your target market — who they are, where they live, what they buy and what motivates them.

Reach, frequency, timing and placement

If a tree falls in the forest and there is no-one around to hear it, does it make a sound? Think of your ad as this tree. You don't want it to fall flat without anyone even noticing it. You want it to stand out from the rest of the advertising clutter. And you can do this in two ways — by having an outstanding creative ad and by placing your ad frequently in the right place over a significant period of time.

Here are some things to consider in placing your ad:

✔ **Reach:** How many people will see your ad? *Reach* refers to the number of individuals or homes exposed to your ad. In print media, reach is measured by circulation.

The Australian Press Council issues an annual report on the state of the press in Australia, which covers the circulation rates of all national, metropolitan and local publications. Check out www.presscouncil.org.au, or www.presscouncil.org.nz for the New Zealand Press Council. For example, I easily found out the circulation of my local magazine, *Beast*, is 61,120. On TV, reach is measured by ratings, and www.oztam.com.au and www.nielsenmedia.co.nz are the official sources of television audience measurement.

✔ **Frequency:** How many times will people see your ad? *Frequency* refers to the number of times your ad will be placed and seen. If, for example, you were advertising on a radio station, you might want to air the ad 10 times every day over a period of three months, so your ad would appear around 900 times. Frequency increases the likelihood of your ad getting noticed and responded to. It also helps to embed your brand, tagline and product in the minds of your customers.

✔ **Timing:** What day or time will your ad run? The timing of your ad can make the difference between sale and no sale. If you're running radio ads targeted at busy professionals, you want your ad to air during drivetime, not in the middle of the morning.

✔ **Scheduling:** How long will your ad campaign run? No small business has the budget to run ads 24/7 for 52 weeks of the year. You want to map out the year ahead and advertise when you're likely to get most response. If you sell reverse-cycle air-conditioning, advertising heavily in the lead-up to summer would make sense, and then again in the lead-up to winter. If you're launching a new product or service, your media schedule would probably start heavy and then may stop for a while before you do another blast.

✔ **Placement:** Where will your ad run? Placing your ad in the right section of the paper or in the right program on TV is critical to hit your market. Asking for a preferred position (usually lower bottom right-hand corner for papers) is a good idea, as is finding out what ads will be placed next to yours and what stories or articles might feature around it. If you're a concreter, you probably wouldn't need to advertise in the early general news section of the paper, but at the back of the paper in the trade and services directory, where people search for the kind of services you offer.

If your budget is limited, use fewer media and higher frequency, rather than trying to spread your message thinly across lots of different media. You'll be able to negotiate better rates, reduce production costs and get a greater response.

Developing the Creative Idea

Having your ad in the right place at the right time isn't enough. Your ad has to be powerful enough to make even the toughest critic stand up and take notice.

Creative without strategy is called 'art'. Creative with strategy is called 'advertising'.

—*Jef I. Richards, American advertising professor*

Developing a creative strategy that works across each of the media you choose is critical. If your ad appears on a website, in the *Yellow Pages*, on radio and on a big billboard, for example, you want to be sure they're all working together to reinforce your unique selling proposition, or USP (flick back to Chapter 9), and get people buying.

Before doing any creative brainstorming, you need to get clear on your strategy by completing a simple one-page creative brief. Your advertising agency should take the brief from you and will want to know about your target market, USP, points of difference, your offer, product or service features and benefits, and any substantiating facts and figures you may have available. And, most importantly, they'll want to know what response you want, and what enquiries and sales you expect to generate so you can measure the ad's success.

Golden rules of the creative process

When the brief is done and signed off and everyone is happy, the creative agency can get to work. And, if you're like me, you'll probably also be lying awake at night trying to come up with a great creative idea too! Here are my five golden rules for making sure you end up with the best creative idea possible:

  ✔ **Stick to the brief.** Review the brief and your USP from time to time to make sure your creative ideas fit the strategy.

✔ **Take your time.** Allow yourself enough time to come up with ideas, and then filter them out until you get the best one. Tight deadlines can sometimes force you to accept ideas that might not float.

✔ **Get out of the office.** The best creative ideas rarely come from sitting in front of your computer. Make time for creative dreaming while on your morning run or on a walk by the ocean.

✔ **Check out other great ads.** Great ideas can be sparked by other great ads. Read the publication or monitor the media outlet you're planning to be in and pull out the ads that really appeal to you.

You can also check out sites like www.bestadsontv.com for some inspiration.

✔ **Don't filter.** Let yourself free-fall during the creative process and don't eliminate any ideas at first. The silliest idea, with a bit of tweaking, may end up having real merit when you've had time to massage it a bit.

Understanding the production process

Every advertising agency follows a process from the time of taking a brief to the time your ad goes to market. Understanding the process is important so you end up a happy camper with an ad campaign you can be really proud of. Figure 10-3 sets out a typical production process.

As you see, there is a lot to be done to get it right, and the timeframe from Step 1 to Step 10 (see Figure 10-3), of course, depends on how big and sophisticated your advertising program is. If you're doing TV ads, it could take up to three months to get it right, whereas a simple print ad campaign could be up and running within a month.

Testing your ads

One of the biggest mistakes you can make in advertising is to assume that you and the agency have got it 100 per cent right and to just hit the launch button. If you're spending lots of money on your ad campaign, it's worth spending just a bit more to make sure the ads will get the response you want, before they go live, by running some tests with prospective customers.

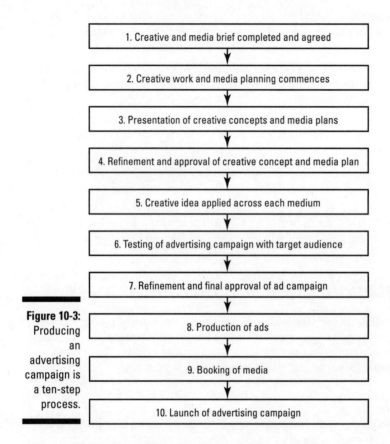

1. Creative and media brief completed and agreed

2. Creative work and media planning commences

3. Presentation of creative concepts and media plans

4. Refinement and approval of creative concept and media plan

5. Creative idea applied across each medium

6. Testing of advertising campaign with target audience

7. Refinement and final approval of ad campaign

8. Production of ads

9. Booking of media

10. Launch of advertising campaign

Figure 10-3: Producing an advertising campaign is a ten-step process.

Here are a few ways you can test your ads:

- ✔ **Hold focus groups.** Gather up to ten people who sit smack bang in the middle of your target market to present your ad idea around the table. Ask a series of targeted questions to get them talking about the ad and giving you feedback. Does this ad make them want to buy this product? If not, why not? If so, why? Focus groups are best conducted by a third-party person who is skilled at drawing out audience response.

  Note: I am personally not a big fan of focus groups. I've witnessed groups where one or two strong individuals can dominate the group thinking and subjectively influence the overall findings.

- ✔ **Send out your ad via email to a trusted target group.** Ask some trusted business associates and customers for their informal feedback. Be careful who you ask for feedback. If your family members aren't the target market for your product or service, don't ask for their opinions.

✔ **Use an online survey.** You can use a format like those provided on www.surveymonkey.com to test your ad more broadly among your customer base. Offer an incentive for them to provide feedback, such as the opportunity to go in the draw to win a weekend holiday.

✔ **Run a pilot campaign.** By airing a few of your ads for a short period you can test the real live response. When customers call or contact you in response to the ad, ask them which specific ad they've seen, what they liked about the ad and what caused them to pick up the phone. This sort of intelligence is invaluable for helping you refine or tweak the ad campaign even further.

When you analyse the feedback, you need to look for patterns that repeat themselves. For example, if you've run a radio ad and 80 per cent of the respondents say how annoying the voice of the announcer was, you might consider trying some alternatives. But, then again, you may not. The annoying voiceover may be the very reason they remembered the ad and called!

Creating Great Print Ads

When you've settled on a great creative concept, you need to apply it across the different media you'll be advertising in. The best print ads (whether for newspapers or magazines) have a great headline, powerful imagery, strong copy and a call to action.

If your print ad budget is very small, opt for frequency over size, and match the size of the message to the size of the ad.

Working up a grabbing headline

Your headline is the best chance you've got to grab your readers' attention. Follow these headline tips:

✔ **Use a question.** Address a major problem with a question, such as 'Would you like to get fit and look fabulous in just 30 days?'

✔ **Lead with your most powerful and obvious benefit.** A headline like 'Lose 5 kg in 5 weeks' gets to the point immediately.

✔ **Keep the headline short and powerful.** But don't make it so short that it could lose its meaning.

✔ **Make it stand out.** Use a large typesize, and bold font and colour.

✔ **Be believable and credible.** Don't promise something that will make people sceptical about your offer.

✔ **Use positive can-do language.** Negative language is a turn-off. For example, 'Get fit and lose weight now' empowers people, as against something like 'Tired of feeling unfit and overweight?'

✔ **Avoid technical jargon.** Jargon just loses people, and so do unnecessary or long words. Compare the punch of 'Get a slimmer waistline' with 'Reduce your kilojoule intake by consuming less saturated fats to decrease your abdominal measurement'.

✔ **Use power words.** They may sound a little clichéd, but words like *save*, *free*, *new*, *improved*, *discover* and *win* do motivate people.

Writing strong copy

The headline grabs attention, no doubt, but the words that follow are what makes people want to keep reading right to the very end. Your ad must build credibility and trust, convincing readers they need what you've got. Here are some tips for writing good copy:

✔ **Tell people the facts.** Don't embellish them. Tell your reader what benefits they'll get for what they pay and how much it will cost.

✔ **Include a story.** Put in testimonials from happy customers or a story of a satisfied customer and how you have improved her life. You could even use a celebrity or well-known identity to endorse your product or service.

✔ **Tell them what you want.** Include special offer deadlines and include toll-free numbers, websites or coupons for them to cut out and mail in.

✔ **Include facts and stats.** Figures that support your copy work wonders in establishing credibility.

✔ **Get legal advice and approval.** This should cover off the small print for any claims, disclaimers, special offers or competitions.

If you're running a competition of any sort in Australia, it's important to get a lotteries licence. These are applied for from a specialist department within each state government. It can be time-consuming, so check out the procedure before you go too far with the planning. In New Zealand, you don't need a licence but you do need to comply with the Gambling Act. Contact the Department of Internal Affairs (www.dia.govt.nz) for information on gaming compliance.

Putting together a winning design

A picture is worth a thousand words. When a great image is combined with a powerful headline and compelling copy, you'll have an award-winning ad that turns heads. Here are some tips on designing the ad:

- ✔ **Include great images.** Use photographs from websites such as www.istockphoto.com or have some professionally shot. You could even consider using cartoons or drawings. You can show the product in use or show the people who use it. If you're advertising gardening services, for example, show a picture of a family enjoying themselves in a beautiful garden rather than a picture of a static plant.

- ✔ **Use lots of space.** Don't put in so much content that your ad becomes confusing and messy. Keep lots of space between the ad copy and the outline and the edge of the page. If you have the space, borders can work quite well to frame your ad.

- ✔ **Make it easy to follow.** Use bullet points or numbers to guide people through the ad and end with a clear statement on what you want them to do and how they can buy.

- ✔ **Don't forget your branding.** Be sure to include your company name, logo, contact details and, of course, your phone number and website in big bold type.

- ✔ **Use the right typeface.** The font you use for the headline and the copy needs to be sympathetic to the environment you're advertising in, the reader and the message. Use clean, simple and easy-to-read fonts like Helvetica or Verdana and increase the font size where necessary to reinforce key messages.

- ✔ **Stick with the look.** When you have your ad look and feel, stick with it. You may need to make minor alterations as you go, but every time a potential customer sees the same ad, you create greater awareness of your business, even if they're not in the market for what you offer right now.

When in doubt (as to whether to put something in an ad), leave it out. Too much information only confuses and alienates the reader. Unless it absolutely has to be in, forget it.

Getting the print ad produced

You've got a great-looking ad and you're champing at the bit to get it out there. You still need to do a few things before it goes to print:

- ✔ **Check the lead times.** Magazines have much longer lead times than newspapers, so you need to be sure your ad is done and ready to go way before the publication is actually printed.

- ✔ **Request preferred placement.** If you really want your ad to run in a certain section and on a certain place on the page, you can request it. For example, your ad may feature a coupon that you want people to cut out, so you might prefer the bottom right-hand corner of the page to make it easy for people to cut out.

- ✔ **Check the ad proof.** Before your ad appears, you need to check a proof of your ad. Two heads and eyes are better than one, so make sure you and a friend or staff member check the ad for *typos* (typographical errors) and that the contact details and fine print are all correct. Surprisingly often, errors in large type also get missed, so check your headline carefully too.

- ✔ **Get the colour right.** If your ad is black and white, then you don't have too much to worry about. Full-colour ads, however, are printed in what is called a *four-colour process*, using cyan, magenta, yellow and black. And some ads can include spot colour where the ad is essentially black and white with some bits of colour. When proofing your ad, check that the colours are right and are in the right places (called colour *registration*).

- ✔ **Check the rates and size.** Print media use lots of unusual terms in sizing up your ad, like *column centimetre*, *cost per thousand (CPM)*, *frequency discounts* and many more. My advice is to just get out the ruler and make sure you know exactly what size the ad will be before approving.

- ✔ **Get copies of the ad.** When your ad appears and, if it's full page and really dynamic, you may want to reproduce copies of it to use as mailers or to give to people.

Directory ads

Many years ago, before the World Wide Web, the only real directory most small businesses advertised in was the *Yellow Pages*. If you've decided directory advertising is a must for your business, here are some steps to follow to create powerful ads:

✔ **Choose the right directory.** Be sure it is the right one for you. Do your homework and get some references from other customers before committing.

✔ **Choose the right classification.** Make sure you're firmly listed in each of the categories you want to be in. For example, if you're an accountant, you might want to list under accounting and taxation services.

✔ **Choose the right size and placement.** Take a look at the ads from the previous year's directory and see where you were placed against your competitors. Then agree on the size and place you want to be listed.

✔ **Choose the right words.** People using directories are looking for a local business they can trust to solve a problem. No matter how big or small your ad, you need to treat it as an opportunity to solve their problem and create trust, rather than a mere listing of your business name and contact details. The same copy rules apply to a print ad you might run in the local paper.

Beware of pushy directory salespeople. Ask for facts and stats to support their claims of advertising success. Just because they say your competitors are placing a bigger ad doesn't necessarily mean you should too.

Creating Great TV Ads

If you're fortunate enough to have the big bucks you need to produce professional TV ads, this section is for you.

If you don't have the big bucks, still read on, because you might learn some neat tricks to help you create low-budget but relatively high-quality ads for YouTube or your own website. Most of the big advertising pros would slap my wrists for even suggesting this and argue for slick production and feature-film quality. I reckon the internet has changed the rules of advertising forever. In thousands of cases people have made their own ads and become famous via YouTube or by sending out their ads virally.

If you run a charity or other not-for-profit organisation, you may find that television stations will do a reasonable deal for cost-effective production of community spots or advertising. Some of the larger ad agencies may also be interested to sponsor advertising production for a charity.

Getting help with your TV ad

Your creative agency (if you have one) will take a detailed brief from you and drill down to find your unique selling proposition (USP) before starting work on the ad.

When I was in the advertising game, the agency wouldn't start work on a TV ad until the brief had passed the *Mum Test*. If your mother couldn't read the brief, understand it and be inspired by it, then it was back to the drawing board!

When you've agreed on the brief, the agency gets to work on the big idea and puts it into a sequence of storyboards so you can get a good feel for the content and flow of the ad. When you've agreed on the ad concept, the agency sources the professionals required to help make it, such as:

- ✔ Actors or talent for the ad
- ✔ Animators
- ✔ Copywriters
- ✔ Costume and set designers
- ✔ Lighting and equipment providers
- ✔ Music or jingle writers
- ✔ Recording specialists
- ✔ Video producers and editors

If you want to use video footage or music that has been produced by another company and is legally owned by them, make sure you get a licence to use it. The fee could be high, so do your homework before you set your heart on the latest greatest hit.

Television stations (and radio stations) use lots of terminology such as *availability*, *network affiliates*, *flight*, *spot*, *increments*, *sponsorships*, *total audience plan*, *gross rating points*, *target rating points* and more. Do a web search for **TV Terminology Wikipedia** to access a full list of terms so you appear informed and up-to-date during your negotiations. And, when dealing with your media agency or direct with the stations, be honest and ask them to explain the terminology and exactly what it means for your advertising campaign so you know exactly what you're getting and what to expect.

The ingredients of great TV ads

Television ads that are emotional, compelling and talked about are very rare. So, before producing any ads, I suggest you trawl through the internet and watch a lot of TV ads to pick out the good ones for inspiration. Here are some top tips to help you create a great ad:

- ✔ **Start strong.** Use a powerful opening message.

- ✔ **Get to the main point quickly.** Don't leave the viewer wondering. Repeat the point often to ensure the message is loud and clear.

- ✔ **Be proactive.** Demonstrate how your product or service will change the viewer's life.

- ✔ **Use powerful music and sound.** Image-provoking music and sound effects create impact.

- ✔ **Work on stirring the emotions of the viewer.** Make them laugh, make them cry, make them sing and dance; just don't leave them yawning or, worse still, switching off.

- ✔ **Use a strong voice.** If you use a voiceover, make sure the voice is strong and commands respect and attention, and that it reflects your target audience.

- ✔ **Use great talent and actors.** Make sure they directly reflect the audience you want to attract.

- ✔ **Don't forget your brand.** Leave no uncertainty that the ad is for your company by including your business name verbally and visually. I've lost track of the number of times I've seen a fantastic ad but can't recall who it was for.

- ✔ **Ask for action.** Tell your viewers exactly what you want them to do, such as ring a toll-free number, register their details on your website or SMS a special code to you.

- ✔ **Place your ad in the right place.** Make sure you choose the right stations, the right programs and right ad breaks to hit your target market. And make sure you run them often enough to get attention. Your media buying agency can recommend the best scheduling and weighting for your ad and manage the booking and placement.

Infomercials

Infomercials are an option to running advertisements. They are more of a program-style ad where you personally promote your product or services direct to viewers via a demonstration. The infomercial can be prerecorded or run live to air. Check out the shopping channels on TV to get a feel for infomercials.

Infomercials can work well for companies that sell products or services such as beauty items or homewares, sports equipment or self-help programs. Perhaps you remember Big Kev's Cleaning Products and how well he used infomercials to market his company.

Good infomercials do the following:

✔ Position your product as the one and only choice

✔ Demonstrate the product in use

✔ Include satisfied customer testimonials and stories

✔ Focus directly on the features and benefits to sell the product

✔ Ask people to act immediately through special offers and discounts

✔ Offer flexible payment options and money-back guarantees

Creating Great Radio Ads

Radio ads are a cost-effective option for many businesses that don't have the big TV ad budgets. In 30 or 60 seconds, a good radio ad aimed at the right target market can grab attention and get people engaged. However, a plethora of very bad radio ads is out there. You can most often really tell the ones that have been hastily put together and thrown on air. Of course, this won't happen to you, because by reading on you'll know exactly what to do to create great radio ads.

Great radio ads are not written, but spoken. Here are some tips for producing a great radio ad:

✔ **Get your listeners' attention.** Make the first sentence sound like an announcement: 'Announcing the launch of the all-new white power cleanser ...'

✔ **Keep it simple.** Use straightforward, modern, friendly and simple language that people use in everyday conversation.

✔ **Use appropriate talent.** Hire the best voice talent you can afford if it will be prerecorded and make sure the voice talent matches your target market. If your market is young kids, use a young kid for the voice talent. If your market is the elderly, use an elderly person for voice talent and so on.

Consider having the radio announcer read your ad live, but only if you can be sure they represent the right market and will add real credibility to your ad. Some announcers will add their own endorsement also.

✔ **Get the pace right.** Speak at the rate that people generally talk — not too fast and not too slow, and include pauses so people can digest and think about what's being said.

✔ **Use power words.** Make the sentences short and punchy, and use power words like *save, free, help, discover, bargain, breakthrough, new, now, yes, life, secrets* and *you*.

✔ **Don't talk about** *we.* Talk directly to the listener like you're having a one-on-one conversation with them: 'Are *you* ready to get rid of your money worries forever?'

✔ **Stick with a theme.** Focus on your USP and stick with a single theme for the ad. You have only 30 or 60 seconds to make an impact, so don't blow it by trying to squeeze in too many messages. Two words per second should be the maximum.

✔ **Make it active.** Include a call to action and make a simple offer: 'Phone 1300 Get Now and go in the draw to win a car.' Offer free estimates and free appraisals and no-obligation information or brochures to be mailed.

✔ **Don't forget your contact number.** Repeat your company name and phone number during the ad. Don't just stick it in at the end, like an afterthought. Make sure the number is easy to remember.

✔ **Use a catchy tune.** Try to create a mental image in people's minds by combining powerful words with a great jingle or music. Use music that is sympathetic to the genre of music on the station.

✔ **Leverage other advertising.** Refer to other forms of advertising. For example, if you want your audience to fill in a coupon on your ad in the paper, tell them exactly where and when they can find it.

✔ **Limit your disclaimers.** Long, hastily mumbled disclaimers can ruin an ad. If you need a long disclaimer, then you probably need to go back to the drawing board and review the ad altogether.

When you have an idea of the radio stations you should feature on, listen to the station for a few days and write down a list of companies that appear to have followed the preceding checklist. If the ads really appeal to you, contact the company and find out who did the ad.

Many of the same production timeframes that apply to TV also apply to radio. Review the section 'Creating Great TV Ads' earlier in this chapter to find out what resources you need to make it work for you. Although it won't be as expensive and the lead times will be way shorter, doing it properly is still vital, so you'll have an ad that works for the long term.

Creating Great Outdoor Ads

I'm personally a big fan of outdoor advertising if it's well placed and targeted, and particularly if it's supported by other kinds of advertising like print. (Check out the pros and cons of outdoor advertising, or out-of-home advertising, in Chapter 9 to see if it suits your product or service.)

Outdoor ads can include anything from the biggest billboard in the CBDs of major cities right down to branding on takeaway coffee cups at the local café in the smallest regional town. So, unfortunately, a one-size-fits-all approach doesn't work. Here are a few tips to work out if outdoor advertising is for you and how to go about it:

- Use your creative ad agency and media buying agency if you plan on spending up big on it. An agency will probably drive a harder bargain with the media than you can and they know what you really should be paying.

- If you don't plan on using an agency, do your homework before committing to anything. Get all the ins and outs of the deal and pricing and don't talk price until you're 100 per cent sure.

- If you're targeting a specific billboard site, for example, make sure you get exact figures on pass-by traffic, response rates and references from other advertisers so you can call some shots.

I could probably write a whole *For Dummies* guide on the world of outdoor advertising, it's so huge! Bring in the experts and get advice before leaping in.

Chapter 11

Getting the Message Out

. . . .

In This Chapter

▶ Getting yourself organised for the campaign

▶ Making the most of your advertising campaign

▶ Giving your customers what your ads promise

▶ Assessing the campaign's success

. . . .

You've put in the hard yards to develop your advertising campaign, and you're about to hit the launch button and send your ads out to the universe. Now you can sit back and relax and wait for the phone to ring, right? Wrong!

Great ads raise awareness of your business, and get people interested and enquiring, but they don't make the sale for you — unless you happen to be promoting a product for people to buy directly online.

Throughout the development of your advertising campaign, you need to also develop the plan to launch and deliver on your advertising promise. In this chapter, you discover how to get the most out of your ads and turn them into sales.

Getting Your Advertising Strategy Organised

Before you can actually launch your campaign, you need to ask the following questions to get yourself organised:

✔ What other marketing tactics should you use to support your advertising campaign?

✔ How do you advise your existing customers, prospects and contacts of your advertising offer?

✔ How do you get your staff involved and motivated to support the advertising? What incentive (if any) will you offer to get them on board?

✔ How will you handle enquiries? What will your sales script be?

✔ What will your tracking and follow-up process look like?

✔ What information should you collect from the customer and what will you record on your database?

✔ How will you fulfil product and service delivery and timeframes?

✔ How will you follow up enquiries that are not an immediate sale?

✔ What will you measure to determine the success of advertising (number of enquiries and actual sales)?

✔ How, when and to whom will you report this information?

✔ How regularly will you review the different ads and refine them if you need?

Launching Your Advertising Campaign

You've spent lots of time and money on developing the ad campaign already, so why not spend that little bit extra to make sure it goes off with a *bang* and launch your campaign in a fun and engaging way that takes your staff and customers along for the ride.

Many ad campaigns fall flat because they aren't supported by a program that inspires and creates opportunities for your audience to engage with you, even if they're not buying right now.

Leveraging your campaign with other marketing tactics

Good ad campaigns work best when supported by other marketing tactics. For example, if someone has seen your ad a few times and then receives a cold call from your telemarketing team, he's more likely to be aware of you and predisposed to accept the call.

Try adding at least three tactics such as letterbox drops, direct mail and even cold calling to support your advertising campaign. (See Chapter 8 for more on tactics like these.)

The staff-led campaign

Many years ago in a past life, I worked for a company managing their three-month print and outdoor campaign. We were spending up big, with full-colour ads in major papers and billboards at the airport. At the time we had about 130 staff.

We spent as much time engaging staff in the ad campaign and getting them behind it as we did working with the ad agency to develop the ads. This paid off in spades. The staff were excited to see their company name up in lights and, because they knew all about it, as well as when and where the ads would appear, they were actively telling their family, friends and customers about it. Our ad campaign created powerful word-of-mouth business via staff.

Imagine you own a car accessories warehouse called CarStop and you've just relocated to a great new site two kilometres away from your old premises. You've expanded your product range and are offering a new range of car-washing and detailing services. You need to let your existing customers know about the move and your new services, as well as attract new customers and drive-by traffic. Your ad campaign includes radio, the local newspaper, well-positioned outdoor signs and an online campaign. Here's what you decide to do to support the launch of the campaign:

- ✔ Take your staff for a weekend of go-kart racing and give them customer service training, tell them about the ad campaign and set them sales targets.

- ✔ Host drinks for your VIP customers the night before you open to the public and announce a special VIP program.

- ✔ Produce copies of the print ad and do a letterbox drop the day you open.

- ✔ Send out a postcard offer to customers on your database announcing a special loyalty offer.

- ✔ Hire an actor to dress up as a racing car driver and hand out flyers at the front of the shop and at the nearby shopping centre.

- ✔ Contact a popular radio station and offer to do an interview (and maybe expand to a weekly spot) on the importance of car maintenance and how to go about it.

Brainstorm with your staff ideas on how to get the message out on the ground. Tell them your budget, timeframes and how many customers you want to get and by when, and see what they come up with.

Getting your staff on board

Putting out a campaign and not having all your staff on board, including your mailroom people and office cleaner, is one of the biggest mistakes you can make in getting your ads out to the market. Your staff are a walking, talking billboard and they need to be actively engaged from the time you agree to go ahead with advertising to the time it hits the streets and way beyond.

Here are some ideas on how to get staff engaged:

✔ Give them a copy of the ads and the advertising schedule that shows when and where the ads are going to appear.

✔ Have a team meeting to tell them the overall sales targets you want to achieve and set individual targets with incentives.

✔ Have a celebratory dinner the night before the ad's launch to thank them in advance for their support.

✔ Give them training on how you want them to respond when someone says to them, 'I saw your ad in the paper this morning . . .'

✔ Develop a flowchart, process and script for how you want your sales people to handle all enquiries. Make sure they ask every person enquiring how they heard about you and where they saw the ad. Ensure they are trained to collect essential customer information that you might want, such as name, postcode, phone number and email address.

✔ Hold weekly meetings to update staff on how the ads are going, to report on sales results and seek feedback on where things could be improved.

✔ Develop a daily sales chart or competition for staff to record their sales results.

✔ Celebrate big wins throughout the ad campaign.

Getting your customers on board

The purpose of advertising is not just to attract new customers. It's to keep in front of your current or past customers to let them know you're still here and to tell them about new products or services. Your existing customers are your best source of new business because they already know, like and trust you, and are therefore more likely to give you repeat business — and, importantly, tell others about you.

Here's how you can use your ads to market to your existing customers:

- ✔ Produce copies of your print ad and give them to customers as they enter your store or put them in their shopping bags as they leave the store.

- ✔ Play your TV ads on a big screen in-store so people can see them. Recently I was at the head office of a major bank where they were playing their ads and running interviews with staff on a looped program on a big plasma screen in the foyer.

- ✔ Use your ad in a mailout with a covering letter to the customers on your database and follow it up with a phone call.

- ✔ Train your staff to ask customers who call or enter the store if they've seen this week's ads in the paper and if the offer is of interest to them.

- ✔ Send an email to your customers through your database telling them about your ad and offering them a special discount as a loyal customer if they respond by a certain date.

Don't ignore your existing customers at the expense of new ones. Get them coming back and buying more, and ask if they'd be kind enough to tell a friend. There's no harm in asking, if it's done with a smile and gratitude.

Fulfilling Your Advertising Promise

Has this ever happened to you? You've been surfing online and come across a compelling ad and you want to find out more. There's a toll-free number to ring or an online enquiry form to fill out. You ring the toll-free number and an automated voice responds with a menu of numbers to choose from that would fill a phone book. Frustrated, you hang up and decide to try the online enquiry form. You fill it out, send it off and then ... nothing. Nil response!

This has happened to me more than once and it's caused me to wonder why the heck the company would bother even advertising in the first place! Don't let it happen to you. If you're going to spend valuable bucks on advertising, be ready, be willing and be able to respond and deliver.

Handling responses

Recently I was looking for a web developer and customer relationship management (CRM) system on behalf of a customer. I did my research and worked out what database systems would be most suitable, making contact with ten companies. Five of the companies I chose from an internet search (I figured if the companies were well found on Google, then they knew a bit about internet marketing) and the other five were recommendations or people I had worked with previously.

I phoned each company to ask about their business and discuss what I was looking for. Of the ten people I contacted, only three were able to actively engage me in a meaningful conversation about my needs and how their service could assist. Another three were just a bit above average with their response and the final four were no less than woeful! Not one of the ten appeared to follow a proper process or script to seek the information they needed from me. Only three even bothered to take my name and contact details, with the other seven assuming I'd remember to send the email with the request for proposal (RFP) I had promised (refer to Chapter 10 for more on these requests).

You can have the best ad in the world, but if you or your staff blow the first point of contact, whether face to face or over the phone, you can kiss your potential customer goodbye! Table 11-1 gives you a model for handling that ever-important first contact.

Table 11-1	Response-Handling Process
Step	**Action**
1	Answer call in three rings. (If the enquiry is by email, respond by both email and phone if you have the number.)
2	Answer with 'Welcome to XYZ company, Mary speaking.' Get their name: 'May I ask who I am speaking with please?'
3	Respond with, 'How can I help you today John?' Listen to customer response.
4	Feed back to them what you have heard them say: 'So you are interested in the . . .'
5	Ask them how they found out about you and which ad they might have specifically seen that caused them to call. Record this information.
6	Create a conversation — about them not you! Ask more questions like: What features do you like specifically? How does the price fit with your budget? How do you think our product might help you? Are you interested in buying today (if so, perhaps we can offer you a special deal or a discount)? Do you want any more information on our company/product/service to help you make a decision?

Step	Action
7	Ask for their contact information — full name, phone number, email, company name, postcode and mailing address (or whatever else you might want to collect, within reason of course). Ask if they would like to be added to your mailing list to receive information from you via email or direct mail.
8	Ask for the sale! Would you like to buy now or arrange for a free no-obligation quote (or whatever your desired response to the ad is). If you don't ask, you most often don't get!
9	If you get a sale, complete the order and arrange fulfilment. If no sale, ask when and how you can contact them again to see how you might be able to help.
10	Record all customer information, contact notes, sale details and so on in your database and diary to follow up at a suitable time to the customer.

A *no* from a first-time prospect doesn't mean *no* forever, it just means *no, not now*. If the prospect truly is a warm one and has potential down the track to become a customer, make sure you have a process in place to record in your diary to follow them up.

Delivering on your promise

A prospect has responded to your ad and you've made the sale. You're happy and the customer is happy, and she can't wait to get the package by courier within three days — just like you promised.

You send the order through to the warehouse and, as far as you know, the warehouse has received it and is shipping it off right now. Done and dusted. Next prospect please. Five days later, however, a very annoyed customer rings to find out where her order is. Has this ever happened to your customers?

A very important part of the advertising process is the delivery process, from the time you take the enquiry right through to sale, to despatch, delivery and follow-up. A flowchart of your fulfilment process and the time taken for each step should be prepared and agreed with all staff before making any promises to the customer. If your ad says 'Overnight Delivery with Money-Back Guarantee', you'd better have processes in place to ensure you can deliver on your promise.

Be careful about promising anything that may not be within the control of your business. For example, if you rely on lots of other suppliers or contractors like fulfilment houses or couriers to deliver, and you don't have tight contracts or deals with them, you may find yourself over-promising and under-delivering.

Keeping records

Keeping records is a critical part of providing a seamless experience for your customers. Refer to Chapter 2 to get savvy on what information you might collect for your database and how to use it. Records of conversation, dates of order and despatch, and diary calls to follow up are all critical. And, if you haven't got with the program yet when it comes to a database, at least make sure your paper files are easy to follow, well ordered and easy to access by anyone in your office.

The more information you record and keep on your customers and their orders with you, the better opportunity there is to market to them in the future and sell them other services and products.

I once came across a law firm that had thousands of customers who had only ever used the company for one service, despite it offering up to eight different kinds of legal service — everything from defending drink-driving offences to filing a divorce. By reviewing its old customer files, which had been kept in meticulous order, the firm was able to go back and contact old customers to remind them they were still there, and have a meaningful conversation about their old case. Calls to a hundred of these past customers netted nine new pieces of business.

Following up

One of the simplest and most obvious, yet the most ignored, parts of the advertising and customer service process is following up. By *following up*, I mean contacting the customer for no other reason than to find out if he's happy, if he received the goods, if he needs any help on how to use the product, or whatever.

Imagine if you'd just been to the doctor with a very sick child and the doctor actually called you a week later to find out how she was. Imagine if you got your mobile phone back after extensive repairs and the mobile phone shop actually called to make sure it was okay. Imagine if your florist actually called to let you know the exact time the flowers you ordered for your mother's birthday were delivered. Imagine if your trip to the dentist to have all your wisdom teeth out was followed up by a call from the dentist's receptionist or the dental nurse to see how you are. Imagine if the restaurant owner rang you the day after you dined there to thank you for coming and to get feedback on your dining experience. You get the picture.

If you're saying, 'That's all very well and very nice, but we don't have the time,' think again. If you made an unexpected follow-up call to the customers who generously responded to your advertising to show you care, do you think they'd remember you and come back? Do you think they would tell other people about you?

This is a simple technique and one that is not often used. Think about what a little follow-up call could do to keep your product, service or business in the hearts and minds of your customers.

Evaluating Your Advertising

How many ads did you hear, see or watch today? How many do you remember? I'm betting you've been exposed to hundreds and that you'd be lucky to remember more than three. To make sure you're one of the three, you need to constantly evaluate how well your ads are responded to and what sales they result in.

Measuring return on investment

If you're spending $100,000 on your ad campaign and spending that again on employing people to manage the calls and fulfil your promise, you want to see a real return on investment. There is no general rule on what to expect, as, of course, the margins on each sale will vary, depending on your product costs and other overheads.

In briefing your ad agency staff, let them know how many enquiries you expect to receive from your ads and what percentage of those you expect to turn into sales and revenue. Remember, marketing is a numbers game. It's about generating enough leads and enquiries to convert a decent number into sales.

If possible, set up a separate toll-free phone number (refer to Chapter 6 for details) or a separate web page (see Chapter 17) for your advertising campaigns so you can measure the exact number of enquiries generated by your ads. That way you can work out your conversion rate and return on investment.

Evaluating what worked and what didn't

At the end of any ad campaign (and, indeed, during the campaign) you need to evaluate what worked and what didn't, so next time your ads will have even more impact.

Here are the types of things you need to evaluate:

- ✔ How many enquiries did you get?
- ✔ Which ads got the best response?
- ✔ Which medium worked most effectively — radio, TV, newspaper, outdoor and so on?
- ✔ What traffic did you get to your website? How many visitors left information on your site or ordered online?
- ✔ How well did you respond to enquiries and convert them to sales? How could you do it better next time?
- ✔ What general feedback did you get on your advertising, your product or service offer and your business in general?
- ✔ How could you improve your advertising campaign next time? Consider creative aspects, the media schedule, fulfilment and after-sales service.

The most important questions to ask at the end of the campaign are: If you had your time over, would you advertise again? Was it really worth the effort? Are there any other marketing tactics that would work better?

Considering a rerun

If your advertising worked for you, you'll almost certainly want to consider a rerun. A rerun gives you the opportunity to refine your ad campaign and get it bringing in even more revenue. In addition, you'll have learned the tricks of the trade in dealing with creative agencies, media planners or the media companies direct. All this means (hopefully) that you're able to drive a harder bargain in your media buy.

For any marketing activity to really work — and that includes advertising — you really need to commit to it for a reasonable length of time and you need to run a decent number of ads to make any sort of impression.

If you have a media buying agency, work with the staff to delve into the reach and frequency data for each medium so you can make informed decisions on where and when to run your next ads and how often to run them.

Establishing an annual advertising program

When you know advertising is the marketing tactic for you and that you're going to do it regularly, develop an annual media plan. Depending on the kind of business you're in, your plan may include a *go-heavy* advertising period and a *go-light* or a *no-go* advertising period. For example, if you run a giftware shop, you might advertise heavily around occasions such as Mother's Day, Father's Day and Christmas, and lightly throughout the rest of the year. If you're a tax specialist, you might advertise heavily in July through to October, and not at all during the remainder of the year.

Chapter 12

Mastering the Basics of Publicity

. . . .

In This Chapter

▶ Getting to know how publicity works

▶ Examining what's good and bad about different media

. . . .

*W*hat is publicity? *Publicity* is the deliberate attempt to manage the public's perception of you, your business and your products or services through the media. Two myths need to be blown about publicity way up-front. Publicity is not about pulling the wool over people's eyes and it is not free advertising.

Be warned, if you approach publicity in the same way you approach advertising, expecting it to directly sell your product or service, forget it. Product pushes, even subtle ones, are quickly sifted out by journalists. You must approach your publicity strategy with a view to adding value, raising awareness of a problem or highlighting a fun or interesting story to your audience. The fact that your business or service happens to help the audience is secondary, and you have to be prepared that your business name, product, service or contact details may not even make it to print.

I get many business owners ringing me for a referral to a publicity expert. With some careful questioning, I can usually find out what their understanding of publicity is and how they think it can help their business. I reckon four out of five people want publicity because they think it's a free way of advertising their business. And most people have a misperception of what it really takes to make a business a publicity magnet. Many times I've advised people to forget publicity and explore other promotional tactics.

Having said that, publicity can work for many businesses if you're willing to work on it for the long haul. This chapter helps you come to the decision as to whether publicity is for you, and sets you straight on how you need to approach it and get the help you need.

Understanding How Publicity Works

No doubt, getting your business in the media is a powerful way to enhance the profile of your business and bring in new enquiries. Good publicity can position you as a leader in your field. Bad publicity can destroy you.

Publicity is much more than just writing a media release and sending it out to a predetermined list of journalists in the hope they'll find it interesting enough to report on. Publicity can work really well if you have a story that is groundbreaking, unrivalled, newsworthy and has wide public appeal. It can also work well if you're an expert in your field or industry and you want to position yourself as a thought leader and sought-after media commentator.

To make publicity work, just like advertising, you need a good, simple plan. In many cases, a publicity plan can work very well alongside your advertising plan.

Publicity versus public relations

Publicity is about the deliberate attempt to create a favourable story about you or your business in the media, but the scope of public relations is actually much broader.

Public relations (PR) refers to the practice of managing communications between a business and its public, and creating a favourable relationship with the different parties your business success depends on. PR can be used to build rapport and establish relations with a whole host of organisations and people, such as:

- The media
- Employees and unions
- The local community and community groups
- Local councils and government bodies
- Voters
- Shareholders
- Customers and prospective customers
- Industry bodies and employer associations

Imagine you're a property developer and you've just bought a big block of land in the city to develop into apartments. You're going to need a serious public relations plan to communicate with the many stakeholders in the project, including the local council, infrastructure consultants such as traffic specialists and engineers, local shop owners, local residents, community groups that might be resistant to development, the local papers, prospective buyers, real estate agents, suppliers and more. In fact, for a property developer, public relations (and publicity) is probably the single most important marketing and communication activity you need to undertake, from the time the land is bought until after the apartments are sold.

If your business is going to have a major impact on a variety of stakeholders and negative backlash is a potential problem, you definitely need a PR consultant or contractor on board. She'll develop a plan for you to deal with and diffuse potential negative relations and ensure you send out consistent positive messages.

PR is not about *spin-doctoring*, which is more about fudging the facts and blurring the bounds of truth. PR is about telling the truth and genuinely caring about what your audience thinks and feels, and positioning your business in a light that shows this. If you feel you need a spin doctor to cover things up a bit, have a think about your business ethics.

Publicity and small business

Unlike big business, small businesses can't afford to have teams of media relations and PR experts beavering away observing and monitoring the media, managing the distribution of media releases and keeping relationships with journalists and various publishers in check.

If you use publicity as a promotional tactic for your business, you need to either have the skills to do it properly yourself — and be serious about making the time for it — or recruit the services of a publicity expert or PR consultant. Read this chapter and the next one, and then you can make a decision as to whether to take a DIY approach or bring in the big guns.

For more information on courses available in PR, how to best choose a PR consultant and a directory of consultants in Australia visit the Public Relations Institute website at www.pria.com.au, shown in Figure 12-1, and in New Zealand www.prinz.org.nz.

Figure 12-1:
The Public Relations Institute of Australia can help you choose a PR course or a consultant.

Choosing a PR or publicity agency

PR and publicity agencies vary enormously in size and capability. They range from one-man-band practitioners to industry specialists, from small local businesses to huge global companies with offices and affiliates around the world. The process of selecting a PR person is no different from the process of selecting an ad agency.

Create a shortlist of consultancies that appear to meet your needs by reviewing the PR association websites noted in the previous section or doing an internet search. Check out what other businesses appear to be doing well in the media and ring them to find out who does their PR or publicity, or ask some business associates for a referral. Prepare a request for proposal (see Chapter 10 for more on RFPs), phone the companies you've listed and ask if you can meet with a representative.

When you meet, you need to find out a few things, such as:

✔ What is their background and experience?

✔ How much work have they done in similar areas to yours?

✔ Do they have any case studies on these projects?

✔ Do they work with any other business that offers what you do; that is, your competitors?

✔ How do they charge — by monthly retainer, by the hour, by the project or on agreed success objectives?

✔ Who would be working on your project (if not the person you're meeting with)?

✔ What are the methods of reporting — a report after each meeting or a monthly or quarterly report?

✔ What is their guarantee that they can deliver the media coverage you wish to get?

When they have all responded to your RFP and you've selected the best agency, you might want to agree on a three- or six-month trial to test the response to your PR activities.

Tips for getting publicity

Whether you take a DIY approach or work with an agent, in working with the media and journalists to get publicity you need to focus on a number of vital aspects. Here are some you just can't ignore:

✔ Determine specifically what media your target market is reading, listening to or watching. For example, if you specialise in wedding invitations, focus your attention on the media that targets young brides-to-be.

✔ Remember, the media today is very broad and encompasses TV, radio, newspapers, magazines, industry journals, websites, online radio and much more. Some media will be easier to get into than others.

✔ Do your research on the top 10 to 20 media outlets you would like to appear in. Subscribe to them or listen to and watch them, so you can identify what they report on and what kinds of stories they might be interested in.

✔ For each media outlet, find out who the editor or program producer is, any specialist or freelance journalists they use and what their deadlines are. Develop a contact list to add to a database.

✔ Determine what you're going to offer the media. You must have a strong angle. A news release on the opening of your new office is just not going to cut it. The media looks for interesting stories or articles that are well written and answer the key questions of who, what, where, when, why and how in the first few paragraphs.

✔ Remember, journalists are busy people with deadlines, and editors breathing down their necks, so don't waste their time with boring drivel — make your story topical.

✔ Always look at ways you can add value for the journalist or program producer. Offer to do a regular freelance article for him or to manage his online forums on a particular topic, or to write the answers to an 'Ask Dave' column.

✔ Keep in mind that the media love statistics, latest research findings, real-life stories and case studies — anything that sells papers or improves ratings!

✔ The best way to get your story out is to have a personal conversation with the journalist and offer her something she can't refuse and then fax or email the story to the editor or journalist. If you really want your story to get noticed, send it in print with a box of donuts.

Setting your expectations

I'd be doing you an injustice if I didn't set your expectations, up-front, about how difficult it can be to get your business up in lights using publicity.

Publicity is not like advertising. When you want to advertise (and pay good money), the media throw their arms open wide and embrace you. When you want publicity, on the other hand, 99 per cent of the time the media run away, unless your story happens to be so powerful (negative or positive) they can't afford to ignore it.

> *If at first you don't succeed, try, try again. Then quit. There's no point in being a damn fool about it.*
>
> —*W. C. Fields (1880–1946), American comedian, actor and juggler*

It pays to have a really thick skin in dealing with journalists. You'll get lots of knockbacks, and unreturned emails and phone calls. But try, try again and only give up if you've gained enough wisdom and insight to know that your time, effort and money would be best put into other promotional tactics.

Looking at the Pros and Cons of Different Media

Every media outlet you work with has its own life, rules, nuances and deadlines. Radio and television are often live, which means you need to be an eloquent speaker or presenter and a quick thinker, whereas newspaper and magazine articles are usually written after an interview or adapted from a version of the story you submit.

Whatever the media you decide is best for your business, you need to spend time getting acquainted with each one and making sure you have the appropriate skills. In Chapter 9 I look at the advantages and disadvantages of advertising in the different media. In this section I delve into what makes or breaks publicity in each medium. Check out Tables 12-1 to 12-5 thoroughly before you decide where you want your story to appear.

Watch out for stage fright!

Some time ago, I released an e-report entitled *Top Ten Marketing Mistakes to Avoid When Times Get Tough.* I wrote it at the time of the looming global financial crisis as a way to encourage small businesses to keep marketing and stay positive. I offered it on my website to subscribers and I sent it to the relevant small-business journalists and magazines.

The *Daily Telegraph* picked it up and ran a huge article. The producer of *Mornings with Kerri-Anne* noticed the story and invited me to appear with Kerri-Anne Kennerley. It was my first live TV interview. I look back on the recording of that interview now and cringe. I

had prepared extensively and knew exactly what I wanted to say; however, when I got into the hotseat ... Now, normally I'm a woman who can think and speak on her feet and sound half-reasonable, but there was something about being live on TV that put the wind up me!

I tell this story to demonstrate that every medium is different. The way you work with it, interact with it and get your story out differs completely for each one. Appearing in the newspapers is far easier than appearing in a live-to-air TV interview.

TV publicity

Appearing on TV can be challenging, as personal experience has taught me (check out the sidebar 'Watch out for stage fright!'). Hopefully, by understanding the pros and cons in Table 12-1, you won't make the same mistakes I did. But television appearances aren't always as scary as a full-on interview. You could simply be asked to give an expert opinion on camera for a news or current affairs program, and often the journalist will use only 20 seconds of you for the story.

Table 12-1	Pros and Cons of TV Publicity		
Advantage	*Why*	*Disadvantage*	*Why*
Mass audience	TV publicity can be great for building your reputation quickly in front of a large audience. If you happen to live in a regional area and appear on local TV, you could become a celebrity overnight.	Difficult to achieve	If you manage to get yourself on TV, give yourself a pat on the back. It's usually the most difficult medium to get a gig on and requires a fair degree of tenacity and confidence to make it happen.
Emotional appeal	People can get to know, like and trust you far better on TV than any other medium, especially if you have great presence and the ability to tell a story and be genuine.	Live interviews	Unless you're a seasoned expert, doing live interviews can be nerve-wracking and, if you make a mess of it, you can't retract it. If the interview is prerecorded, at least it can be edited.
Short lead time	Most programming is not done too far in advance. If you have a great story and contact the media with it one day, you could find yourself on TV the very next day!	Cluttered environment	Unless your story truly is breaking news for the nation, you may find it or your interview lost among the day's news, ads and other interviews.

Advantage	Why	Disadvantage	Why
Personally fulfilling	Becoming a good presenter on TV is personally really rewarding and can force you to improve your presentation skills and the way you look.	Appearance	It's sad but true — people will make a judgement on how you look and this will affect their feelings towards you, your message and your company.
Experience	Being on TV is a fun experience. You get to see how a program is produced and meet the stars (and maybe even make friends with them).	Location and time	Unlike other media, if you're doing a live-to-air interview or even a studio-recorded one, you need to travel and devote time to it.

Radio publicity

Getting your dulcet tones heard on radio doesn't involve quite the same stress levels associated with TV, but it still requires some skill. You might be invited in for a full-length studio interview or simply to speak to an interviewer over the phone, either live to air or prerecorded. Alternatively, a journalist might interview you and take a ten-second *grab*, which is media talk for the portion of what you've said that is selected to be broadcast to demonstrate a point. Check out Table 12-2 for more on radio publicity.

Table 12-2	The Pros and Cons of Radio Publicity		
Advantage	*Why*	*Disadvantage*	*Why*
Targeted audience	Radio is a great medium if you want to get your message across to a targeted audience such as the elderly, who are generally active radio listeners.	Live interviews	Doing live interviews can be nerve-wracking, so you need to try to find out what questions you'll be asked so you can be prepared. If it's prerecorded, the producer can do a small amount of editing.

(continued)

Table 12-2 *(continued)*

Advantage	Why	Disadvantage	Why
Expert opinions in demand	If you happen to be an expert in a specific field and have a great radio voice and interview well, you may be able to get a regular program as, say, the finance expert, gardening expert or property expert.	Distracted audience	When listening to radio, people are often on the move and flicking stations so they may not even take much notice of your interview or story.
Short lead time	Radio is a pretty instantaneous medium. You could pitch your story to a radio station today and find yourself on air tomorrow.	Non-retractable	Once you've said it, you can't take it back. Be very careful what you say, but not so careful that you don't make an impact on your audience!
Can be done anywhere	Some radio stations will require you to come into the studio, but most won't. You can do a phone interview live to air while sitting in your living room.	Cluttered environment	Your story will be competing with other stories, breaking news and lots of ads. That's why it's important to be engaging, a good storyteller and even humorous to get people's attention.

Talking up travel

Nick Bowditch is a travel consultant based on the Central Coast of New South Wales and is an expert in family travel. He features weekly on a program of the local ABC 92.5 radio station, where the host of the show interviews local people in a glass booth located in a busy shopping centre.

Nick decided he wanted a regular gig on the show, so he got on the station's website and sent an email to pitch his idea of a weekly travel segment. And he got it! He loves doing it every Tuesday at lunchtime for 15 or 20 minutes.

He finds many people stop to watch and listen, and will then wait around to ask him travel questions after the interview. This alone has got him new business. The interview is always about a predetermined travel destination chosen by Nick, and one that he has obviously been to and can talk authoritatively on. He writes a lot of notes for the interviewer to follow so he can see clearly what Nick will be discussing and the direction he wants to take. The ABC being a non-commercial radio station, Nick is unable to promote or advertise his business, but he does find that it gives him

credibility as a travel expert due to the ABC being very non-partisan and unbiased.

Nick is unafraid to be a little controversial and, in fact, recently did a segment on the top ten most overrated tourist destinations in the world. The goal was to create interaction between himself and the audience, and quite a number of people reacted by phoning in to give him their opinion.

Nick is also a master at using these interviews in all of his other marketing activities and in positioning himself and his business. He includes 'as heard on ABC' on his business cards, on his website (www.nickbowditchtravel.com) and even at the bottom of his email signature. Each week, a podcast of the interview is sent to him and he places it on his website and announces it on the various social sites he belongs to, such as Twitter and Facebook. Before each show he puts a teaser out to his database of clients and social media followers to inform them of this week's topic, inviting those people who have travelled to the destination to send in ideas, questions or stories of their experiences.

Newspaper publicity

Most people tend to associate publicity with newspaper stories for some reason. No doubt, getting into the paper can be easier than being interviewed for TV or radio, especially if you happen to live in rural areas where local and community papers are always looking for stories and content. But newspapers still have their good points and not-so-good points, as detailed in Table 12-3.

Table 12-3	The Pros and Cons of Newspaper Publicity		
Advantage	*Why*	*Disadvantage*	*Why*
Short lead time	You can ring the editor or journalist of the publication one day and have your story printed the next.	Limited lifespan	Newspapers are usually read and discarded as they are replaced by the next edition, which means, if people don't read your story first up, they're unlikely to return.
Engaged readers	Unlike radio, which is targeted at people on the move, people reading newspapers are more likely to be reading the paper at a leisurely pace and, if they're interested in your story, will read on.	Cluttered environment	Your story will be competing with other stories (maybe even from your competitors) and ads on the same page, which could mean you get overlooked.
Engaging stories	Papers are a great medium to tell people a story and back it up with a great photo. You can also get your audience engaged through such mechanisms as an 'Ask Mary' column or letters to the editor.	Accessible	Journalists have tight deadlines and editors to please. If your story is a good one and you can make the journo's life easy by giving her great information and photos, you have a better chance of getting your story into print.

Magazine publicity

You can choose from literally thousands of magazines to approach for publicity. I recommend selecting the top five you want to be seen in and focusing your efforts consistently on them over a period of time, so they get to know you and may eventually be inspired to tell your story.

If you're really media-savvy or have a good PR agency on board, you may be able to tailor your story in different ways for different magazines and get coverage across different markets. Table 12-4 gives tips on the pros and cons of magazine publicity.

Table 12-4	The Pros and Cons of Magazine Publicity		
Advantage	*Why*	*Disadvantage*	*Why*
Long lifespan	Most magazines are kept for a long time, read at leisure and passed on to friends and family, giving your story more opportunity to be read.	Long lead time	Magazine editors work to very specific production schedules, often months ahead of the release date. So, if you want your story to feature, you need to understand the deadline.
Niche markets	If you have a highly defined target market, such as car enthusiasts, you can really focus your publicity efforts on niche magazines such as *Wheels,* or, if your market is small-business owners, then *My Business* might do.	Passive readers	Unlike other more instant media like radio, magazines often don't provoke an immediate response from readers. They can be rather passive and, depending on the magazine, may not even pick it up for weeks or months after they've received it.
Emotional connection	Magazines include stories and feature interesting articles and lots of photos rather than tell you the news. You have a lot more opportunity to paint a picture, engage your readers and get them involved.	Difficult to access	Most magazines have a theme or predetermined idea of what articles they want to feature in their magazine so, unless your story fits, you might find it tough going.

Online publicity

You can gain online publicity in two ways. The first is to be interviewed by a journalist or writer from a specific media website and for him to write the story and publish it on the site. The second is for you to write your own stories and articles, and publish them online yourself.

Here are some of the ways you can publish online:

✔ Write a blog

✔ Post the article or story on your own website

✔ Respond to other people's blogs

✔ Send the article to media websites for them to publish

✔ Send the article or story to other businesses you know with the same target market and ask them to publish it on their site and send it out in their e-newsletter

✔ Submit your writing to article directories like www.ezinearticles.com or www.goarticles.com

✔ Write your own e-book or e-paper for subscribers

✔ Send an e-newsletter with the article to your database

In Chapter 18 I discuss how to publish online in great detail. First, check out Table 12-5 for the advantages and disadvantages of online publicity.

The world of online publishing is huge and can become very time-consuming. Be very clear on what you want to achieve before you jump in, and get an expert to help or advise you.

Table 12-5	The Pros and Cons of Online Publicity		
Advantage	*Why*	*Disadvantage*	*Why*
Fast	An interview or story can be up on the web instantly, driving traffic to your website and creating interest.	Cluttered environment	Making your message and article stand out, not only from the competition but also from all the other bloggers and opinion makers out there can be difficult.

Advantage	Why	Disadvantage	Why
Rich media	You can tell your story in many ways and get your audience interacting and engaged. Try podcasting (audio), vodcasting (video), forums, blogs and more.	Fickle audience	The internet world is fast-paced. If you don't capture users' attention in the first one or two lines of your story, they're likely to move on.
Feedback	Unlike most other media, you can get an instant response and feedback from your audience.	Time-consuming	Publishing online and responding to feedback and monitoring what's being written or said takes time.
Viral marketing	One click of a button is all it takes for your article or story to be sent on to thousands of people, creating a viral campaign without you doing a thing.	No control	If an unfavourable story is published online and distributed widely over the net, you can have very little control over where it ends up and what impact it may have.
More likely to buy	Consumers who go online to specifically research the type of product or service you offer will be more predisposed to buy from you if they can read articles about you and establish what kind of reputation you have.	Limited knowledge	Most business owners find the world of online publishing confusing and don't know where to start. If you're serious about it but aren't interested in mastering it, you need to be prepared to bring in the experts.

Chapter 13

Planning for Publicity Success

*T*he media have just two simple objectives — to inform and entertain their audience, and to sell more papers and magazines or get more people tuning in.

I have two simple rules for seeking publicity:

1. Have something worth telling the world about! If your story doesn't help the journalist or producer bring something useful or interesting to his audience, then you simply won't get your toe in the door, let alone see your name up in lights.

2. Put yourself in the shoes of the editor or journalist. Have you ever wondered what it would be like to spend a week in the shoes of an editor or a journalist of a major daily paper? Can you imagine how full-on her job would be?

Before preparing your plan to get publicity for your business, ponder these two rules.

Got it? Great. Now's the time to get a plan and make it happen. In this chapter, I tell you how.

Getting Your Story in the Media

Achieving publicity has a lot more to it than just ringing up a journo, pitching your story and hoping he'll give you a plug. To start, you need a simple plan that outlines

- ✔ **Your specific objective for getting in the media.** For example, to position yourself as an expert in your field, to let people know about a groundbreaking discovery you've made or to inform them about a major issue affecting consumers.

- ✔ **The media outlets you want to target.** If you're also running an advertising schedule, these media will be a great start.

- ✔ **Your contacts.** Get the names, email addresses, and phone and fax numbers for the editors, journalists and program producers of each media outlet.

- ✔ **The theme of your stories or articles.** Develop ten ideas to pitch at the media and then fine-tune them down to a few. Photos, statistics, research findings and real-life stories help to back up your story.

- ✔ **How you'll target your contacts.** Work out what best suits your contact and your story — phone, fax, email or hard-copy release, or all of these.

- ✔ **A script for what you're going to say.** However you make contact, you need to get the journo interested enough to do a story.

- ✔ **A media release to send as a follow-up to your initial contact.** This would include a paragraph on your company and contact details.

- ✔ **A program for your follow-up.** It might take more than one call to find out if they're interested, but please don't hound them.

- ✔ **What other marketing and advertising efforts will be supported.** You need to work out how to make the most of the publicity when you get it.

Targeting your audience

Target markets and targeting your audience are recurring themes in marketing. That's why I talk about them so much. And here it comes again.

In getting publicity you have two audiences to consider. The first audience is, of course, the reader, listener or viewer (take a look at Chapter 2, which talks about who your market is).

If you don't have a PR company or publicity agency on board and you have no media experience at all, you need to make an educated guess at the kinds of media your target market is consuming, and then narrow that down to the top 20 to 30 you'd like to appear in. For example, if your target market is young women, you can pretty safely assume they read magazines like *Marie Claire*. When you have your list together, buy a copy of the publication (for print media) and contact the advertising manager to find out the demographics of its audience.

The second target market to engage in getting publicity is the editor, journalist or program producer. You need to do your homework on who this person is — find out all you can about her — and, of course, get her contact details.

If you really feel you have the potential for widespread and long-term publicity, you have no option but to engage a PR specialist. If you try to tackle it yourself, you'll most definitely run out of steam and it will become ineffective for you.

You can find a complete list of the media by purchasing the Media Monitors *Media Directory* at `www.mediamonitors.com.au` or `www.mediamonitors.co.nz`. (From the Services dropdown menu choose Target the Media and then select Media Directory.) The Yahoo! Directory is an online resource at `http://dir.yahoo.com` (select News & Media from the left-hand menu). Another great guide that's been around for a long time is *Margaret Gee's Australian Media Guide*. Check it out at `www.crowncontent.com.au` (select it from the list of directories). The Crown Content site has some other useful resources also.

Niche versus mass media

As with advertising, I'm a big fan of niche media (refer to Chapter 10) for publicity, as it is highly targeted and generally easier to get into than the mass media — provided, of course, that you want to position you and your business as an expert or specialist provider in that field.

When I was working extensively with small businesses in the banking, financial-planning, mortgage-broking and investment industries many years ago, my stories regularly appeared in *Your Mortgage Professional*, *Australian Broker*, *Money Management* and various banking magazines. Over time, as my interest expanded into other professions and small-business industries, I had to redefine my positioning and target more broadly the small-business sector, and the publications and media being consumed by them. When it comes to the media, small-business owners are still a niche market, but obviously much broader than finance.

If you feel it would be too limiting to focus on just one niche audience and media type like I did at first, why not consider targeting a few niche audiences? Choose the niche media publications in industries that you have direct experience in and can talk about with authority. You may find this then lends itself to publications with broader or mass audiences over time (if that's where you want to expand into, of course).

Finding the angle

Before working out your angle, you need to understand the difference between a media release and a feature article. *Media releases* are used to make an announcement, and are usually short and sharp, dealing with topical news. *Feature articles* or columns are much longer than media releases and are designed to be educational and informative, and to demonstrate your expertise and experience.

Say you're a psychologist specialising in working with female breast cancer patients. You might send out a media release on the findings of some of your recent research to coincide with the media stories being featured during Breast Cancer Awareness Week. And, if you want ongoing media coverage, you might write a regular column for a women's health magazine or a weekly blog giving women (and their loved ones) practical advice on how to deal with breast cancer.

Whatever your business, here are some ideas to help you find the angle to excite a journalist and motivate the audience:

✔ Read, watch or listen to the media you want to be in, look for the hot topics people are responding to and find an angle that fits for your business.

✔ Brainstorm a list of the top five or ten issues associated with your field of expertise and write an article that addresses these issues in a practical way for your audience.

✔ Do a competitor analysis of your products or services, feature by feature, and send it to the specialist media focusing on your field.

✔ Gather facts and figures from the internet or from research with your customers and write a media release quoting the findings.

✔ Write a story using a customer you've worked with and ask if he's happy for you to use his story and photo for an article.

✔ Film a short video of yourself presenting directly to the camera on your topic of expertise and send it to the online media you're targeting.

✔ Offer your services to the media to be the resident expert in your area of expertise. You could land a regular radio spot, run a regular column or answer readers' questions.

Whatever you do, make sure you tailor your media release or article to the audience, avoid the hard sell (that is, don't write like you're advertising yourself), avoid hounding the media and aim for quality coverage not quantity!

Writing media releases

Writing a great media release is both an art and a science. You already know that it must be newsworthy and devoid of ad talk. Here are some other tips for writing a media release:

✔ Put 'Media Release' at the top and date it.

✔ Use a powerful headline to summarise the story. For example, 'Five Things You Must Know about How to Deal with Breast Cancer'.

✔ Cover the who, what, where, when, why and how questions in the first couple of paragraphs to encourage the journalist to read on.

✔ Mention your name and your company name early in the release.

✔ Be clear and concise and use simple language. Avoid clichés and jargon.

✔ Try to keep the media release to one page.

✔ Use quotations where possible and statements from yourself or the people you're featuring in the release.

✔ Ensure you have a third party check it for flow, grammar, punctuation and newsworthiness.

✔ Use a large font and double-spacing if possible.

✔ Write from the perspective of the audience and the benefit to them, rather than from your own point of view.

✔ Write in the third person, referring to yourself by name, rather than using *I* or *we*. For example, 'Ms Bright Spark of Fantastic Electrics said that ...'

✔ Make the story local and highly specific to the reader, viewer or listener.

✔ Don't assume the audience has prior knowledge. Refer to other articles or information they may know.

✔ Send in interesting and professional photos or offer an exclusive photo opportunity for the media outlet to send its own photographer.

✔ Finish with a paragraph demonstrating your expertise and experience, and a one-liner on your business.

✔ Include your contact details and website address.

Writing content and articles

Although most of the tips for writing a media release also apply to writing an article, you need to use a quite different approach. An article heavily features your opinions, experience and advice, and gives readers a how-to guide on your topic. Articles often feature real-life stories — the secret ingredient to getting most articles published.

One thing I've learned since being in my own business is that the power of the story is what sells you like nothing else. It establishes your credibility, gives people hope and a real idea on how they might approach their own individual problems.

To make the distinction between a media release and an article simple, consider it like this. Media releases have a short life and are focused on topical news and what's happening right now. Articles, on the other hand, have a long life and can be used again and again to get your message out. I personally favour articles over media releases any day.

Understanding what journalists want

The only way to get your story into print, or on TV or radio, is to know what will push the journalists', editors' or producers' buttons. Put yourself in their shoes. They get hundreds of people trying to sell them stories every day.

'John's Diary'

Imagine you own a personal training business. You write a regular article for your e-newsletter that is also posted on your blog and sent to a health and fitness website that has commissioned your articles each day. Your articles follow the day-to-day progress of one of your very overweight customers and how he has lost weight and drastically improved his fitness.

You interview the customer and write about his daily weight loss, vital measurements and how

his attitudes and emotions have been affected. Your article is entitled 'John's Diary: My Road to Recovery'. Each article gives a daily account of what he has eaten, his exercise program that day, and how he feels before going to bed and on getting up each day. He openly shares his feelings with you and the audience.

Now, if you really wanted your article to have impact, you could film it and post it as a video (as long as John was comfortable with that, of course)!

Here are some things you need to consider in working with journalists, editors and program producers:

- **Find out their area of specialty.** Most journalists (except in small community or regional papers) specialise in writing on topics of their expertise, such as finance, law, gardening, food, wine or architecture. Find the journalist who specialises in your field in the media you want to appear in, rather than attempting to contact the editor or producer who oversees everything.

- **Understand their deadlines.** Deadlines for stories differ depending on how often the paper publishes or the program airs, so be sure to find out what their deadlines are and make it easy for them to use your story in their next edition or program.

- **Appreciate their pressures.** Sourcing and preparing stories or articles and getting them produced in time can be a headache for many journalists, particularly with editors breathing down their necks. Make it easy for them by providing facts, figures and real-life stories they can write up quickly with a minimum amount of research required on their behalf.

- **Don't hound them.** Journalists hate pushy people who want to sell their story relentlessly. When speaking with journalists, ask them what you can do to help them and listen to their response. If they say, 'We can't report on your idea or story this month, but maybe next month,' ask if it would be okay to call them next month and what would be the best day for them. And, of course, do it!

- **Earn their respect.** If you can become a credible source of information, or the *go-to* person, in your field, over time you'll earn their trust and build relationships with them.

One of the best ways to get to know journalists is through reading their stories and articles. When speaking with them you can refer to the article and have an intelligent conversation about it. And if your opinion differs from theirs, don't be scared to express it. There are no prizes for being a shrinking violet.

Establishing contact with the media

You've written a great media release and now it's time to get it out and into the hands of the journalists. You can either send it yourself to your own list of media contacts, get your PR consultant to do it or use a reliable news distribution service. You need to weigh up the pros and cons of each, depending on how far and wide you want your story seen.

A number of media distribution companies exist that can handle the distribution for you, whether you want to send your release across New Zealand, Australia or the world. Check out http://ozmedia.com for one.

Now, if you're doing the distribution yourself, using a combination of two or three methods of sending out the story is a good idea — phone call, fax, email or mail. I've emailed media releases in the past and got nil response. On the other hand, when I've called the journalist and been able to establish rapport and ask what sort of stories she needs for the next edition, I've had a great response. I've not even required a written media release or article. I've just thrown the journalist some great ideas and offered to give her some case studies and stories to help out. I often find the more casual, friendly approach works well. Every journalist is different. Some want to go through the list of faxed or emailed releases trawling for good news. Others want the personal touch, so you need to be prepared to be flexible in your approach.

Emails can get filtered out into spam boxes or lost in the thousands of emails that come in. Faxes can get lost in the pile that comes through every day. Mailed media releases in an 'express delivery' envelope marked private and confidential to the journalist probably get noticed the best.

If you've made it clear you're available to the media for interviews, make sure you are 100 per cent available to drop everything if they call you. Tell your staff to put the call through, no matter what. And, if for some reason you simply can't take the call, phone them back as soon as possible.

Sending your media release with a case of wine and a chocolate cake won't make any difference if your media release has no news value!

Maintaining contact

Congratulations, the media has picked up your story and it's running. Now is not the time to move on to greener pastures. Now is the time to keep in touch and thank the journalist for the story with a simple thank-you note, phone call or email. Tell him you'd be happy to help him any time, then note in your diary to follow up again at a reasonable interval with a new idea or story.

If your story didn't get picked up, don't give up. Make sure you continue to maintain contact and offer ideas. It might take five or six goes before you get the gig.

Always ask journalists, 'How can I help you do your job?' and be genuine in your offer. They are people like you and me, and have a tough job to do.

Becoming a Media Expert

Establishing myself as a media expert has been one of my own promotional strategies for more than seven years now and it's been one of the most enjoyable and rewarding ways to market my business. It has helped me establish credibility, build my reputation, secure speaking gigs and ultimately help me bring in new business. In fact, it was the reason the good people at Wiley contacted me to write this *For Dummies* book for you.

In the early stages of being in business, when things were a bit quieter, it was nothing for me to spend one or two days a week writing articles and media releases, and chasing the media. I now spend less time on it, because I've got to a point where many of the media know me now and will ring me for an opinion rather than me chasing them. It's taken seven years to get to that point and, to be very honest, I've probably taken my eye off the ball a bit as I pursue different interests.

To be a media expert you need to be:

✔ Prepared to appear in any and all media

✔ Trained and skilled up to handle live TV and radio interviews

✔ Committed to being a thought leader in your field

✔ Available to the media for comment or interview 24/7

✔ Well read and up-to-date with what's happening in the media generally and in the media that hits your target market

✔ Seen as a sought-after adviser by influential parties such as the government or lobby groups

✔ Abreast of the latest research, reports and news regarding your field of expertise

✔ Aware of the personal biases and writing styles of each of the journalists you may interact with

Becoming a sought-after media expert is not for the faint-hearted. Think long and hard about it before committing. You may want to revert to other promotional tactics that get the message out without putting yourself on the line.

Staging media conferences

If your news really is big enough, you might want to stage a media conference, invite the media to attend and make your important announcement directly to them. Politicians and government representatives hold media conferences regularly to get their message out, so they can be sure all media receive the same information at the exact same time.

Most journalists and editors sigh at the thought of having to take time out of their busy day to attend yet another media conference. Unless your news is absolutely groundbreaking, you'll probably find it tough to get them there.

You should hold a media conference for any one of only three reasons:

✔ When you have vital news that absolutely must be announced simultaneously to all media

✔ When news is best told in person and needs to be backed by visual imagery or video footage, and you know the journalists will have lots of questions

✔ When you're featuring important speakers or celebrities who are a big drawcard

Managing media interviews

Report me and my cause aright.

—*William Shakespeare (1564–1616), English poet and playwright*

Whether you hold a media conference or whether you get invited in to do a radio or TV interview, you want to be sure that your cause, message or story is recorded and aired as you meant it to be. The only way that can happen is if you are well trained and skilled in handling interviews. I thoroughly recommend getting some media training skills.

Media training courses abound. Do an internet search in your local area for media training to find out more. Check out www.editorgroup.com or www.media-associates.co.nz, for example.

Even if you've done some training and are fairly confident in your skills, it pays to bear in mind the do's and don'ts listed in Table 13-1.

Table 13-1	Do's and Don'ts of Media Interviews
Do . . .	**Don't . . .**
Ask how much time is scheduled for the interview.	Ramble on or talk about yourself.
Ask for a list of likely questions so you can prepare for the interview.	Criticise the competition or be slanderous.
Speak slowly using simple language.	Lie or make up answers. Be honest and say you don't know, if that's the case.
Make your important points at the beginning.	Answer questions that might recriminate you or dig you into a hole.
Keep your comments brief so they can be easily quoted.	Pick a fight with the journalist.
Ensure the interviewer has your name and company name correct — both in spelling and pronunciation.	Say 'No comment.' If you really feel you shouldn't make a comment, provide a brief friendly answer instead.
Ask for your web address to be mentioned or shown at the end of the story.	Say anything you wouldn't want to hear or read later.
Be genuine, warm and caring.	Show bias or preference to the interviewer — remain impartial.
Smile, nod and acknowledge the journalist by name during the interview.	Swear or make overly colourful or outrageous statements.
Ensure you get a recorded copy of the interview.	Be boring. I am all for playing it large and creating a memorable impact!

Handling Negative Publicity

Some industries are more prone to receiving negative media attention than others. If you happen to be in banking, finance, property development, real estate, financial planning or car sales, you may be more likely to receive negative publicity than businesses in fields such as medical research, childcare or food (unless, of course, you've been involved in a major harmful incident).

It wasn't our fault!

Imagine you own a restaurant and one of your customers slips on a cracked tile on the way to the toilet and breaks her arm. You happen not to be on duty that night so one of your staff has to handle the situation. They panic and simply don't know how to handle the crisis.

Luckily the ambulance comes and the customer is okay, but later, when she recovers, she is annoyed at the way it was handled and wants to seek compensation from you. She decides to call the local paper, who is

desperate for stories that day, and you know the rest.

How do you handle the negative media attention? Do you angrily respond to the paper, saying it wasn't your fault, that the customer was drunk and that's why she slipped? Or do you respond with a media release acknowledging what happened and explaining that you have met with the lady and agreed to help her on the road to recovery by delivering her a free weekly dinner to her home?

If you're in an industry prone to negative media coverage, consider putting in place a crisis management plan to deal with it. This simple plan needs to cover the scenarios or topics you might receive negative media about and an action plan on how you will deal with it, as well as who will respond and what the message will be.

If you are clever and sensitive, you can always find a way to turn negative publicity into a plus (see the sidebar 'It wasn't our fault!'). Simply consider whether it should be dealt with as an opportunity or a threat.

Making the Most of Your Media Coverage

Well done! You've got a three-page article and photos in the *Australian Women's Weekly* and a live radio interview on 2Day FM. So what now?

Without sounding too crude, my advice is to milk it for all it's worth.

If you've sent out mass-media releases and want to get copies of all the resulting stories, you can pay a media-monitoring company such as www.mediamonitors.com.au or www.medaimonitors.co.nz. These services trawl through the media every day for articles or stories you feature in and send them on to you. Big businesses all use media-monitoring services to keep an eye on the media coverage and to ensure their reputation is kept intact.

I've had friends call me to say, 'I read your interview or a quote in blah, blah publication,' when I hadn't even done an interview with that paper or sent them a story. They'd picked it up from another media source and just decided to run the story.

Remember to seek copies of your interview or article from the journalist after it appears. The *Daily Telegraph*, for example, always send me lovely PDF copies of my articles. Thank you!

When you have a presentable copy of your article or interview, you can use it very cleverly in the following ways to promote your business long after the story appears:

- ✔ Post it on the homepage of your website or in a section on your site entitled 'In the News'.
- ✔ Add a link to the article on your site as a promotional line at the bottom of all your email signatures.
- ✔ Print copies of it to include with requests for tender or give it to customers as you meet them.
- ✔ Put it up in your shop window with an 'As seen on . . .' sign.
- ✔ Include it in PowerPoint presentations to your audience.
- ✔ Mail it with a covering letter to the customers on your database.
- ✔ Send it to other journalists on your list to whet their appetites for your story.
- ✔ Include it in your printed newsletter or e-newsletter.
- ✔ Post it on your blog, Facebook, Twitter and any other social media you use.

Most media stories are here today and gone tomorrow. It's up to you to give yours a long life and use them in all your communications.

Part IV
Relationship Marketing

Glenn Lumsden

'Maybe you should get someone else to do point of sale.'

In this part ...

Relationship marketing helps you to retain and attract customers through activities that allow you to get in front of people and build direct relationships, which generate positive word-of-mouth referrals.

In this part, you discover why relationship marketing is critical to business success and how to build a variety of relationship-based activities into your marketing plan. Work out how to build alliances with other business owners, how to run a successful sponsorship, how to host a business event, improve your public speaking, make a splash at trade fairs and much more.

If you're not so good at relationship building, make a commitment to start now. It can be the difference between life and death for your business.

Chapter 14

Introducing Relationship Marketing

*T*ake some time to think about your circle of business friends. Which ones seem to have the most successful businesses? Which ones are great communicators and connectors who seem to know everybody? Which ones don't seem to do much advertising yet always seem to have floods of customers? Maybe this person is you or your business partner or a staff member? Or maybe this is the missing ingredient in your business — someone who is superb at relationship marketing.

When I first jumped ship from the corporate world and started my business many years ago, I knew very few other small-business owners. I knew that being in business for myself was going to be lonely, so with the support of two friends, Neen James and Alison Hanlon, we started a networking group for small-business owners in the marketing and communications field. Together we brainstormed a list of all the people we knew were working for themselves as marketing consultants, in copywriting, advertising, PR, graphic design, photography and more. We emailed people and called local businesses and invited them to our launch party. No less than 80 people turned up on launch night. And that was the start of my relationship-marketing program.

Today I have no less than 5,000 significant relationships with small-business people (and from big business as well), including customers, suppliers, and those from networking groups, the media, industry associations, community groups and more.

Any business owner can build a relationship-marketing program from nothing, if she's got the gumption. In this chapter, you find out how to go about it. Personally, it's one of the most rewarding ways to market your business.

Understanding Relationship Marketing

I define *relationship marketing* as the process of attracting and retaining customers through activities that allow you to build direct relationships, resulting in positive word-of-mouth referrals. These activities may be a little outside normal business activities, such as belonging to networking and community groups, and hosting customer seminars and asking them for referrals.

Understanding how relationship marketing differs from other forms of marketing, such as advertising, publicity or internet marketing, is important. Advertising and publicity are about getting the message out to people you can't realistically or physically connect with face to face. Relationship marketing is about establishing and leveraging the relationships you have to generate positive word-of-mouth business for yourself.

I recommend devoting 75 per cent of your marketing effort — dollars and energy — to activating a word-of-mouth network.

—Tom Peters, author, and father of the post-modern corporation

On the upside, relationship marketing is generally low (or even no) cost and is virtually impossible for your competitors to imitate. It also works well for the long term and can bring in new business consistently, unlike advertising, whose ability to bring in business tends to experience peaks and troughs. It can also be very personally satisfying and open up a whole new world of business possibilities and partnerships you may never have thought possible.

The downside to relationship marketing is that it takes time to build and also takes up time in your busy week if you want to seriously do it properly.

If you're looking to start working more *on* the business, rather than *in* it, start by taking a look at your relationship-marketing strategy.

Making relationship marketing work in a small business

Relationship marketing is the secret weapon of small business that big business doesn't seem to have. The bigger the business, it often seems, the worse they are at relationship building!

As a small-business owner, you are the face of your business, whether you like it or not, and the buck starts and stops with you. People want to do business with a great guy or gal, regardless of what you're selling. So, by building relationships, you're building your reputation and hopefully securing a steady flow of new business leads.

Relationship marketing is not a one-way street. It's about asking how you can help others, and taking action to get involved and support others. This is why it can be such a rich and rewarding experience.

For relationship marketing to work in your small business you need to get clear again on your target markets. Find out what organisations these people belong to and what events or conferences they attend. You then need to choose two or three tactics and develop a simple plan to develop your relationships and make the most of them.

A colleague of mine who is a consultant in the financial-planning industry attends every Financial Planning Association conference. Before going, he works out his purpose for attending and develops a list of the people he wants to personally connect with there. He offers the conference organisers his speaking services and has a booth at the conference to promote his business. He also invites some of his customers and prospects to be his guests at the conference dinner.

Relationship marketing do's and don'ts

The core of relationship marketing is about making genuine connections with the right people in order to form mutually beneficial relationships. It's about having the personal skills required for people to get to know, like and trust you so they're comfortable referring and recommending you, even if they don't personally become your customer.

The sad fact is that not everyone can be good at relationship marketing. Go through the list of do's and don'ts in Table 14-1 to understand how to make it work most effectively for you.

Table 14-1	Do's and Don'ts of Relationship Marketing
Do ...	**Don't ...**
Be willing to devote at least four hours a week to building relationships.	Jump in with your sales pitch every time you meet someone.
Find out who will be attending events beforehand if you can.	Be late for events or leave early. Make the most of your time there.
Be warm, friendly, engaging and genuinely interested in every person you meet.	Talk about yourself all the time.
Be ready to give referrals and connect people in the room.	Drink too much or be rude or ask inappropriate personal questions.
Develop great conversational skills. Talking about the weather is something only boring people do.	Sit with your friends or one person the whole time. Make sure you move around and meet a range of people.
Be prepared — take your business cards, a notepad, pen and even some giveaways.	Take business cards and just add them to your mailing list without the person's permission.
Think about how you might be able to help whoever you're meeting during your conversations.	Try to meet as many people as possible. A few meaningful connections are far more valuable than lots of meaningless ones.
Add them to your database and make a diary entry to follow them up.	Give out your business cards willy-nilly to every person you meet.
Follow up with a nice email, card or phone call to arrange a meeting, if that's appropriate.	Ask a person for their card, unless you've made a genuine connection and have a reason to follow up.

Considering tactics that work for you

Not all relationship-marketing tactics will suit you or your business. You need to consider what you're comfortable with, the industry type that you're in and how your business operates.

Here are some of the relationship-marketing activities you could undertake for your business:

- Attend networking events
- Build referral alliances with other business owners
- Develop customer referral programs

- ✔ Establish loyalty programs
- ✔ Exhibit at expos and trade fairs
- ✔ Get actively involved in a community group
- ✔ Host your own networking events
- ✔ Run educational seminars or lunches
- ✔ Sponsor an event or organisation
- ✔ Support a local charity or community program
- ✔ Take on public-speaking engagements

These activities have one thing in common. They are about eyeballing the right people in order to make a genuine connection so that, one day, you can earn the right to ask for their business, seek a referral or help them generate word-of-mouth business for you.

In Chapter 15, I examine more closely what it takes for each of these tactics to be successful. In the meantime, choose no more than three of them and consider how you could do them really well rather than doing bits and pieces of each one poorly.

Using Combined Marketing Tactics

Successful businesses need to adopt at least four marketing tactics to work in tandem in order to generate a consistent flow of quality new leads. The list of possible tactics actually runs into the hundreds — far too many to delve into in any detail here — so you're actually spoiled for choice, and limited only by your imagination!

Combining your relationship-marketing tactics with others you might choose, like direct mail, publicity or advertising, is advisable. So, if you've chosen supporting a local charity as a tactic (see the sidebar 'Feelgood tactics that work'), you may like to combine it with a tactic like publicity, for example.

You might argue that supporting a charitable cause shouldn't be about marketing or making money. Of course, you must do it for genuine altruistic reasons first. However, a major benefit of your involvement is that you and your business gain a favourable reputation in the eyes of the community, the people you help, the media, your staff and your customers. A pretty compelling reason to put a charitable program in your business and marketing plan.

Feelgood tactics that work

Imagine you're an electrician. You notice an article in the paper that a local group is setting up a program to help disadvantaged youth by using the local community hall for respite and counselling services. However, the hall is in disrepair and requires major work for the program to happen.

You decide to help, and approach the local group to offer to coordinate a major overhaul of the hall, which is gratefully accepted. You call on all the tradespeople you know in the local area to give their time and equipment for free, and most of them want in. You set a deadline of two months to complete the work required.

To get people engaged, you contact the local paper and convince them to run a series of articles on the different tradespeople who have so far agreed to be involved and to invite more. The result? A united community. A renovated hall. A place for kids to get help. Great publicity — for the program, for you and for everyone else involved. And a really good feeling!

Getting Your Staff Involved

Your staff can be involved in almost every aspect of a relationship-marketing program. If you decide on a charitable program, your staff may want to be part of it and invite their friends to join in also. If networking is in your program, why not get your staff to attend local business events with you or on your behalf, if they love that sort of thing? If one of your staff has children at the local school, why not agree to sponsor the school fete? The staff member could even manage the sponsorship program.

If you're asking your staff to contribute to the marketing and business development of your business, make sure that's written into their employment contracts with you or their goals and objectives, and that they're regularly reviewed. You may also agree on an incentive payment for bringing in new business.

Your staff need to have the skills and abilities to carry out relationship marketing well on your behalf. You may need to coach them to ensure they are giving out the messages you want for your business. Who knows, if your staff are getting a bit bored with their jobs, it may just be the ticket to keep them motivated.

Every one of the people who work for you is a walking billboard for your business. Give them the encouragement they need to make them a billboard that attracts new business, not one that goes completely unnoticed!

Reviewing and Refining Your Relationship-Marketing Plan

Like all good plans, your relationship-marketing plan needs to be reviewed and refined at regular intervals to ensure it's reaping the results you expect. If you don't know why you're doing a particular activity or what results to expect, then you can never measure its true value to your business.

For example, if networking is a strategy you've adopted, then you need to work at it consistently and be prepared to make the commitment to attend events every week or two, even if at times you feel you can't be bothered. Of course, if you've worked hard at it and haven't been getting the results, then you either need to find a new strategy or ask yourself why it's not working for you. It could be that you're networking in the wrong places, that you're not following up properly or that you just simply don't enjoy it.

The secret to making your relationship-marketing strategy a success is to actually love doing it. It really shouldn't feel like work. If it's a chore you would rather not do, drop it. You may be doing you and your business more harm than good!

Chapter 15

Putting Relationship Marketing to Work

*I*f you've decided that relationship marketing (refer to Chapter 14) is an important part of your marketing plan, you now need to work out your tactics.

In this chapter, I highlight the tricks of the trade and show you how to build a step-by-step plan to put your relationship marketing into practice. I cover everything from how to build a customer referral program to how to make sponsorships work and how to host successful events.

Of course, every business is different and some tactics will work better than others for you. Some will resonate with you personally. Others won't. My one caveat for taking on any of the tactics discussed here is that you ensure you are personally comfortable with it. If the thought of networking leaves you in a cold sweat, for example, don't do it. If, however, you really like the idea of getting involved in a local charitable program, get creative and start brainstorming ideas on how to go about it for your business.

Building a Customer Referral Program

A *referral* is when someone, particularly a satisfied customer, suggests or recommends your services to other buyers. It is one of the most powerful and underutilised tactics in your marketing toolkit, yet many business owners leave the whole referral process to chance. Like anything you do in business, developing a referral program is a process, not an event. It takes time to iron out your program and get it working effectively, and to see the results. However, referrals are an almost free way to market your business.

Your customers are the best source of referrals because they've already had firsthand experience with you. If you give them a WOW experience and go beyond the call of duty, they'll give you referrals without even being asked.

If you're not getting referrals from people (whether you ask for them or not), ask yourself (and your customers) why not. It could be that you're not measuring up and need to improve an aspect of your business.

Here's a good approach to take to generate more referrals for your business:

- ✔ **Build a referral program.** Develop a step-by-step process for seeking and acknowledging referrals. Set referral expectations early, in writing, verbally and throughout the process of dealing with customers. Use a script to ask for a referral and practise it. 'Your referral would be our biggest compliment' is one of my personal favourites. And make sure all your staff follow the program.

- ✔ **Build business alliances.** Look for alliance relationship opportunities. Start by focusing on the business owners who offer a complementary service to you and who also have the same target market. Look for a win–win opportunity to cross-refer.

- ✔ **Get active.** Develop a list of active referrers. Review your database and make a list of family, friends and business associates who actively refer you. The 80:20 rule applies here — 20 per cent of your referrers will refer 80 per cent of your new business.

- ✔ **Get formal.** If appropriate, formalise the referral arrangement. You could make your referrers into a sales force by putting an agreement in place and offering financial incentives.

- ✔ **Keep the relationship alive.** Keep in touch via email, calls, invitations, e-newsletters and cards, and by sending them quality information and links to your website.

- ✔ **Make contact.** Ask all new customers how they *first* heard about you. Delve deep to find out who referred you. It could be that you don't even know this person. Find out his contact details so you can thank him and add him to your database.

✔ **Scratch their backs too.** Give your referrer a referral. This is the most powerful thing you can do in the whole referral process.

✔ **Set goals.** Set a target list of calls to make to customers, even if it's just five calls per week. Make time for it and allocate at least 15 minutes per call. Make sure you record conversation details and follow-up notes on your database.

✔ **Talk to your customers.** Call your customers and have an open and honest conversation with them. Ask how you can help them. Then tell them you're looking for more business and that you're calling to discuss if they can help. Tell them about your referral program and the kinds of customers you'd like to attract.

✔ **Thank them.** Thank them for referring, by sending them a card or gift — a book, an e-report, movie tickets, wine, a picnic hamper — just do it consistently!

Referrals can, of course, come from many other sources too, such as family and friends, business associates, other professionals, mums and dads at school, your church group, sporting colleagues and so on. Don't forget to add these people to your referee list and treat them just as you would your customer referrals.

Asking for a referral is something I personally find difficult to do, so I've developed a little Tell-a-Friend card, which is the size of a business card (see Figure 15-1). I give it out to customers and to audience members when I speak, and send it to people when they order books or DVDs from me. And it works fabulously.

Ready to get a referral program in place for your business? Don't wait, you can start today!

Figure 15-1:
Handing out a Tell-a-Friend card can work wonders for referrals.

Hi, I'm Carolyn Tate, the small-business marketing expert. I don't spend much money on expensive ads to get more business. My business is built on my reputation, relationships and referrals. So, if you've benefited from working with me and have a friend who could also benefit, please pass on this card and encourage them to contact me or subscribe to my website. I'll do everything I can to help them be brilliant at marketing so they simply get noticed and get more business! And if I can help you too, please give me a call.

Please tell a friend . . .

Networking to Get More Business

Your networks are equal to your net worth! *Networking* is the interaction between people who share a common interest or goal. It can be done face to face at the footie, on the beach, at the dog park (one of my personal favourites) and at business-networking events. And, of course, networking can take place without even having to leave the comfort of your office or lounge room, via sites like Facebook and LinkedIn.

Networking is about opening up the opportunity to get to know someone better so you can establish a relationship for mutual benefit. On a business level, networking is about getting to know someone well enough to earn the right to ask for her business or for her to refer another person's business to you and vice versa.

Here's how to go about building a networking strategy for yourself:

- **Get a networking plan.** To be a great networker you need to understand why you're networking, who you want to network with and what you want to achieve from it. And you need to be prepared to invest the time, money and energy in becoming great at it.

- **Develop a list of networks.** Do your research in your local area or in the community or industry type you want to network within and prepare a list. For example, if you're a corporate travel consultant and you want to build relationships with the heads of sales (sales teams can do a lot of travel), find out what associations they belong to and industry events they attend, and go along.

- **Combine personal and professional networking.** Consider networks that can combine a personal interest with business opportunities, such as the local Surf Life Saving Club (SLSC), Rotary branch, chamber of commerce, sporting groups or the school parents and friends committee. Belonging to at least one personal and one professional networking group is a good move.

- **Find the right networking events.** Always attend a few functions of the networking group or association before committing to membership. You need to make sure it's a good fit for you first and that you'll be regularly networking with your target market.

- **Get the networking skills.** Not everyone is great at networking. It requires a set of interpersonal skills that may need polishing up. Refer to Chapter 14 for a list of do's and don'ts of relationship marketing to see if you've got what it takes. The more you network, the better you get, of course.

- **Be prepared.** Before attending any event, have your business cards, notepad, pen, attitude, prepared questions, verbal brand (or elevator pitch — refer to Chapter 7) all ready to go. Read up on the day's news, and on the company and people hosting the event. Dress appropriately, arrive early so you can meet the host and be there to greet people as they arrive. Scan the nametags at the front desk for other people attending so you can identify those you want to connect with.

✔ **Make quality connections.** During the event, don't try to meet everyone; just connect with a few. Have at least five quality conversations and try to engage with the movers and shakers, particularly the host and the speaker. Ask for their business cards and seek permission to follow up. Be the last to leave and offer to help the host clean up.

✔ **Follow up.** Networking has little point if you don't follow up the people you've met. Always follow up with something that adds value to the relationship, not a sales pitch! Don't overuse email to follow up. A personal card might work for you, or an email with an article or introduction to another person can work, or a phone call to organise a cup of coffee or an invitation to an event. Remember, always ask their permission to add them to your mailing list.

If you lack a bit of confidence with networking but are committed to getting better at it, find someone who is great at it and ask him to be your networking mentor. If he agrees, stick to him like glue, observe and copy him, and in no time you'll become a master networker too.

Building relationships face to face has no real substitute, in my personal opinion. However, if, for example, you're a busy mum and after-hours networking just doesn't work for you, you can be just as effective at networking online. You need to do it well, though. Chapter 18 covers how to use social media for effective networking.

Building Alliances with Other Businesses

Smart business owners (like you, of course) spend as much time on building alliances with other business owners as they do on marketing direct to the end consumer. Alliances are developed through establishing deep relationships with other business owners who offer a complementary service and who also have the same target market as you.

The purpose of the alliance is for you to support the growth of each other's business through a steady flow of cross-referrals. A significant side benefit is that your customers love the extra value you add by being able to refer them to other quality businesses like yours.

Striking up alliances

Imagine you've just set up shop as an interior decorator. You'd probably be looking to build alliances with architects, builders, feng shui consultants, landscapers, homeware and furniture stores, handymen and painters, and so on. You make a list of 100 businesses in your local area that could be a source of referrals and send them a brochure with a covering letter. You then follow up the letter with a phone call to see if they would be open to a coffee to talk about whether there is an opportunity to help each other. The 100 contacts could net ten meetings and five alliances. Not a bad strike rate!

An alliance relationship can take many forms, from an informal handshake to a formal joint-venture agreement. Trust is the single most important ingredient for an alliance to work.

Follow this process to build business alliances:

- **Get a list.** Start by developing a list of complementary industry types that you could connect with to refer each other business. Be creative. When developing this list, ask yourself who has the same target market as you do. If you're an accountant, for example, the list might include lawyers, consultants, real estate agents, mortgage brokers, financial planners and more. Be creative — it could even include your hairdresser!

- **Get specific.** When you've identified the different industry types, make a list of the actual business names that might fit the bill. Do a web search, ask your customers, friends and networks for ideas or recommendations, and even walk the street and check out the names of the businesses in the area.

- **Make contact.** Send a letter, call or drop in on the business owners and ask if you can meet for a coffee to discuss an opportunity for cross-referrals. If they don't have time for a coffee, ask if you can just pop in to see them for five minutes. Be ready to discuss how you can help them and your referral idea. Be the first to refer.

- **Hold initial meetings.** The first stage of the alliance-building process is to get to know each other and establish trust to be sure the other party can deliver (and vice versa, of course). Organise a couple of meetings so you can tell each other about your business and the kinds of customers you serve, and introduce your staff.

✔ **Conduct a trial.** When you've got to know another business owner, agree to give each other a trial referral or use each other's services, if possible, so you can get an insight into the way she operates. Remember to seek feedback from all parties after business takes place to be sure you're both comfortable with the service and outcomes.

✔ **Set targets and review.** When you're 100 per cent sure the customers are happy with the service provided by your alliance partner, and you've agreed to the referral alliance, organise to meet regularly to set referral targets and to agree on objectives and the number of referrals sought. Be sure to meet regularly.

✔ **Make it formal.** If the relationship progresses nicely, you may want to establish a more formal referral agreement where you pay each other a referral fee.

✔ **Be flexible.** As with any type of relationship, some alliance relationships will stop dead in their tracks, some will slowly fade away and some will last a lifetime. Be prepared to let them grow organically as you both change and grow in your business direction. Always allow for either party to opt out and be sure to celebrate successes as they occur.

In many cases, through no fault of either party, the flow of referrals can be one way. If this happens, discussing a financial incentive for the referral may be wise. Financial incentives can no doubt influence referrals. This is quite normal business practice and above board, under one proviso — that the customer is made aware of the referral fee paid. Transparency is paramount!

Although you might feel uncomfortable cold-calling alliances, it's very different to cold-calling prospective customers (refer to Chapter 8). You're not trying to sell them anything, you're trying to establish a mutually beneficial relationship for cross-referrals of business. So, just do it!

Developing a Sponsorship Program

A good sponsorship can be worth its weight in gold. I reckon it's one of the most undervalued and underutilised marketing tactics there is.

Before I go any further, it's important to set you straight on what a sponsorship actually is. It's not about giving your local footie club $300 to have your name on the footie program. In my books, that's a donation.

A *sponsorship* is a commercial arrangement where you give a certain amount of money for rights to an event or organisation that results in increased brand awareness — and, most importantly, new business. If you're not getting new business from a sponsorship, then you might as well just call it a donation!

Sponsorships are a great way of establishing relationships with the community, and building your name and brand among your target audience to get new business. The secret ingredient to making a sponsorship work is the relationships that you build from being a sponsor.

The most successful sponsorships combine a personal passion with business. For example, if you're passionate about golf, and golfers happen to be your target market, you have a great combination for a successful sponsorship because you're most likely to put your time and energy into it.

Here's how to find a sponsorship that's a good fit for your business and get it happening:

- **Be proactive not reactive.** Look for (or even create) opportunities to sponsor community groups that exactly fit your target market and marketing strategy. This may be the SLSC, bowls clubs, the local chamber of commerce, women's clubs or Rotary. Most businesses just look at sponsorship requests that float across their desk rather than actively looking for opportunities.

- **Do your homework.** When you've found what looks like a good sponsorship opportunity, do your homework on what the sponsorship is worth financially and the benefits, or *entitlements*, it offers to you.

- **Get an agreement in place.** Have an official agreement drawn up to ensure the organisation or group you're sponsoring will deliver on the entitlements you've agreed on. Think creatively about the entitlements you'd like and negotiate them up-front. Entitlements might include exclusive naming rights, exclusivity in your industry, free admittance, the right to present and make awards at events, inserts and ads in newsletters or mailouts, acknowledgement in media releases and at events, editorial content in newsletters, promotion on the website and more.

- **Negotiate payment options.** Maybe you can make the payment for the sponsorship in instalments (particularly if a large amount) or tie it to the agreed measurements of success and the amount of new business you gain. For example, if you were a mortgage broker you could sponsor your local golf club and pay a lump sum for naming and branding rights, and then a bonus of $200 for every new customer you get.

✔ **Manage and review the sponsorship.** When your sponsorship is in place, manage it carefully and do regular reviews to make sure both parties are happy. Make sure you have an opt-out clause in the agreement, if for some reason the sponsorship isn't working for you.

✔ **Have a contingency fund.** For every dollar you spend on a sponsorship you need another dollar to make the most of it. For example, if you host a seminar for members, you may also want to print a brochure with special offers or pay for branded giveaways and banners.

✔ **Get actively involved.** Remember, the sponsorship is about building relationships with members and event attendees, so you need to be prepared to attend events, make awards, and meet and greet people.

✔ **Be creative.** Getting people to sit up and take notice of the fact you're a sponsor and to then go to the next step of buying your services or products is often hard. Do something a little unusual or fun that gets people talking about you.

The best sponsorships go for years, not months. Getting traction and making an impact so you're seen as a real partner takes time. A good term might be three to five years.

If you get a sponsorship request, but you decide it's not for you, be courteous and decline it within five days of receiving it. You can still use it as a good public relations opportunity by offering alternative services to the organisation seeking sponsorship.

As a member of our local SLSC and with an involvement in the kids' side of the club, the Nippers, one of the best sponsorships I've seen is from our local Ray White real estate agent. Craig Sewell is a great guy and actively involved in Nippers, attending every week with his children and making the most of it with branding, awards and much more. If I ever buy or sell my home, I know who I'll call on!

Generating Community Involvement

As the world becomes more global, it's also becoming more local. People are looking for ways to connect with their local community, support local charities and improve the environment. They're looking to interact with like-minded people, whether that's through the local tennis club, the surf club, the school, arts festivals, the dog club, book clubs or through groups who serve the community such as Lions and Rotary. Getting involved in your local community makes you feel good and can be extraordinarily good for business.

If you want other local businesses and the community at large to support you, you need to demonstrate your commitment to your community first.

Here are some ideas to consider to show your community commitment:

- **Build on your current activities.** Consider what local community activities you're already involved in. Think of ways your business can support these by donating prizes, offering sponsorships, speaking at events or volunteering your time and expertise. Maximising your involvement in current activities makes sense.

- **Create your own community group.** If you don't have the kind of community support group you'd like to belong to, another option is to create your own community group. For example, you could create your own group for mums in business so you can get together weekly to talk business, and strategies for juggling family and work.

- **Develop a charitable program.** It feels great to support an organisation that supports those less fortunate than you. If every small business in Australia did this, think what a difference could be made! And it's not just about giving money. It's about supporting a local charity with your hands and heart too. It's about being an ambassador for the charity and volunteering your time and skills to make a difference. Charitable programs are great for staff to get involved in too.

- **Get onto boards, committees and advisory groups.** You can make really meaningful connections by getting onto the board of a charitable organisation or local business, becoming a local councillor, getting involved with the local chamber of commerce, joining Rotary or Lions and so on.

- **Live local, shop local, eat local.** By supporting other local small businesses, eventually you get to know, like and trust each other and, importantly, find out what each other does. Personally, I met my hairdresser at the dog park, my plumber at Nippers, my landscaper through local friends and more. You get the picture.

The primary objective of getting involved in your local community is not to get business (except in the case of sponsorship, which is a commercial venture), but to give something back. In doing this, business will flow back to you.

Smile and say hello to everyone you meet in the course of your day. Where possible, strike up a conversation. You'll make someone's day and you never know what it may lead to!

Hosting Events and Seminars

Holding an event is a great way to build deeper relationships with customers, alliances and potential customers. It's an opportunity for you to get up close and personal with people and, at the same time, demonstrate your expertise and what you offer. Events can take many shapes and forms, from educational seminars to a long lunch or a cocktail party.

Events can also cost you money or be cost-neutral if you charge a small fee. I recommend you hold regular smaller events with fewer people rather than big one-off events, as their ultimate purpose is to build deeper relationships (which is difficult to do when you have large numbers present).

Here's how to hold an event to get people talking about you:

- **Establish your event program.** Determine how many events and what type of events you want to run this year. For example, you may want to hold one each quarter to include three educational lunches and a Christmas cocktail party.

- **Put the dates in the diary.** Make a commitment to the dates and lock them in your diary. You need to promote your calendar of events to the people you want to invite. Put them on your website, send out invitations via email or by a personally printed invitation. Tell them what's coming up and ask them to put it in their diaries.

- **Prepare for the event.** In preparing for each event ask yourself the following questions: What is the purpose? Who is the audience? What are my lead and new business targets for the event? What is the theme or topic? Who will I invite to speak? When will it be? How long will it last? What will be the format? How many people will I invite? Where will I hold it? What catering is required? How will I invite people (mail, phone, email, printed invite or a combination)? What audio and video equipment do I require? Will I charge? If so, how much? What budget is required? Can I get sponsorship? What will the format of the event be? What will people take away with them? Can I get door prizes? Will I get feedback forms completed? How do I plan to follow it up?

- **Be organised.** On the day of the event, make sure you leave plenty of time to set up the room, test equipment, rehearse your presentation, set up the welcome or registration desk, prepare nametags and brief people helping you.

✔ **Communicate with the participants.** Ensure you have someone to help register and welcome people so you're free to network and mingle. Welcome people as they arrive, register them, give them a nametag and introduce them to each other. When you get started, make a short introduction speech to let them know what's coming up, invite their involvement and point out facilities. Be natural and involve the audience as much as possible. Always stick to time. Ask people to complete the feedback form before doing the door prize. Thank them for their participation and let them know you'll be in touch with them in the next week to follow up.

✔ **Follow up.** Evaluate the event the day after. What worked? What didn't? Would you do it again? What was the feedback like? Which people will you follow up and what will you talk to them about? Update your database and make notes to contact people who need following up at a later date. Send people who attended a thank-you card or email. Measure your current or likely return on investment for the event.

Remember that people are busy and get invited to lots of events. If you're asking them to take time out of their busy work and personal lives, you need to make your event stand out. Here are some creative ideas to make your event special:

✔ Consider the personal interests of your customers in developing your events program. Are they golfers, art lovers, wine buffs or music lovers?

✔ Make it a stand-out, exclusive event they can't afford to miss. Limit the event to a small number of people.

✔ Invite a well-known local businessperson or a celebrity to open the event or speak at it.

✔ See if you can get media interest in the event. Send the media an invitation and an interesting story to go with it.

✔ Ask your alliance partners to speak and/or invite their customers. Perhaps they could co-host the event with you?

✔ Be creative and fun by stimulating all the senses. For example, if you specialise in teaching Spanish, invite a local Spanish guitarist to entertain the audience.

✔ Invite your best customers and ask them to bring a friend so you get exposure beyond your current customers.

✔ Leave plenty of time for networking and mingling before and after the event.

✔ If you're not confident in presenting, get the skills. (See the next section, 'Becoming a Confident Public Speaker'.)

✔ Take photos at the event. It's a great way to follow up by either emailing participants their photo or even getting it printed and framed for them. You can also put photos up on your website, use them in newsletters, send them off to the local paper or use them in later marketing activities.

Events are a great way to demonstrate your expertise and connect with lots of people. The best events leave people buzzing and talking about you and your business.

I once hosted an evening cocktail event with about 50 people. I invited a speaker who was ill-prepared and very flat in his delivery style. I could see the audience very quickly became disengaged and fidgety. Rightly or wrongly, I ended up interjecting to add some ideas and try to get the audience engaged and participating with questions. While I knew the speaker personally, I had never really seen him speak. So beware, if you invite someone to speak at your events, your reputation is on the line, so do your homework and make sure you have personally seen the speaker presenting before you book him.

Becoming a Confident Public Speaker

Being invited to speak at public events or speaking at your own events is a great way to promote your expertise and business — that is, of course, if your number-one fear is not public speaking (as it is for many people)! Know what you want to speak about, who the likely audience is, what lasting impression you want to leave and what action you want the audience to take as a result of listening to you speak.

When you've really mastered public speaking, you may even want to add it to your relationship-marketing and business activities, and put yourself on the speaking circuit.

Preparing to speak

Congratulations, you've got a speaking gig (even if it's at your own event)! Now, here's what you need to do to be a great and inspiring speaker:

✔ **Define your topic and think about your audience.** Consider the kind of people you'll be talking to and what's likely to appeal to them. You need to have something engaging to say, so choose a topic you're passionate about that reinforces your expertise and what you have to offer. If the topic's already chosen for you, angle it towards your favourite topic, as long as it engages the audience and informs them.

- **Prepare a speaker's introduction.** Develop a two-paragraph introduction to send to the event organiser to be used by the host to introduce you just before you jump on stage.

- **Get your presentation together.** Lots of words on PowerPoint is not recommended and will only bore your audience. Instead, use great photos of people, music, video footage and interviews with people to inspire and engage your audience. People like getting information in bite-size pieces, so use topic headings like: 'Top Ten Things to ...' or 'Seven Secrets to ...' Always have a structure around the presentation and notes in dot-point form to back you up — index cards are good for this.

- **Get some help.** Professional speakers have had years to master their craft. So, if you're just starting and you need to improve your speaking skills, invest some time and money in it. The National Speakers Association and Toastmasters are organisations that can help here (the websites are at the end of this list).

- **Practise, practise, practise.** You really want to make an impact, so you need to gather your stories, facts and figures, and rehearse your presentation. Although a bit confronting at first, try filming yourself and reviewing the video. This helps you to improve your performance as you pick up things like ums and ahs, and words you use all the time, so you can try to limit them for the presentation.

- **Let people know you're available to speak.** If you're comfortable in front of an audience, and the audience gives you positive feedback, you may want to let specific people know you'd be happy to speak at their events. Don't push it too much to start with, or you may find yourself overwhelmed (or you can take it a step further — see the next section, 'Marketing your speaking services').

- **Engage your audience.** Be early so you can greet individuals as they arrive and get to know them before you speak. When you're up on the podium, imagine you're speaking to each member of the audience in turn and talk directly to them. Ask questions of them and get them interacting with each other. Use stories and paint colourful images in their minds. Above all, be genuine and real. Your audience will connect with you even if you aren't the world's best speaker.

- **Keep connected with your audience.** If you're organising the event yourself, at the end of your talk ask for people's contact details so you can follow them up. A good way to do this is to offer a door prize. Get them to put their business cards in the prize-draw box and pull out a winner. You could also promote a special offer at the end of your speech (you should also mention this during the speech so it's not a surprise at the end). Tell everyone you'll send them some information as a follow-up, unless they don't want to be added to the mailing list. Even if you're a guest speaker rather than the organiser, make sure you have plenty of business cards or brochures to hand out to those who request it.

✔ **Follow up.** Call the event organisers for feedback to ask how your presentation was received and how it could be improved. Ask if you can provide anything else to help them follow up, like an article. If it's appropriate, call those in the audience who you had a meaningful conversation with.

✔ **Leverage your content.** You can use many strategies to get more interest and engagement using the content of your presentation. Often it can be used as the basis of content for articles, e-reports, short video clips and blogs.

Check out the websites of these great support groups to help you become a great speaker at www.thoughtleaders.com.au, www.nationalspeakers. asn.au and www.toastmasters.org.au or www.toastmasters.org.nz.

Speaking is not for everyone. If you're no good at it and never will be, or you simply don't want to do it — don't! You risk the possibility of doing more damage than good if you do.

Marketing your speaking services

If you've decided this speaking gig is really for you, consider if you have the time to offer your services on the speaking circuit. You can treat it as a great relationship-marketing activity or even as a new aspect to your business. Some public speakers earn lucrative incomes in this way. But do think about the effect this may have on your core business.

You should still follow most of the tips in the preceding section, especially in preparing your presentations, but you now also need to market your speaking services.

✔ **Prepare a speaker's bio.** A one- or two-page document that outlines who you are, your experience and background, your area of speciality and the topics you can speak on is a great way to get your own ideas focused and to let people know you're available. If possible, have yourself filmed speaking, put it on YouTube and provide a link in the biography and on your website. Include some testimonials from customers and a picture of yourself in it. You may need to get it professionally written and designed.

✔ **Contact likely audiences.** Send your bio out to local groups or organisations that may be interested in having you speak, such as Rotary, Lions, chambers of commerce, business-networking groups and any other organisations that host regular speakers. Be sure that the audience is your target market. Another good source of speaking opportunities is to offer to speak to the clients of your business alliance partners.

✔ **Prepare your presentation.** Have a few presentation options and topics available, and be prepared to fine-tune your presentation according to the needs of the event organiser. If your presentation normally takes an hour, be prepared to do an abridged version if you're only given half an hour.

✔ **Keep connected with your audience.** Make sure everyone leaves with something that includes your contact details. A postcard with a beautiful image on it, your business card, a brochure or even a giveaway squeezy ball or fridge magnet.

Capitalising on Exhibitions, Expos and Trade Fairs

Exhibitions, expos, trade fairs and large-scale conferences are a great opportunity to exhibit and promote your wares to lots of people (both attendees and other exhibitors) under one roof. Beware though, they're not for the faint-hearted! They can be costly and time-consuming. Before jumping in, work out if it really is the best way to market yourself.

Here are some tips to help make your exhibitions, expos and trade fairs really reap the return on investment you're looking for:

✔ **Do your homework before committing.** Hundreds of exhibitions and trade fairs are held every year across Australia and New Zealand. Identify the ones that target the market you're after. Find out the following: How many exhibitors will be attending? How many visitors are expected? What type of people attend? What does it cost to be there? What is your space allocation? What does the organiser provide (things like partitions and signage)? Where is your stand located? Can you run competitions and special offers? What information can you distribute? Can you get a list of other exhibitors? How many staff passes do you get? What advertising and marketing is being done by the organisers to attract the punters? (*Note:* This last question is critical. I've heard many an exhibitor complain about low attendance rates seriously affecting their potential for sales.) In addition, if you'd like a speaking spot (most exhibitions have a speaker's corner), ask for one.

✔ **Do a cost-benefit analysis.** Work out the total cost (including your time) to be at the exhibition. You need to add in costs like signage, tables, banners, computer screens, staffing costs and more. Determine what number of new leads and conversions you need in order to make it worth your while.

✔ **Plan for the exhibition.** If you decide to proceed and book space at the expo, you need to invest some time in planning for it. Work out the theme of your stand. What will your special offer be? (Make it unique and ensure your stand is not next to a direct competitor.) How will you collect names and addresses of people visiting the stand? What staff do you need to host the stand? What skills do they need?

✔ **Market your presence at the exhibition.** Don't rely on the exhibition organisers to do all the marketing. Ask for some free passes for your customers. Let your customers and everyone else on your database know you're exhibiting and invite them along to your stand. If you have a special offer going, let them know what it is and ask if they want to take advantage of it.

✔ **Train your staff.** Having well-trained, assertive and engaging staff can determine the success or failure of your involvement. Staff need to be able to talk to anybody and everybody, and have the knack of getting people buying. You need to set sales goals and ensure your staff know what to say and what to ask.

✔ **Make a splash.** Your stand must be attention-grabbing and create interest. An interactive experience ensures people engage with you. DVDs, competitions, giveaways and interactive games are great ways to get people engaged. Shoulder massages, golf competitions and face painting or funny balloons for the kids are good ideas. Make sure you collect the contact details of people visiting your stand. Be different and fun!

✔ **Follow up.** Being at an exhibition has no point unless you follow up with every contact you make. This should be done within a week of the exhibition, while you're still fresh in their minds. The best way to follow up is through a combination of phone calls and emails. Make sure you record all their details in your database and diary to follow them up.

✔ **Do a post-exhibition evaluation.** Hold a team meeting to discuss what worked, what didn't and what you would do differently next time. Measure the number of leads and likely conversions. Ideally, you want conversions to happen within three months of the expo — any longer than that and they may be lost forever.

Although exhibitions can be really tiring, they can also be lots of fun. As the business owner, make sure you have lots of great salespeople to staff your stand so you have time to interact and engage with other exhibitors and any VIPs at the exhibition, like speakers or entertainers.

At the exhibition, don't do the hard sell. Shoving brochures into people's hands and not bothering to engage with them is the quickest way to turn people off and ensure your brochures end up in the bin.

Part V
Marketing Online

Glenn Lumsden

*'You've got to get a website.
Look! Everyone's got one!'*

In this part ...

Despite the prevalence of the World Wide Web in today's business world, not much more than 50 per cent of small businesses even have a website. Of course, a website is not the be all and end all for every business. You can market your business online in many other ways — you can use email, list your business on local and industry directories or promote yourself via social sites like Facebook.

Every business has a different online marketing strategy, depending on your growth aspirations, the number of customers you want and the type of business you're in. For example, if you're a one-man-band handyman, fully booked and earning enough money, you may find a simple directory listing is enough. If you're a stand-up comedian, you might not even bother with a website and instead build a blog, and use YouTube and Twitter to get your message out.

Whether you have a website or not, this part shows you how to weave and duck your way around the ever-changing, ever-murky world of marketing online. Excited? Take a deep breath and read on!

Chapter 16

Discovering e-Marketing

· ·

In This Chapter

▶ Finding out who's online and what they're doing

▶ Investing time and money in e-marketing

· ·

*T*he internet is here to stay and its use is growing by the second. The World Wide Web has changed the rules of communication and marketing forever. And, if you don't believe me, check out the facts listed in the following section, 'Widening Your e-Marketing Horizons'.

> *The internet? We are not interested in it.*
>
> —*Bill Gates, Microsoft, 1993*

Even wise and rich men of the IT world can be wrong! Before jumping in to build or improve your own e-marketing, take a broad look at the World Wide Web and how it's impacting our everyday lives.

In this chapter, I talk about how people behave online, how they use the internet for communicating, what they're buying, and what kinds of online marketing and advertising they respond to.

Widening Your e-Marketing Horizons

The World Wide Web is a very big world, and getting bigger by the day (if not by the minute). And web users and developers seem to come up with new uses for it all the time. Check out the following facts on current internet and email usage:

✔ More than 70 million websites exist worldwide.

✔ More than 70 million blogs exist worldwide.

✔ Google has indexed more than 1 trillion URLs.

✔ More than 85 per cent of searches in Australia are done on Google.

✔ More than 2 billion searches are done each day on Google worldwide.

✔ Facebook has more than 200 million active users, with 100 million of those logging on every single day.

✔ Around 183 billion emails are sent each day — that's 2 million per second! (Who knows what percentage are spam emails though.)

✔ Users worldwide spend on average 32 hours per week on the internet and about half that time watching TV.

More than 75 per cent of households in Australia and New Zealand have a computer and 67 per cent of households have access to the internet. That's a lot of people spending time online. But what are they doing online? What are they playing, reading and buying online? How are they communicating with each other? What online media are they following?

And why do you need to know anyway?

So you can get a bird's-eye view of the playing field and work out how to position your business on the field. And so you can sharpen your arrow, target your market, generate interest and enquiries — and, of course, sell!

The most important thing you can do before getting started on your e-marketing plan is to get e-savvy and spend some time learning about the internet in its entirety. Dabble on Facebook. Try writing a blog. Subscribe to newsletters and emails from small-business sites. Get on YouTube and check out how the competition is using it.

If you don't know where to start, find some friends who are e-savvy or even ask your kids to give you a guided tour. You'll not only learn lots but also have some fun along the way.

I'm not suggesting that all of the tactics mentioned here should actually form part of your online marketing plan. I'm suggesting that you spend some time playing around with them and seeing which ones you like using, and then work out if they're worth investigating further.

When it comes to the internet, you don't know what you don't know! I suggest getting comfortable with it.

Who's online and what they're doing

Every generation uses the internet in entirely different ways. For example, my 12-year-old son uses the internet for entertainment and social interaction. He buys and downloads games, buys credit for his mobile phone, plays online virtual games with other kids from halfway around the world and uses it almost every day for project research. To him, email is old hat! Instant chat and messaging via Skype and Facebook are his preferred methods of communication. And his Apple Mac is like a third arm.

On the other hand, I (a Gen Xer) use the internet for work, to buy and transact, and a little for social interaction. (Call me old-fashioned, but I prefer face-to-face connections where possible.) I use the internet to send out emails, scan the daily news, buy airline tickets, book accommodation, pay bills, do the banking and conduct research. And I'm increasingly using instant messaging on Skype and Facebook — it's sometimes the quickest way to communicate with my son!

The best way to get the latest and hottest information on who uses the internet and what they're buying is through, you guessed it, getting online. Here is a list of the most reliable websites to get you started:

- ✔ Australian Bureau of Statistics — www.abs.gov.au
- ✔ Statistics New Zealand — www.stats.govt.nz
- ✔ Internet World Statistics — www.internetworldstats.com
- ✔ Experian Hitwise — www.hitwise.com.au and www.hitwise.com/nz

Experian Hitwise is a particularly useful site, shown in Figure 16-1. Hitwise Competitive Intelligence provides insights into how internet users interact with over one million websites across numerous industries. Hitwise helps you understand how people search online, what search engines they're using and what sites they're visiting, and shows their lifestyle and demographic profiles. Hitwise also analyses trends in online activity for specific industries. If you want to get really serious you can engage them to give you specific stats and information on your own website and how you compare with your competition.

To get further information around your industry, product type and target market, do some detailed online research by checking out your competition and looking at what the big companies in your field are doing. Also look at the overseas trends and follow the blogs of opinion leaders in your field.

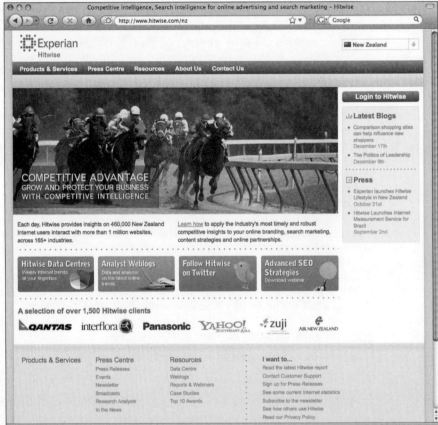

Figure 16-1:
The
Experian
Hitwise
New
Zealand
website.

Understanding the internet for small business

If you're keen to find out where you sit in the online world for small-business owners, you can find some great information in the Sensis e-Business Report. The research is conducted annually with around 1,800 owners of Australian small and medium businesses.

Check out the Sensis website, shown in Figure 16-2, at www.about. sensis.com.au. Click on Small Business in the menu bar and select Sensis® e-Business Report from the dropdown menu.

Figure 16-2:
Sensis
conducts
annual
research to
produce its
report on
e-business.

Interestingly, according to the 2009 Sensis e-Business Report, 97 per cent of Australian small-business owners have a computer and 95 per cent use it for email. The single most important use was to access the internet for email. The second most important use was to look for information about products and services, and the third reason was to get reference information and data.

In 2009 Sensis also found that 57 per cent of Australian small businesses have a website and 12 per cent are planning to build one in the next 12 months. Around half of the small businesses with a website actually use it to sell products and services online. And 71 per cent said that their website had increased their business effectiveness, making it easier for people to be more informed about their business.

Whether you are one of the 57 per cent or the 12 per cent, every business can improve its online presence — not to just inform people about your business but to generate positive response and sales.

Navigating the murky world of e-marketing

Before going much further, you need to make sure you're familiar with some of the common terminology and definitions used on the World Wide Web. Table 16-1 gives just some of the terms you're likely to come across.

Table 16-1	Some Common Web Terms
Term	**Meaning**
affiliate marketing	A revenue-sharing arrangement where two companies agree to link to one another. If someone clicks from Site A to buy something at Site B, Site A gets a commission on the sale.
blog	A *website* or section of a website where users post a chronological e-journal entry of their thoughts, offering readers the opportunity to respond to the writer or converse with other commentators.
browser	A program required on your computer to allow you to access and use the internet, such as Internet Explorer, Mozilla, Firefox and Safari.
click through	When users click on a link to your site from an advertisement, a directory listing, an article or an email you may send out.
email marketing	When you send a promotional mail message electronically from your computer to other people's computers or to groups of people on your database. Can be in the form of a simple email with links to your site or in an *HTML* newsletter format.
e-marketing	The broad term used to cover any marketing you might do via the *World Wide Web*, from *websites* to *blogging*, emailing and more.
e-commerce	Any online selling where consumers purchase products for shipment.
forum	An online community where users read and post comments on topics of common interest.
Google	Founded in 1998 by Larry Page and Sergey Brin, Google ranks the results that match your keyword search according to best fit and popularity. At last count, more than 76 per cent of searches in Australia and are done via Google (www.google.com.au).
Google AdWords	A means of paying to advertise your business on *Google* using short headlines and promotional words. On Google they appear as sponsored links across the top of the page and along the right-hand side. Google ads can also appear on other *websites* that hit your target market.

Term	Meaning
hypertext markup language (HTML)	A computer language used to tell web *browsers* how to structure text into headings, paragraphs, lists and links. You can see a web page's HTML code if you select View Source from the view menu in your web browser.
landing page	A page on a *website* to which people are referred via links from other websites, especially from advertising banners.
Really Simple Syndication (RSS)	A web format for gathering and distributing content from different web sources, including newspapers, magazines and *blogs*.
search engine	A web program that indexes and locates desired information by searching for the keywords that you type in. Common search engines are www.google.com.au and www.yahoo.com and www.bing.com.
search engine optimisation (SEO)	The process of selecting targeted keywords that reflect the content of a *website*, placing them within a tag that is recognised by *search engines* and then testing the search engine results to make sure the site is well positioned, based on these keywords. An SEO specialist can be paid to help you get well ranked.
site navigation	The set of directional tools, links and buttons presented on a *website* that, when clicked, take you to other sections of the site. The names on a navigation bar are usually determined by the titles of the sections within a website.
social media	The many different forms for communities with common interests to interact online including social-networking sites like Facebook, MySpace and Twitter, *blogs* and vlogs (video blogs), forums, podcasts, wikis and much more. It's a huge area that is constantly evolving.
subscriber	A person who has opted in to receive emails, newsletters and regular information via a *website* or *blog*. Subscriber details are usually collected on a database as the basis for sending out regular information.
uniform resource locator (URL)	The location or access address people use to locate a *website*. Your URL address is very important as it points people to your website. A URL is what a telephone number is to a telephone, for example.
website	A place on the web where a business or organisation is featured, consisting of information that is organised into files. A site can contain a combination of graphics, text, audio, video and other dynamic or static materials. It's similar to any other medium, like TV, but is presented on a computer screen to market your business.
World Wide Web	A collection of graphical pages on the internet that can be read and interacted with by computer. To access the web you need a computer, internet *browser* and some specialised programs.
Yahoo!	The second most popular *search engine* after *Google*.

For a full list of web terms, check out `www.netlingo.com`, shown in Figure 16-3.

Figure 16-3: The Net Lingo site allows you to search for terms used on and about the web.

Getting started with e-marketing

You have two choices on entering the e-marketing game. You can have a vague idea of what you want and pay someone to do what they think you want — you might be lucky and actually be happy with the results. Or you can do your homework, understand what it is you need and then oversee the work of building your website so it actually works for you.

A customer came to me recently after spending more than $5,000 on a new website. He wasn't happy! He'd had a friend's cousin, who was supposed to be a bit of an IT guru, build his website for him. At first he was happy and he liked the site, but after three months he'd had exactly three enquiries from prospective customers, of whom exactly zero had turned into business. An audit of his website revealed poor design, navigation and copy, and no search optimisation at all. In fact, the whole site was simply not up to scratch. But that wasn't all. The website developer had decided to take a job at a big corporation and he didn't have the time (or, frankly, the interest) to continue helping his customer to get the website fixed (if, indeed, it was even repairable). The website had become null and void, and he simply had to start all over again.

Now it would be easy to blame the website developer, but, in fact, I lay equal blame on the customer himself. He hadn't done his homework and he didn't know what he needed or choose the right supplier in the first place.

I reckon, on average, three in five small-business owners will relate to this story. They've either had it happen to them or they know someone who has. And this is why so many people are wary of the World Wide Web (and rightly so). Becoming e-savvy before you jump in pays off. Knowing what results and return on investment you should expect, what you should spend and how you can make your online marketing work for you on a daily basis is priceless.

If you want to waste money on e-marketing, just pay someone a pile of it to build you a website and leave 'em to it! If you don't want to waste money on e-marketing you need to get e-savvy and project-manage it. That doesn't mean you have to do the work. It just means you need to know what your web developer is doing and why, and what results to expect.

Remembering to use a database

When you're in the formative stages of building your online presence, you need to remember how important it is to attempt to collect visitors' contact information via your website. Some visitors may wish to subscribe to your regular e-newsletter. Others may just want to buy or enquire and not subscribe. Whatever you do, your most important task is to use your website, and any other online marketing you do, to collect prospect contact information so you can keep in touch. (Refer to Chapter 2 for methods of collecting information using a database.)

Not every customer wants to buy right at the point of visiting your website, but they may be willing to be added to your database so you can connect later.

Don't add people to your database for marketing purposes unless they specifically opt in to receive information from you.

Investing in e-Marketing

Now you've got a handle on the basics of the internet and e-marketing, it's time to find out how to go about establishing your own business online. Investing in e-marketing means more than just coming up with the dough to get a good website. It's about making time for it, having a plan and taking a strategic approach.

Depending on the type of business you're in, I recommend spending around 30 to 50 per cent of your total marketing time, energy and money on your e-marketing activities.

Getting help and advice

Never underestimate the importance of good advice and expert assistance. And, remember, that doesn't mean you can just hand over the lot to an expert. You, also, need to know *what to do*, though not necessarily *how to do it*.

So, when it comes to the web, the best investment you can make before leaping into building your online presence is to get the right advice and help — not just in the website-building process, but in all things e-marketing. And, to be honest, getting the right advice and help can be tricky, as every person you speak with seems to have a different opinion on what works and what doesn't. That's why you need to do your homework and find the best person to help before jumping in. In Chapter 17, I write about what to look for in a good web developer and how to know if you'll get the results you want.

Many receive advice, only the wise profit from it.

—*Publilius Syrus, Roman author, first century BC*

How much time should I invest?

Like any goal worth achieving, mastering the world of online marketing takes time (and a big dose of patience).

Although you can employ a web developer and search engine optimisation (SEO) specialist (refer to Table 16-1 for an explanation) to build your website and make sure people online can find it, that's really only the starting point. If you want to continue to get your website ranking well and get people buying, you need to update your content regularly, create reciprocal links to other sites, advertise, update your directory listings regularly, use some of the social media out there, write articles and much more.

If this level of maintenance sounds exhausting and it's not something you personally have the time or appetite for, you might consider using your web company or even a part-time uni graduate to do it for you. The long and the short of it is you need to invest time in continually managing and upgrading your online presence.

The biggest mistake you can make is to build a website and then do nothing with it for two or three years until you realise it's out-of-date and broken. However, most websites probably need to be rebuilt every two to three years because of continual technological advancements. In fact, blogs seem to now be taking over the world and in many cases replacing websites — so who knows what will be next!

How much money should I invest?

Ah, the million-dollar question! In my experience, if you get a web developer to build your site, you won't get much for less than $3,000. Depending on your business and needs, of course, you could be paying anything between $3,000 and $50,000! And that's just for the up-front build.

Of course, you have other costs to consider, such as website hosting, URL registrations and e-commerce costs like online payment gateway fees and credit card merchant fees (if you happen to sell online), Google AdWords, directory listings and other advertising costs.

When working on a website project for a customer recently, I went out to the market with a request for proposal (RFP — refer to Chapter 10) and had four companies tender. The cheapest came in at around $12,000 and the most expensive came in at around $40,000! And two in the middle range came in at around $25,000 each. The cheapest company won, and price was only the third reason we chose it. The company's services included not only website development but also ongoing SEO work and support for 12 months and much more. We liked the people and their approach, the size of the company, the platform they used (www.businesscatalyst.com) and more.

Do a spreadsheet that itemises all your web-associated costs over a year and then work out what number of new enquiries and sales you need to make sure your investment pays off. Don't forget to cost out your time and include that too.

Evaluating your online activity

Whether you market your business on Twitter, YouTube, your blog or your website, be sure to measure what traffic and enquiries your online activity generates. Remember to collect information at the time of enquiry as to where they first heard about you online.

The true test of your online success is not how much traffic you get or the number of enquiries you generate, but how many convert to customers. Having only a hundred highly qualified prospects come to your site, with ten turning into customers, is better than having 1,000 unqualified prospects, of which only one turns into a customer.

If your conversion rate is very low, take a look at your packaging, pricing, messaging and your whole offer, as well as the kinds of enquiries coming through. You might need a refresh.

Chapter 17

Developing a Great Website

In This Chapter

▶ Setting website objectives

▶ Project-managing your website build and launch

*W*hen speaking at seminars on the topic of websites, often new business owners approach me and say, 'I've just started a new business, and I need a website ASAP — can you tell me where to get one?'

When I ask them more about their business, very often they're still unsure of what their business actually is, what they want to offer to the market and even if the market wants it. Before getting a website, get the basics right first. Then ask yourself, 'Do I need a website?' In most cases the answer will be a big *yes*, unless you have a steady flow of customers and no desire to grow bigger, or if you happen to be a convenience store with a steady flow of walk-in customers, for example.

If you need more business and your potential customers are likely to be searching for your type of service or product online, a website is really an essential cost of being in business. A good website tells people you're serious about what you're doing. It helps people find you and interact with you. It can also inform, educate, inspire and connect prospects, customers and the public at large. And it can act as your sales force and make you money while you sleep through online sales. (Doesn't everyone want that!)

If you're just starting in business, this chapter gives you a step-by-step guide to getting a great website. If you already have a website but want to improve it or build a new one, you still need to take the same approach.

Defining Your Website Objectives

Many people find the process of getting a website daunting, and I don't blame them. Thousands of so-called web gurus are out there offering all sorts of packages and deals, and finding the best help can be tricky. Take heart — it's not that hard. If you're informed, know what you want and have the right people on board to help, you can have the best website around.

A website usually has two overarching goals — to attract new customers and to retain your existing customers. Don't make the mistake of simply thinking about your website as a way to attract more business. Your best source of new business is actually your existing customers. So, if your website is informative and worth going back to, they'll hopefully buy more and be willing to refer their friends to your site.

You need a strategic and staged approach to your website development. It's a bit like trekking up a huge mountain. You need to make sure you're well prepared before you start and then you need to do the trek in stages while always keeping the pinnacle in mind (even if it's out of sight) during the journey.

Quite a few business owners spend days, weeks and even months online building their own websites and setting up social media connections on every social media known to humanity — without any real end goal or objective in sight. Unless you plan to become an online guru and that's actually your core business, then be aware you're probably just wasting your time. This book doesn't cover how to build your own website — that's another whole *For Dummies* book on its own! In fact, if you want to go down that road, check out *Web Sites Do-It-Yourself For Dummies* by Janine Warner, *Building a Web Site For Dummies*, 3rd Edition, by David A. Crowder, or *Building Web Sites All-In-One For Dummies* by Claudia Snell and Doug Sahlin (all from Wiley Publishing Inc.).

Your first objective is to find the best web developer who can interpret your overall business objectives and goals, and then help you shape your website objectives accordingly. Read on to find out what you need in a web developer, and what you need to do first.

Matching your business objectives to your website

If you have a clear picture of your business objectives, then (with the right web partner) you'll end up with a website that delivers exactly what you want, with no nasty surprises.

Before searching for a web developer, prepare a one-page summary of your business and be clear on how you see your website supporting you in achieving your business vision and goals. Refer to Chapter 4 for some good tips on goal setting and planning and then check out the next section before looking for the best developer.

Planning your website strategy

Whether you already have a presence online and need a refresh or are starting from scratch, you need to go through this checklist of questions:

- ✔ **Target market:** Who are you trying to reach online? Is your target market existing customers, brand new customers or a certain kind of prospect? Where are they located? How old are they? Where are they currently buying services like yours? What are their internet usage patterns? Where might they look for your kind of services or product? Would they buy what you offer online?

- ✔ **Competitors:** What are your competitors offering online? Where do they advertise? What do they sell? What are their messages and points of difference? What information can you find out about their traffic and success online?

- ✔ **Environment:** What are big companies in your industry doing online? What's happening in global companies that are like yours? What government resources and tools are available and a good fit for your business? What other complementary businesses are operating online? How are they selling online?

- ✔ **Website:** What is the goal of your website? To attract new customers? To get old customers to buy more? What messages do you want to convey? What specific outcomes do you want from the people who visit the site? A phone call? Enquiry form completed? A sale? What impression do you want to leave? What keywords would people be using to search for your services?

- ✔ **Spreading the word:** How are you going to get your website found by your target market? What needs to be done to get your site found on search engines? What social media sites might you use to drive traffic to the site? Are you going to use articles, news updates and blogging to get people engaged? (For more on this check out Chapter 18.)

- ✔ **Resources:** How much money do you have available to spend? How much time do you have available to spend on building your website? Who will you get to build your online presence and do search engine optimisation (refer to Chapter 16 for an explanation of this and other web terms, and Chapter 18 for how to go about it)? How will you keep your online presence fresh and current? What else will you need to manage your website on a daily, weekly, monthly and yearly basis?

✔ **Measurement:** How many people do you want to visit your site? What will be the key pages they should visit? How often do you want visitors to return? How many people do you want posting comments on your site, subscribing to it or enquiring about your services? How much do you want people to spend online? How will you track where enquiries come from?

It's okay by the way, not to know the answers to many of these questions. A good web developer should be able to help you at least make some intelligent guesses at the answers.

Finding a good web developer

Many web developers build from scratch and/or use their own content management systems to build your website, whereas others purchase licences to build your website using an off-the-shelf system.

Literally thousands of these systems are on the market, such as www.wordpress.com, www.businesscatalyst.com, www.eknowhow.com and www.joomla.com, and no one system is perfect for every business. I recommend scouting around and checking a few out before settling on a developer.

Follow this process to find a web developer:

✔ **Do your research.** Look at competitor websites and find out who built them. Ask friends or colleagues who have successful online businesses who built their sites and if they would recommend them. Do a search on, say, **web developers (your city/town)** and see who comes up. If they're easily found on a search engine like Google or Yahoo!, then they know a thing or two about e-marketing. Narrow down your list to around six developers.

✔ **Make contact.** Meet the developers for a coffee or talk to them over the phone. Make sure there is a fit between your business and theirs before you ask them to tender for your business.

✔ **Be prepared.** Have a list of questions on hand. What system do they use to build their websites and why and how easy is it to use? Can you update your own content once they've built the site? How long have they been in business? Who are their customers? How big is their team of people? What ongoing support do they offer with your e-marketing? What is their track record with search engine optimisation? Is that included in their services? What is their typical price range for a website? Do they offer other services to complement their online services? (Many web developers also do brand and print work.) Can you have three references for customers you can call? What results have they achieved for their customers? What process do they follow in helping ensure that you end up with the best solution?

✔ **Listen and observe.** Depending on their answers to the preceding questions, you'll be able to quickly gauge their professionalism and ability to deliver. Also watch for the questions they ask you. They should want to know more about your business, your target market, what you want to achieve online, what your budget is, what your timeframes are and more.

✔ **Narrow it down.** Once you've narrowed down your list to three, ask if they would be prepared to present a proposal to you based on your very carefully prepared request for proposal (RFP). Refer to Chapter 10 to help you prepare the RFP.

✔ **Make a choice.** When they present their credentials to you and their response to your RFP, ask yourself some questions. Which one do you like and trust? Which one has a track record and a good list of customers? Which one shows genuine interest in your business? Who can you see yourself working with in years to come?

When selecting a developer, look at the total cost anticipated over a year, not just the up-front build cost. While the least costly ones may be appealing, you may find yourself paying more in the long run.

Never choose a developer on cost alone. Ongoing support and service, track record and a bit of good old-fashioned gut instinct should be considered in your final selection.

Developing a project plan

Your role in getting your website built is to be an excellent executive. Trust that you've chosen the experts to build your site and meddle only if alarmed (which, hopefully, if you've done your homework, won't happen).

A simple project plan is required so that both you and the web developer are on the same page as to the expected outcomes and delivery deadlines. It also helps you plan for the launch and hopefully increase the enquiries and business that present themselves after the site is launched.

The best executive is the one who has sense enough to pick good men to do what he wants done, and self-restraint to keep from meddling with them while they do it.

—*Theodore Roosevelt (1858–1915), 26th US President*

Attributes of a good website

Good websites are warm and engaging, and keep people coming back. You need to provide practical attributes to encourage your customers to use your site for information and purchases, fun stuff to keep them entertained, and maybe even links to social-networking and other useful sites.

As the proprietor of Happy Hounds Mobile Dog Grooming, here are some of the different attributes you might consider to make your website interesting and fresh:

- **Buttons:** Include a few simple 'share with a friend' or 'make this your homepage' buttons.

- **Contact us:** Make it really easy for people to buy from you. Include your phone and fax numbers, email and address (whichever suits your system), and make them bold on every page.

- **Eye-catching graphics:** Use rotating banners or buttons with pictures of cute dogs to highlight different products or services rather than lots of heavy written content.

- **Frequently updated information:** A static homepage is boring. Keep it up-to-date with the latest news on dogs needing rescuing or an invitation to your doggie Christmas party.

- **Forums:** Set up a forum where users can post comments about a topic such as a new regulation on dogs set by the local council.

- **Opinion polls:** Get people interacting with you by asking them to complete a simple opinion poll or survey to rank the best dog park in your local area.

- **Pictures:** Take photos of dogs and their owners and post up a dog-of-the-week picture on your homepage.

- **Podcasts:** Record interviews with famous dog lovers talking about their dogs and post them on your site.

- **Resource library:** Have a section that includes links to websites about places you can take dogs for holidays or dog-friendly beaches, articles or tips on dog grooming and behaviour, and links to great doggie books you might recommend.

- **RSS feeds:** Really Simple Syndication (RSS) feeds allow you to automatically feed in stories and articles on dogs from other sites that fit with yours.

- **Secure log-ins:** Some businesses may find it useful to provide a section of their site for customers only. Banks do this for online banking and airlines do it for frequent-flyer programs. (Not sure that a mobile dog-grooming business would need this, but you never know!)

✔ **Social media links:** Set up a Doggie Lovers Facebook or Twitter page and include buttons on your site to allow people to click through and follow you.

✔ **Subscription access:** Offer users the opportunity to subscribe to your Doggie Doings e-newsletter or email updates, or to receive a copy of your free Top Ten Doggie Holidays e-report. You can then set up your site to auto-forward these items via email to subscribers.

✔ **Testimonials:** Obtain real testimonials from satisfied customers, and get their permission to use their picture and name on the site.

✔ **Video content:** Film yourself with your own dog, highlighting your approach to grooming, and put it on your site or even post up funny doggie YouTube clips. You could also film the Happy Hounds mobile dog-grooming van in action.

Now, I'm aware that's a mighty long list of things Happy Hounds could do and it might not be possible to do them all. A good web developer should help you sift through your ideas and give you some direction.

Building good content for your website

When referring to the web, *content* is a general term to mean the words (copy) and images on your website, including articles, blogs, forums, resource libraries, videos and anything else included on the site that a user can read or engage with.

Spending all your money and time on the look of a site and not enough on the content is committing website suicide. Your website is not a mere online version of a printed ad. It's a powerful tool that, with deep and rich content, will get you found where and when no print ad possibly could.

In the Happy Hounds Mobile Dog Grooming hypothetical in the previous section, I give you some ideas on what type of content could work well for your site.

The other consideration when it comes to content is the copy you include about your business and products or services. Writing powerful copy is both an art and a science and I recommend using a professional web writer. When writing, you need to be mindful of frequently including the keywords that will get you found on the web (more on this in Chapter 18). You can also include articles and stories on your site to increase its credibility.

Content must be highly relevant. Just adding in any old stuff to pad your site out has little point. Your users are pretty good at weeding out the fluff.

For a great example of how to build content for a website, check out `www.dsbn.com.au`, shown in Figure 17-1.

> *If you build it, he will come.*
>
> —*The Voice, from the movie* Field of Dreams, *1989*

Build good content on your website and many will come!

Figure 17-1:
The Dynamic Small Business Network website is very user-friendly.

Site navigation and usability

Another important consideration in building your website is the usability and navigation of the site. By *navigation* I mean the set of directional tools and buttons that, when clicked on, take you through to other pages on the website. *Usability* refers to how easy it is to switch across to other pages and generally move around the site, to subscribe and purchase online.

Poor navigation and usability is a major reason for people to leave a site. If pages take too long to download or annoying pop-ups keep appearing or click-throughs result in a 'sorry this page is not available' or if there are too many click-throughs to buy online, users become frustrated and don't return. They opt for another site that is easier to use and you've lost a potential customer forever.

Before launching your new site, test and test again how easy it is to use. Doing this is critical. Ask a few people in your office to go through your site. Stand behind them to watch how they interact with the site, and get their direct feedback on how it could be improved.

Selling from your website

Every business has the potential to sell online, even though some businesses find it more appropriate than others. For example, if you're a tax accountant, you'd probably find it hard to sell your traditional taxation services online. However, if you decide to run paid workshops or events, or to offer online tutorials or software, then you need to consider how to set up a buying facility, commonly known as a *shopping cart*, as part of your website.

In addition, you need to set up a *payment gateway facility*, which enables a secure payment method for your customers, like www.paypal.com or www.gopay.com.au, which I've used for many years and have found very reliable. You also need to ensure you're set up with your *merchant provider* so people can pay by credit card (Visa, MasterCard, Amex and/or Diners).

Setting up your shopping cart, payment gateway and credit card facility isn't hard to do; it just takes a bit of organising. Your web developer should be able to show you what needs doing.

You also need to set up a process to follow, from the time of sale to dispatch, to ensure that every online sale is handled efficiently. This includes everything from automatic electronic tax invoicing to delivery.

To work out how to sell online and the steps you should follow, take a good look at how the airlines and other companies that sell successfully online go about it.

Before going full-steam ahead and spending the money required to sell online, you need to go back to your business objectives and determine if your target market is likely to buy online.

For a great example of a website that sells products and services online, check out this occupational health and safety company site at www.safetyculture.com.au, shown in Figure 17-2.

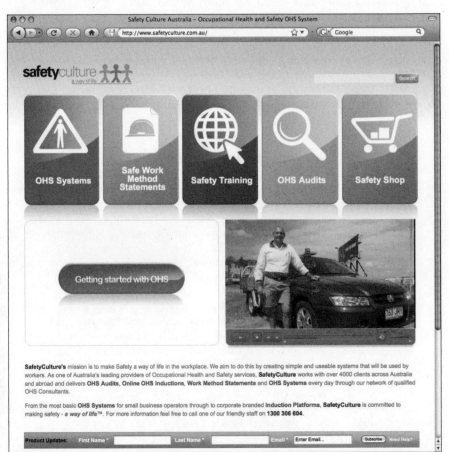

Figure 17-2: The Safety Culture website is focused and uncluttered, making it easy to purchase products online.

Building and Launching Your Website

If you've read the previous sections of this chapter, you should have a good idea of what goes into building a good website. It's time to get started and go for it. Set yourself a schedule by working backwards from your proposed launch date, and then work like mad with your web developers to make it happen, following a staged approach. Plan your launch party and tell people it's happening and when they can expect to see you online.

Stages of building your website

Actually building the site follows a fairly standard and logical process. Here are the stages your web developer is likely to use to get you up and away:

- **Proposal:** Before getting started you and your web developer should sign a simple agreement outlining delivery date, payment terms, stages of delivery, and support and training provided.

- **Brief:** Your developer then clarifies with you your website objectives, brand, design and navigation requirements, photography or image requirements, e-newsletter requirements, shopping cart needs (if you plan to sell online), keywords you want to include and more. Part of the brief should include agreeing on URLs you currently have registered or want registered.

- **Site map:** The developer then produces a *wireframe*, or *sitemap*, to give you an overall picture of the navigation, dropdown menus, buttons and functionality.

- **Design:** Next he may give you a couple of homepage and secondary page design options for you to select from before he starts building. You have the opportunity here to ask for modifications to the design. This would include e-newsletter templates too.

- **Build:** He then starts building the site for periodic review and testing. This includes setting up a shopping cart and payment procedures, and any other add-ons you may want.

- **Content:** Writing good content is as critical as navigation and design. You can either do it yourself or outsource it to a web copy specialist (which I recommend). It's important to have content in tip-top shape and proofread before you send it to the developer to upload to the site.

- **Testing:** Once the site is built you need to check all links, click through all buttons, proofread the copy, make sure the shopping cart and subscribe buttons are working, and generally ensure anyone using the site is going to have a first-class user experience.

✔ **Back end:** If you're buying an all-in-one solution that has a customer relationship management (CRM) system and more, you need to test this is also working effectively. Refer to Chapter 2 for more on CRM systems.

✔ **Training:** When the site is ready, you need to get training on how to upload content and keep the site fresh and maintained.

✔ **Launch:** You're now ready to launch. Have a party and send your website link to everyone!

✔ **Ongoing support:** Various things will always need tidying up from time to time or you may want to give the site additional functions at some stage. Make sure you know how to get the support when you need it. This includes helping you drive traffic to the site with search engine optimisation (SEO), which I detail in Chapter 18.

Launching your website

Getting a new website is no small feat, so, like any milestone in business, celebrate it and tell your customers, prospects and friends all about it. You might consider

✔ Doing a letterbox drop or plastering your website address on your car.

✔ Getting onto the social-networking media and pointing people to your new website.

✔ Holding a fun cocktail evening with your web developers, staff and customers. (No need to bore them with a huge tour of the site though; just the highlights will do!)

✔ Including your website link on all your customer correspondence and invoices.

✔ Listing your new site on online directories.

✔ Mailing out a postcard or letter to your customers to let them know about the site.

✔ Providing a special limited offer for people who register on your site.

✔ Putting your website address on all your signage and in your shopfront window (if you have one).

✔ Running an ad campaign that encourages people to log on to win a prize.

> ✔ Sending the link to your new site to all your alliance partners and potential referrers, asking if they would like to feature on your site and if you can feature on theirs.
>
> ✔ Sending your very first e-newsletter or email to all your contacts and asking them to send it on.

You can find a thousand ways to direct traffic to your new website, of course (I note some of them in Chapter 18). Consider making a big splash at first and then doing a little to promote your site every week. When it comes to marketing your website (like all marketing), you simply can't just set and forget.

Getting subscribers to your website

One goal to consider is how to get people to subscribe to your website to receive regular emails from you. In the new and novel days of the web, people would subscribe to most things. Now, with all the spam and rubbish people receive in their in-boxes, people take subscribing far more seriously and only do it if they're really, really interested in you and what you promise to send them.

For example, I don't want to receive e-newsletters from my bank, phone company or health insurance company. I do, however, love getting an e-newsletter from my local surf club and my son's school, as well as many of the small-business websites I follow.

To win a subscriber you need to promise (and give) value and quality — a free e-report, invitations to events or latest news. I talk more about this in Chapter 18.

Subscriber bases are best built slowly and steadily over time, based on earning the right to keep communicating. You can damage your reputation hugely by sending unsolicited emails to people who either don't know you or who have not willingly opted in, and you could be breaching the Privacy Act.

Chapter 18

Driving Traffic to Your Website

In This Chapter

▶ Putting the search engines to work

▶ Advertising your business online

▶ Using other clever tactics to drive traffic

*I*f you produced a great new sales brochure, would you leave it in the cupboard or would you look for as many ways as possible to get it in the hands of your prospective customers? Of course, you'd distribute it as far and wide as possible. However, when many people build a website, they post it up on the web and then, for some reason, just hope people will find them. You can't just build a site and do nothing with it. You need to be proactive to get it in the hands (or on the computer screens) of your prospects. In short, you need to *drive traffic* (attract visitors) to your website.

You can choose from thousands of ways to entice people to visit your website. Simply putting your website on a business card and handing your card to someone may result in a visit. Mailing a special offer brochure that directs people to your website may also result in a visit. Plastering your new website address on your car or shop window may also drive traffic. These traditional tactics should all be used; however, the most cost-effective and more immediate way to drive traffic is to use the online medium itself to attract interest and visitors.

In this chapter, I show you how to drive traffic through search engines, online advertising, social-networking media, directories and more. Whether you actively manage your online marketing yourself or pay someone else to do it for you, I also tell you in this chapter how to select the best tactics and put them to work.

Getting Search Engines to Work for You

A *search engine* is actually a web program that catalogues information published on the internet. Search engines attempt to index and classify information so you can easily locate your desired information based on the keywords you type into it. Common search engines are Google, Yahoo! and Bing.

Interestingly, according to www.hitwise.com.au, of the three million Australian internet users in the four-week period to 2 January 2010, a whopping 85.52 per cent of searches were done on Google, 8.77 per cent on Yahoo! and 4.3 per cent on Bing. Similar statistics for New Zealand show 92.99 per cent of searches were done on Google, 2.49 per cent on Yahoo! and 2 per cent on Bing.

Although getting a handle on all search engines is important, clearly the most critical one to master is Google. In fact, if you're not found on Google, your online business simply doesn't exist!

Because Google is so dominant and has so many tools that small-business owners can use, I focus on Google throughout this chapter. If you'd like to know more about the other search engines, check out *Search Engine Optimization For Dummies* by Peter Kent (Wiley Publishing Inc.).

How to get search engines indexing you well takes a bit of trial and error, and consistent effort over months and even years to get it right.

Every business owner needs to get a handle on the free service, Google Analytics (www.google.com/analytics), shown in Figure 18-1. This powerful tool gives you intelligence about how people find your site, how they navigate around your site and how they become customers. You can analyse keywords used and compare your website performance from one period to another to help you improve traffic.

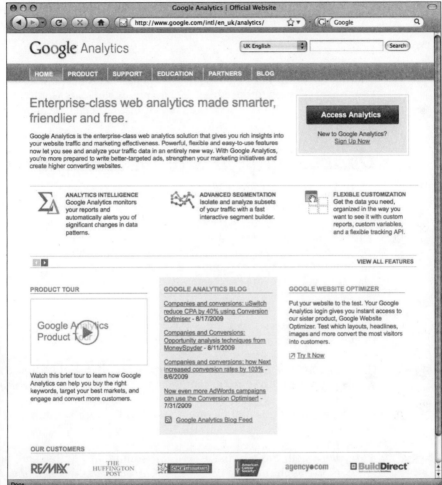

Figure 18-1: Google Analytics offers free tools to improve your online presence.

Registering your site for online searches

An important consideration to getting found online is your *domain name* (the core part of a web address, such as dummies.com) and website address (URL) or addresses you have registered for your business. In most cases, registering many domain names is better than only one or a few. The last thing you want is someone else registering domain names that would be a natural fit for your business and then taking all your potential traffic.

In my case, I've registered every domain name that someone could possibly type in to search for my services including my business name, Connect Marketing, my own name, Carolyn Tate (and previous name Stafford), and the title of my first book, *Small Business Big Brand*. I have registered most of these as `.com`, `.au` and many others too. My main URL is `www.connectmarketing.com.au`, so all of the other domains are redirected to this one, making it easier for people searching for me to find me. Sadly, I was too late to get `www.connectmarketing.com`.

You can check for and register domain names on many sites. I use `www.web central.com`, `www.netregistry.com` or `www.melbourneit.com.au` and `www.domain.co.nz` or `www.nzregistry.co.nz` in New Zealand.

Optimising your site for search engines

After you have all of the most likely domain names pinpointed to your main site, you need to get cracking on being well ranked by the search engines so when people type in the keywords you want to be found for, your business is listed and enticing enough for people to click through to. *Keywords* are the specific words or terms used by a person searching for something on the internet. If you use them in your headings or text they pop up in the search so your website is listed in the search results, hopefully ranking high on the list.

You know you've reached Google heaven if your site is found in its top three to five listings as the result of a search!

Getting a handle on your keywords is critical. You can do a free check of words people are likely to be searching for on the Google Insight for Search site at `www.google.com/insights/search`. Your web developer should have a handle on this and be able to work with you to create your keyword list.

If you were a gift basket business in Christchurch, New Zealand, your keyword list might include *gift, basket, Christchurch, New Zealand, Mother's Day, baby, birthday, wedding* ... You get the picture. You could narrow it down to more specific locations or occasions, depending on your business goals and the services you offer. These words then need to be included regularly in the copy on your site and also in the navigation bar of the website browser (an oversight for many businesses), as *alt-tags* (the words that appear in the little box when you scroll over a picture) attached to images and more.

Most SEO (search engine optimisation) experts would say this is an oversimplified explanation of how keywords and SEO work. And I'd probably agree. I'm not an SEO expert. However, I reckon it gives you a good idea of what you need to consider.

Lots of people pitch themselves as SEO experts, but finding a good one can be difficult. If you're building a new website, find a web developer with a good handle (and track record) on SEO so that it's considered before, during and after you build your site. If your site is already built and you just want to drive more traffic, an SEO specialist can help — just do your homework before appointing one. Most SEO experts charge a fixed fee up-front to set you up for SEO and then a monthly fee to keep you well ranked.

SEO is different from Google AdWords (refer to Chapter 16 for a definition). SEO is generally about getting yourself well ranked in a Google search page. Google AdWords is about paying for ads to be listed as *sponsored links* on a search page, which is usually a shaded area either at the top or side of the search results page.

If you really want to master Google yourself, check out *Google Business Solutions All-In-One For Dummies* by Bud E. Smith and Ryan Williams (Wiley).

Building links on your site

A great way to keep your customers interested in your site is to create links on your site to other sites.

Happy Hounds Mobile Dog Grooming, the business I introduce in Chapter 17, might consider developing a resource library with links. It could consider great dog holiday destination sites, dog advice and tips, links to local vets and pet shops, dog-training businesses, famous dog trainer websites like Cesar Millan (the dog whisperer), sites selling dog books and DVDs, and so on.

Always make sure the links you choose are relevant to your business and your audience, and check them regularly. Also ensure that at any time when users do click on a link, they can easily flick back to your site. You want to be careful not to lose your users in the process.

I've been asked many times if you need to get permission from these other website owners to put their link on your site. It's not really necessary, but I think it's courtesy (and a great marketing opportunity) to call and ask.

Promoting your site on other sites

You can do lots of things for free to get your site on other sites to drive traffic to it, such as:

✔ Post an article with a link to your site on www.ezinearticles.com or www.goarticles.com.

✔ Get a regular column or write articles for the online section of the media in your local area and be sure to include your website.

✔ Respond to blogs or forums on sites that hit your target market, such as www.smartcompany.com.au or www.flyingsolo.com.au and include a link to your site.

✔ Ask business owners with a complementary business targeting the same market in your local area if they would consider reciprocal links.

✔ List your business on any of the thousands of free directories out there — such as www.hotfrog.com.au or www.hotfrog.co.nz.

✔ If you have a product, consider selling it on eBay or other shopping websites.

For a full list of free online directories that might be suitable, check out www.web-directory-australia.info or www.nzdirectory.co.nz.

Advertising Online

Before reading on, I suggest you take a quick look at the sections on online advertising in Chapter 9. They give you a comprehensive overview of the pros and cons of online advertising.

The most common question I'm asked is, 'I know I need to advertise online, but where do I do it and how do I do it — and how much money should I spend?'

If you decide to allocate a reasonable budget to it and are working with a creative or advertising agency, the agency staff should be able to work with you and their media buying agency to recommend a plan. If they haven't even considered online advertising in your overall advertising media plan, the alarm bells should be ringing! Ask why.

If you're doing it yourself (which I don't recommend without some serious advice), go back to the basics, just like you would with traditional print advertising. Who is your target market? What are they reading online? What type of online advertising works best for your audience?

Advertising online can be done in many ways through affiliate marketing, Google AdWords, *rich-media* (video) ads, social-networking ads on sites like Facebook, *banner* ads (horizontal on the screen) and *tower* ads (vertical), and by advertising in directories.

The advantage of online advertising over almost every other form of advertising is that it is immediate, so at little cost you can test, measure and track your traffic and results.

Affiliate advertising

Affiliate advertising, often referred to as *affiliate marketing*, is where two online businesses strike an agreement where one pays the other based on the performance of an advertisement placed on the other's website. Payment is usually made according to the number of purchases resulting from the ad, although it can also be made for click-throughs and leads. Affiliate advertising was actually pioneered by online bookseller Amazon.

Say you own a personalised stationery business, where people can choose from certain designs and order online. One of your product lines is wedding invitations. You decide to set up an affiliate program with other website owners who happen to sell anything to do with weddings, such as wedding car hire, wedding photographers, bridal shops, wedding caterers, bridal expo hosts and more. You place an ad on their sites and then, when a bride-to-be (or groom-to-be) clicks through your ad and orders, you pay the site owner a percentage of the sale, say 15 per cent.

A number of parties (who, by the way, all take a cut of the sale) are required to be involved in affiliate advertising, such as the website you advertise on, your merchant provider, gateway payment people and the affiliate tracking company you sign up with.

Hundreds of affiliate advertising partners and tracking companies that you can sign up with are in operation. One company that provides a good overview on how affiliate marketing works is clixGalore. Check out their website at www.clixgalore.com.au and www.clixgalore.co.nz, and click on More Information in the banner.

Google AdWords

When you do a web search on Google, you often find sponsored links pop up at the top or side of the results page. These are Google AdWords.

The best way to find out more about Google AdWords is to get on it and try some AdWords campaigns and see how they go. And check out *Google AdWords For Dummies* by Howie Jacobson (Wiley) if you really want to get serious.

The process is pretty simple. You sign up to Google AdWords and then create ad campaigns using keywords people might use to search for your type of service or product. When people search for these words, your ad appears (called an *impression*) under the Sponsored Links sections of the Google page. When people click through on your ad, you pay a small amount for each one (this amount is set by you). You also set a per-day limit so you know the absolute maximum charge you'll be up for. At the end of each month your nominated credit card is charged for your advertising.

Creating multiple ad campaigns that run at the same time is a good strategy. Then you can test, measure and compare the impressions, click-throughs and sales results of each one. You can keep and improve on the ones that appear to work and eliminate the ones that don't.

For more information on how to use Google AdWords, check out the website, shown in Figure 18-2, at `http://adwords.google.com.au` or `http://adwords.google.co.nz`.

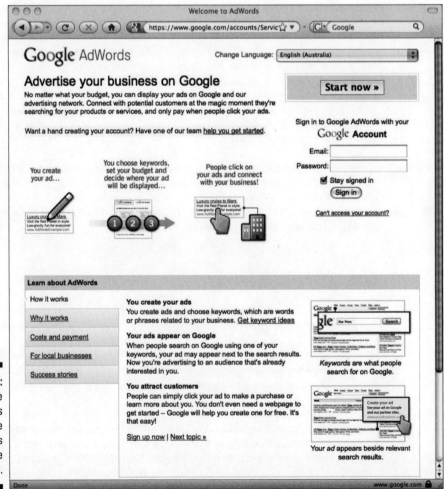

Figure 18-2:
Google
AdWords
gives simple
instructions
to advertise
online.

Other types of online ads

Google ads are only one way of advertising online. You can also negotiate direct with websites to have your ad placed on a site for a fixed fee. You pay a certain amount for it to appear a certain number of times (impressions) over a certain period. Different types of ads include:

✔ **Banner, button and tower ads:** These types of ads use a high degree of design and HTML coding (refer to Chapter 16), and generally include images or photos and animation to capture the attention of the browser. Banner ads appear horizontally across the screen, tower ads usually appear down the right side of the screen and button ads, well, they seem to appear wherever they fit! Figure 18-3 shows the Smart Company website (www.smartcompany.com.au), with banner ads appearing along the top and tower ads on the right side.

Figure 18-3:
Banners and towers — online ads can come in all shapes and sizes.

- **Copy-only ads:** Simple ads with compelling headlines and clever copy that may even appear as an advertorial or article can also work well for advertisers. They work much like Google AdWords.

- **Rich-media ads:** These are like TV ads produced for the online world and can be hosted on sites like YouTube. *Infomercials* (recorded ads with you, the owner, telling people about your business and demonstrating what you offer, and often including testimonials) can also work well for some businesses.

- **Pop-up ads:** These are the ads that pop up on your screen when you least expect it and use images and often lots of long text to get you engaged. Personally, I find these are the most annoying ads of all. One minute you're happily browsing on a website and then up comes some totally unrelated ad selling the latest fat-blasting program!

If you're prepared to invest heavily in this type of advertising, again it's best to work with a media planning agency that can recommend the best sites to advertise for you and get your ads out there.

Directory advertising

I get very mixed reactions from many small-business owners on the value of advertising in directories. The fact is directories can be highly appropriate for some types of businesses and industries, and an entire waste of money for others.

Advertising in online directories at sites like www.yellowpages.com.au or www.yellow.co.nz and even the *White Pages*, or sites like www.truelocal.com.au or www.hotfrog.co.nz and industry-specific sites are all worth considering in your advertising plan.

You need to ask yourself how likely people are to be buying the kinds of services you offer from a directory. For example, if you're a lawyer catering to the wealthiest of the wealthy, you'd be unlikely to advertise in an online directory as most of your business will come through referral. If you're an electrician, on the other hand, it may well be a different story.

If you're in an online directory already, go back and critically analyse which customers came to you directly from it. If you haven't got that kind of information, start gathering it now so you can make a sensible assessment of its value to you.

No doubt directory advertising can drive traffic to your website and your business. Getting on all the directories, including the free ones, can be time-consuming but worth it. If you want to build it into your overall e-marketing plan, get some help to make it happen.

Other e-Marketing Tactics to Drive More Traffic

If you've read the previous sections of this chapter, I'm sure you've got a handle on how much work it really takes to continue to attract visitors to your website. Building a website and not spending time (and a bit of money) on getting it on the screens of your target market is a common mistake.

You can do lots more to drive traffic. Some of it will work — with some real persistence. Much of it won't. Read on to find out if some of these tactics are for you.

Developing landing pages

A *landing page* is just another name for a specific website page to which people are directed after clicking on an online advertisement. Most businesses selling online will design one landing page per ad, so the follow-up content matches the sell on the particular ad. In this way, you can think of the banner ad as the sizzle, and the click-through page as the sell and the call to action.

Here are some tips for creating successful landing pages:

- ✔ Use an attention-grabbing headline that flows from the banner ad that a potential customer just clicked on.

- ✔ Include statements that establish trust. Consider including a photo or personal guarantee.

- ✔ Include a colour photo of the product with professional imagery and captions.

- ✔ Make a clear statement of what the customer gets for how much she pays and how to order it.

- ✔ Include special offers, money-back guarantees, delivery costs and timeframes.

- ✔ Include testimonials, product demonstrations or anything that reinforces a buying decision.

- ✔ Ensure the layout is professional, not too wordy and clearly directs people to take action by filling out an enquiry form or requesting a quote.

Keep the landing page to no more than two pages when scrolling. I know many businesses using *long-copy sales letters* as their landing pages that can sometimes end up being six or seven pages long. I'm not a big fan of these but, if you do decide to use them, you want to be serious about getting a real pro copywriter to do it for you.

Discuss with your web developer whether you need landing pages and what specific product or service you might use them for. If you decide to go that way, have a look at *Landing Page Optimization For Dummies* by Martin Harwood and Michael Harwood (Wiley).

Email marketing and e-newsletters

I could produce a whole book showcasing the good, the bad and the ugly when it comes to email marketing and e-newsletters. And, to be honest, I've been guilty at times of breaking some of the email-marketing rules myself!

Before jumping in and saying, 'Yes, yes, yes, I need to do email marketing to get my message out to as many people as possible,' you need to ask yourself a few questions:

- ✔ **Who do I send it to?** Do people even want to receive email marketing messages from me? Do I send a separate one to customers and another to potential customers? If so, what do they want to know from me?

- ✔ **What do I send them?** Do they want articles and updates on what's happening in my industry or invitations to attend events? Will they respond to special offers and discounts? How will I get them to interact and engage with me? (Follow this general rule with content: 70 per cent information and 30 per cent sell.)

- ✔ **How do I send it?** How do I set up my database to do this? Do I use my own CRM (customer relationship management) program with email capability or do I set up an email-marketing program with a reputable company?

- ✔ **How often do I send it?** Do I send it daily, weekly, monthly, bi-monthly? (I usually recommend monthly for most businesses and in some instances weekly, depending on the business.)

- ✔ **How do I measure it?** How many people will view it? How many people will click through? What enquiries and sales do I expect?

Many companies can help you target, create, send and track email marketing campaigns. Do your research to find a company that might work for you. People Logic is one such company that helps specifically with email marketing. Check out its website at www.peoplelogic.com.au. One of the very few regular emails I receive that I enjoy is from Richard Sauerman's Wake Up Tiger (www.wakeuptiger.org). Richard is a brand strategist and public speaker, and you can sign up to receive his Thought of the Week emails. They have great inspiring messages, are quick to read and, for me, keep Richard's business top of mind. If I want to hire an inspiring public speaker or brand strategist for a client, I'll probably think of him first.

A recent email campaign I sent out to subscribers, 'The Top Ten e-Marketing Must Knows', resulted in a full-page article in the *Daily Telegraph* because the journalist had opted to receive my emails and liked what I wrote. Not everyone who receives your emails actually reads what you send, but it does keep you top of mind and it can pay off in the long run.

Don't add people to your database to receive group emails or e-newsletters without their express permission, and make it easy for readers to unsubscribe at any time. I hate those ones that you need to go back in and reconfirm your email address before you can unsubscribe!

Podcasting and vodcasting

A *podcast* is a free downloadable audio file that you can listen to on your computer and download onto a CD, MP3 player or iPod so you can enjoy it while running that marathon you've always wanted to do or while you're on a long road trip. A *vodcast* is a free downloadable video and audio file such as the videos you see on YouTube. Just like podcasts, you can download them onto an iPod for later viewing.

Podcasting and vodcasting can be very powerful tools to get your message out. They're hosted on your website and also sent in email-marketing campaigns. They are best for entertaining, informing, educating and inspiring your audience rather than direct selling — although this is, of course, the end goal.

You can try it at home, recording and producing them yourself; however, if you're not an expert you can end up looking pretty amateurish. Getting a professional to help tailor your message, film, record, edit and get the end product looking sharp and professional is definitely worth considering. And check out *Podcasting For Dummies*, 2nd Edition, by Tee Morris et al. (Wiley).

A long boring monologue from you could actually do more harm than good. If you're not a natural with a microphone or in front of a camera, you may want to think about getting someone else for the talent — or finding other e-marketing tactics!

Gary Vaynerchuck is the star of Wine Library TV and has an incredible 80,000 people download his wine-critiquing video interviews every day! For some inspiration on what you can do, check it out at http://tv.winelibrary.com.

Infomercials

Infomercials are especially long format TV ads — they can go for 30 minutes or more. They are usually presented as short documentaries with cleverly woven-in sales messages, testimonials and stories to support the sales message.

You probably won't have the big bucks to do this sort of thing on TV; however, it may be something to think about doing online. Infomercials can work really well for a whole host of products and services, particularly if you can demonstrate results with before-and-after scenarios and stories. Some businesses that use infomercials include weight-loss companies, personal trainers, gyms, hair removal products, hair transplant companies, plastic surgeons, cleaning products and cosmetics.

To be honest, a good browse of the internet doesn't really pull up too many great examples of infomercials. Not sure if that's a sign that they don't work or an opportunity.

Webconferencing

Webconferencing is used to conduct live meetings, training or presentations online (sometimes referred to as a *webinar*). People can participate from anywhere in the world from their own computer. They need to register to attend the webconference and, when the time for the conference arrives, they access the meeting by clicking on a link that connects all participants.

Webconferences offer the ability for the hosts to present a PowerPoint presentation where they are visible on screen, while participants can post live comments and ask questions online for immediate response. They're a powerful way to educate and inform people about your area of expertise, answer participants' questions and promote your services.

Imagine you own a financial-planning business and want to keep your customers up-to-date on what's happening in the financial, superannuation and funds management world. You decide to host a monthly webinar on a different topic to do with investing and use the webinar to answer your customers' questions. You ask them to also invite their friends to participate, potentially bringing you new customers.

Many companies offer webconferencing facilities, so you need to do your homework to find the best deal. Check out www.premiereglobal.com.au or www.premiereglobal.co.nz for an idea of what's on offer and what webconferencing is all about.

Blogging

Do you have a blog? If you haven't been asked this question before, then you should be wondering why. The number of blogs in the world has already caught up with the number of websites and could soon outdo it. In fact, the difference between the two is becoming increasingly difficult to define as blogs start to look like websites and vice versa.

A *blog* (short for web log) is virtually an online diary or journal where people post their thoughts and opinions, and publish them to the online world. The postings appear in chronological order and invite readers to comment and interact with the blog publisher. Blogging can be very therapeutic, addictive and fun at a personal level.

Blogs are being increasingly used for commercial purposes to generate online revenue for their creators, but they only help generate enquiries and new business if you're prepared to use your blog diligently and consistently and devote time to it — and if you have a message worth blogging about that people will actually read! If you want to get into blogging, take a look at *Blogging For Dummies* by Shane Birley (Wiley).

For sites used to set up a blog, check out www.wordpress.org and www.blogger.com — they're free.

Darren Rowse is the creator of www.problogger.net (see Figure 18-4), www.digital-photography-school.com and www.twitip.com. Darren has more than three million visitors to his blogs a month! He started blogging seven years ago, when it wasn't a big deal, and has turned it into his business, earning direct revenue from advertising and affiliate programs, and indirect revenue from his book, and consulting and speaking services. For each of his blogs he uses www.wordpress.org and he loves it because he can outsource the design and development while still maintaining complete ownership and control.

Figure 18-4:
Darren
Rowse's
Problogger
website
shows what
can be done
using free
blogger
set-up sites.

Here are some expert tips on how to produce a good blog:

- **Get your message right.** Blog on something people actually care about, and don't be afraid to voice your opinion. Give useful information, solve people's problems, provide a social commentary. Decide what you will and won't blog about. Be careful not to dilute your message or positioning by blogging on anything that comes to mind.

- **Listen to your customers (or blog followers).** When you get feedback on your blog, respond appropriately and create interaction between your followers. Use the feedback to inspire the content of your future blogs. Watch what other bloggers in your field are writing about and interact with them too.

- **Outsource the set-up and design.** If you don't feel qualified to set up your blog yourself (for free), find someone who can set it up for you. Be aware that you may pay blog experts anything up to $5,000 for a custom-made bells-and-whistles blog.

Two excellent sources to find blog design and set-up experts are
www.odesk.com (see Figure 18-5) and www.elance.com. You can employ
people to set up your blog for you from anywhere around the world and
pay as little as $10 an hour (however, I recommend going for a mid rate, say
around $25 an hour for a good finished product).

Figure 18-5:
You can put
an online
work team
together
from sites
such as
oDesk.

Other social media sites

The use of social media is rampant around the world — Twitter, LinkedIn,
Xing, MySpace, Facebook, Digg, Flickr, wikis, blogs and forums. For many of
the oldies like me, the term *social media* itself is enough to send us into a
cold sweat. For the younger generation, using social media is part of their
daily routine, like brushing their teeth. So what exactly is meant by the term
social media?

Social networking takes the cake

Imagine you own a cupcake bakery delivering cupcakes for special occasions to people all over New Zealand. You want to get people talking about your cupcakes, so you set up a blog for cupcake addicts, sharing your recipes and decorating tips. You ask people to share their special cupcake stories and to send in photos, which you publish on www.flickr.com.

You develop a simple survey on www.surveymonkey.com and ask people to rank which of your cupcakes they like best and to give you feedback on your prices, flavours, decorations and delivery. You publish the survey results on your blog and also on your Facebook page and Twitter account.

Put simply, social media is the practice of sharing opinions, experiences and insights with others via online technologies. Social media provide social-networking sites — places for people with a common interest to connect and communicate. They're an online version of face-to-face networking.

The distinction between using social media to connect at a personal level and using it as a marketing tool for your business is a fine line. The rules of blogging apply to all social media. It's about developing a great message and sending it out to the people, while providing them with an incentive to pass the message on to others.

Whole books are devoted to marketing through each of the social media, such as *Social Media Marketing For Dummies* by Shiv Singh, *Twitter Marketing For Dummies* by Kyle Lacey, and *Facebook Marketing For Dummies* by Paul Dunay and Richard Krueger (all from Wiley), so this is not the place to go into each one in detail. The best way to work out which social media might work for your business is to get online and play. Try doing a blog, set up a Facebook account and register for LinkedIn, for example.

For definitions of all the social media available visit www.netlingo.com or check out www.wikipedia.org.

Part VI
The Part of Tens

Glenn Lumsden

*'Before you start distributing these tablets,
have you thought of making them smaller
and mintier?'*

In this part . . .

*B*eing a great marketer requires some fast-paced thinking and an ability to adapt to market forces and consumer needs. Sometimes you need some rapid-fire tips and processes to rejuvenate your thinking to reposition yourself or make the most of new opportunities.

If you need an at-a-glance list of ten ideas to consider, this part helps you out. Follow the tips in each of the last three chapters to help you create a powerful customer value proposition, work out what you should and shouldn't do in marketing and try out some great out-of-the-box marketing ideas.

Chapter 19

Ten Hypothetical Answers to the Customer Value Proposition Model

A *customer value proposition (CVP)* is a statement of the value you offer your customers. It answers ten crucial questions, including who you are, what you offer, who you offer it to and what benefits the customer gets. When you can answer these questions clearly, your customer places the utmost confidence in your ability to deliver on your promise.

This chapter shows you how to get a great CVP and how to communicate it with power and passion to the people. This, after all, is really the heart of good marketing. First impressions count. If you can't convince someone of the value you offer and why they should deal with you, then it's game over and you might as well go and get a job.

In Chapter 2, I give you the CVP model with all its ten questions. Here, I give you a little more explanation of the questions and some model answers from a hypothetical travel consultant's perspective, to inspire your thinking when you're pondering the questions for yourself and your business.

Even in a cluttered market such as the travel business, you can have a knockout CVP with great points of difference by thinking creatively before you answer these questions. Try it with your business and don't limit yourself. Being bland like everyone else is boring. Being different gets people talking about you. Read on for Belinda Moon's take on the CVP model for Off the Planet Travel.

1. Who Am I?

This question is about you, the business owner. You're the face of your business. People buy you first and what you offer second. You need to be able to clearly communicate your personal expertise, background, history, why you're passionate about what you do and why you're in business, and give a personal guarantee about your services, products and advice.

Belinda Moon, who owns Off the Planet Travel, highlights her passion for travel, the places she's travelled to and is an expert on, the relationships she has with travel service providers, her years of expertise as a consultant and the thousands of happy customers she has served.

2. Who Are We?

This one is about your company positioning. It takes a bold company to make a bold statement about who you are. Believe you're the leader in what you do and position your business as the leader. People want to deal with expert people and expert companies who deliver what they promise.

Belinda positions Off the Planet Travel in cruises, experiential travel such as ski holidays, and exotic destinations such as Africa. She is, in fact, the number-one choice for people wanting an amazing African travel experience.

3. What Do We Offer?

This stage is where you let people know what products and services you offer, and communicate the simple processes and questions you use in helping customers make the best choice. Prepare a list of the services and packages you offer. This is also where you can consider the areas you might specialise in. Statements such as 'We specialise in . . .' are good to include in your CVP.

Belinda Moon lists the kinds of travel experiences Off the Planet Travel specialises in for Africa, from organised tours and safaris, to boutique tours, famous train journeys (called Once in a Blue Moon, on the famous *Blue Train*), scenic flights, adventure experiences and more. When customers first visit Belinda's consultancy, she asks them why they want to travel to Africa, what their expectations are, what they want to experience (and what they don't) and what their budget and schedule is. Then she loads them up with information, including a reference list of books, not just brochures, and asks them to have a good think about what they want to include. When they come back to book their travel, they have a meaningful discussion and can make informed choices.

4. Who Do We Do It For?

Remember target markets? The biggest mistake you can make is to try to be everything to everybody, because inevitably you end up being nobody to anybody. Be clear about the kinds of businesses or customers you want to target, whether big corporate accounts within the top 100 companies or small-business owners in particular industries. Ask yourself questions like: Which customers bring in the most profit? Which ones do I enjoy working with? Which ones don't I enjoy working with? Who will pay for my service and expertise? Where is the biggest opportunity for growth? It's okay to have a few target markets, just prioritise them and focus your marketing efforts accordingly.

For Off the Planet's specialty, Africa, Belinda Moon focuses on people in the 35 to 45 age bracket, usually professionals with a healthy travel budget, who like a little luxury along with their adventure. However, she can also accommodate younger people with a leaner wallet, through organised tours and specialty adventures, such as whitewater rafting. People in higher age brackets (and with plenty of expendable income) she directs to the Blue Moon train experience — the ultimate in luxury.

However, Belinda doesn't just focus on African travel. She targets the same adventurous professionals for all sorts of experiential travel, as well as fun cruises with exciting side trips. Some of her packages include different modes of travel for different legs (a cruise to Maui for some trekking and a surfing safari, a luxurious stay in a resort to recover, and return by air, for example) so she can tailor to her markets.

5. How Much Do We Do It For?

Many people buy products and services on price alone. Ask yourself if you want these types of customers. If not, then you need to justify your pricing by the value you add for your customers through your expertise, delivery, product attributes and service. Identify how your pricing is different from that of competitors. Package and price your services in a way that makes them attractive to people and consider creative pricing options like monthly payment plans or discounts for payment up-front. Avoid discounting all the time as you just create a price war and undervalue what you offer.

Belinda Moon's specialty Off the Planet packages don't come cheap. In fact, she focuses on the higher end of the market. But she also doesn't want to cut off her nose to spite that sweet moon face, so she has a few specials that include group travel in order to benefit from bulk discounts.

6. When Do We Do It?

Communicating your operating hours to your customers is important. The old days of the nine-to-five corporate world don't really work for most small businesses and, in fact, don't always meet the needs of your customers anyway. Depending on the type of business you operate, you may want to offer a 24-hour emergency service by phone, after-hours house calls or even a weekend or weekday evening service. It can be a simple way to differentiate your service offering, help you fit your business into your lifestyle and get you more customers because your competitors just aren't as flexible.

Belinda Moon is happy to visit customers at home to present Off the Planet's African holiday options on Tuesday evenings or on a Saturday afternoon. She also opens the office, by appointment, on Sunday afternoons. The office is open Monday to Friday 10 am to 7 pm and on Saturdays from 9 am until midday. Belinda has an offsider to staff the office when she's on call, or when she needs valuable break time, and time to devote to her suppliers.

7. Where Do We Do It?

How and where you operate is important to many people, whether it's from a big swish office in the CBD or your kitchen table at home. I always try to support local small businesses where possible. It's my way of supporting my community and keeping my local economy going. Most businesses can generally attract more than enough work within a five-kilometre radius. Let people know where you operate and how they can deal with you, whether by phone, fax, email or face to face at your place or their office or home. Being flexible in this regard and giving customers as many ways as possible to deal with you makes it much easier for them to buy.

Off the Planet's office is in a lovely old shopping precinct in a prestigious inner-city suburb. It receives plenty of walk-in traffic and isn't too far away from the professional offices of the CBD. The business website has contact details for after-hours emergencies (lost passports, cancelled flights), including the phone number of a friend of Belinda's in Johannesburg, who has kindly agreed to act as a local emergency contact and sometimes hosts very special customers to dinner. Many of the package details are also included on the website.

8. Why Do We Do It?

Your mission statement is a concise expression of the reason you're in business. Have a look at some of the examples of different business visions back in Chapter 1 if you're still unsure. You need to spend most of your time on communicating why you do what you do, because this is where you engage and enthuse your customers to choose you over the competition.

Belinda Moon's mission statement for Off the Planet Travel is: 'My purpose is to enrich the lives of my customers and their families by giving them the ultimate African holiday travel experience.'

9. What's in It for the Customer?

Customers want to know what benefits they get for dealing with you versus the competition. They want to see that you're willing to go the extra mile on their behalf and be assured that your offering is really going to benefit them.

Off the Planet's 24-hour emergency phone service if something goes wrong on holiday already gives a great benefit to the customer. In addition to booking airfares and accommodation, Off the Planet also prepares a full itinerary for sightseeing, arranges visa and travel insurance, offers advice on vaccinations, language tips, festival details and much more. Customers even receive a Lonely Planet guide and a mini travel kit with their booking. The list of benefits goes on. This is where Belinda Moon likes to be really creative in order to stand out. And often it's the little things that count!

10. How Does It Make the Customer Feel?

This area is the most important question of the lot. Customers buy from you because of the experience you provide that invokes a feeling in them. These feelings can include confidence, happiness, comfort, inspiration, motivation, satisfaction and more. Be sure to include in your CVP how the customer will feel from dealing with you.

Belinda Moon's customers feel special and pampered, even before they've left the office. They feel safe and secure when they travel with Off the Planet, and they know they're about to have the holiday of a lifetime, even as they book. How does the customer know that, and how does Belinda know that's how they feel? Off the Planet's website has heaps of testimonials and links to articles written about some of its packages. And Belinda always follows up when her customers return from their travels to find out how they fared, and, of course, their comments (and some of their photos) go up on the website.

Chapter 20

Ten (or So) Marketing Do's and Don'ts

. . . .

In This Chapter

▶ Focusing on your customers

▶ Maintaining your marketing efforts

▶ Setting your targets and keeping up your skills

▶ Developing your marketing plan and your product or service

▶ Targeting your market

. . . .

*T*he best marketers learn from their mistakes and those of others. They continually fine-tune their approach to marketing, and they know what works and what doesn't. This chapter fast-tracks your learning by giving you the heads-up on the do's and don'ts of marketing. I start with the don'ts, the mistakes you can learn from.

Don't Forget Your Customers

Ignoring your existing customers in the hot pursuit of new ones is a big mistake. Talk to your past and current customers regularly. Find out what they want. Ask how you can help. Offer them a reward and thank them for their business. It costs five times as much to acquire a new customer as it does to keep a current customer happy.

You can have the best product in the world and ruin the experience totally for your customers through poor service. Over 80 per cent of people leave a company because of poor customer service, not because of poor products or services. Put your customers at the heart of your business. Every time you make a business decision, ask yourself: How will this affect my customers? Will it improve their experience with my business?

Always talk to your customers and prospective customers with respect and sincerity. Brochures, ads, websites and salespeople that treat your customers like fools do untold damage to your brand and definitely don't bring you any new customers.

Don't Believe Advertising or the Web Is the Nirvana of Marketing

When business is slow, just whacking an ad in the local paper and crossing your fingers in the hope it brings in new business can be tempting. Advertising can be costly and, if it's not done professionally and properly (and repeatedly), you're just wasting your money.

I've also come across many business owners who believe marketing on the web is the golden key to business success. If you're an online web guru and you have a purely online business, then you just might be able to do it. However, 99 per cent of businesses are not going to be this. Avoid the hype and make sure you have a balanced approach to your marketing.

Don't Stop Observing, Learning, Adapting and Marketing

You've built the perfect products and services, have a lot of customers and are earning a nice income from the business. Now isn't the time to take it all for granted. It could all change overnight. Keep doing the following things:

- Improving your product
- Learning and reading
- Getting better educated to improve your expertise
- Watching the competition and what else is happening out in the big wide world that impacts your business

And don't build a fabulous business and hope that people will simply drop by without a persistent and consistent effort with your marketing. Make marketing a habit. Every day of every week, devote some time to it. It can be as simple as attending a networking lunch or phoning three customers or sending an e-newsletter. Whatever you do (and no matter how busy you are), never stop marketing!

Don't Constantly Change Your Branding

Dramatic and regular changes to your brand and logo can be confusing for customers and cause them to wonder if you've changed management or dramatically changed your business in some way. Don't forget that most people don't like change and avoid it if at all possible (not you, of course) so you need to be mindful of your customers' reactions to brand changes (and any other major change for that matter).

Don't Ignore the Numbers or Your Team

This advice is the most important of the lot. Conducting marketing activities when you haven't set your sales and new business targets has no point. For every marketing activity you do, be sure to set targets, measure expenses and work out what your break-even point is.

You've found a good web developer or graphic designer or part-time marketing assistant, you've given them the drill and you can now leave them to it so they can get on with it, right? Wrong. If you've initiated a new marketing project, you need to be a good project manager and not abdicate all responsibility. This doesn't mean you don't delegate; by all means delegate away, but make sure you have the skills to be an excellent project manager and know what your team is doing, so you end up getting the results you want.

Do Get a Marketing Plan, and a Great Elevator Speech

Okay. I am sorry about labouring this but it's so true. I don't care if you have a single-page mudmap or a 50-page fully bound marketing plan. Just get one. But a plan can only be worth more than the paper it's written on if you actually follow it. The number of pages doesn't count. It's your ability to execute and not get sidetracked that counts.

Be sure to have a brilliant response when people ask what you do (one you can deliver in the time it takes to travel in an elevator). Don't tell them literally what you do. Tell them how you help your customers. Make it funny. Make it memorable. Whatever you do, don't let them leave thinking you're boring so they forget who you are, let alone what you do.

Do Make a Good Product or Service and Constantly Add Value

Building a great website or running a brilliant ad campaign has little point if your product or service is shoddy in the first place. Good products speak for themselves and get their customers talking. A great product backed by brilliant customer service is the best marketing tool in the toolkit.

Discounting is one of the worst marketing tactics you can undertake. It can start a price war, undervalue your product or service, reduce your margins and send you under. Instead, look at ways you can add value so people come back. Give them great service, gifts, warranties, money-back guarantees or whatever to avoid the constant discount trap.

Do Have at Least Four Ways to Market Your Business

Using one marketing tactic alone doesn't work. It might work well at first but, when leads dry up, you'll scramble for new tactics to replace them. Take a multi-pronged approach to your marketing and get them working together. Get online, run an ad campaign, host events, start networking or try cold calling. Whatever you do, don't do just one.

Do Target Your Market and Ask for Regular Feedback

Spending lots of money on advertising to the masses can be tempting. Avoid the mass-marketing approach and be specific on who your market is and where they are, so you can focus your marketing very specifically at them. This avoids marketing and advertising wastage, and often makes it much easier to measure return on investment.

Your customers are the best source of new product or service ideas, and the best ones to tell you how you can improve with regards to any aspect of your business, whether it's the service of the girl at reception or the quality of your product. Don't make the mistake of thinking you have to commission a big research project to get feedback. Build it into the everyday processes of your business, during phone conversations, meetings or by simple online surveys.

Do Be Flexible and Pay Attention to Detail

Being flexible is probably the number-one quality required of any business owner. You must be flexible and have an ability to adapt almost overnight to market forces, customer forces and competitor forces. Burying your head in the sand and sticking to the old way of doing things could end up in disaster.

Rough or slip-shod work, not delivering on something you promised a customer, not phoning back when you say you will, sending out letters with spelling mistakes or taking a she'll-be-right approach ends up losing you customers hand over fist. Good marketing is in the detail — from the time you first meet a potential customer and for many years to follow.

Do Celebrate Your Successes

Getting caught up in the constant demands that come with owning a small business can be a tempting trap. Whether you've won a new deal or had a productive week refreshing the office ready for new customers, be sure to reward and thank your staff (and yourself). And, if you've had a failure of some sort, don't take it too seriously. On the other side of failure might wait your biggest success. Something can only be deemed a failure if you don't learn from it!

Chapter 21

Ten Nifty Marketing Ideas That Won't Bankrupt You

In This Chapter

▶ Opening up your creativity to market your business

▶ Looking for ideas that won't break the bank

You can find 101 ways to market your business, and the exciting thing about marketing is that you can be as creative and out-there with it as you choose to be. This chapter gets your creative juices flowing and gives you some fun ideas to work on. These ten great marketing ideas aren't the most common or the most popular — they're in the rest of the book — but these are ideas that won't break the bank and that you can do immediately to generate new business.

For each idea, I use real-life stories or create a hypothetical based on marketing tactics I've seen out and about on my travels and in dealing with my small-business customers. Take some time to think about whether they may work for you and try them out. It's better to give them a go and see if they work than be left wondering.

If I had one more day to write this book, I'm sure I'd come up with hundreds more nifty little ideas to market your business. All it takes is some creativity and, in many cases, a bit of bravery!

The Transportable Sandwich Board

When you're one company among hundreds touting for the same business in an area, especially when the government is offering subsidies for the work by a certain deadline, creativity comes to the fore.

Recently I had insulation installed in my roof. The installer placed a very clever sandwich board advertising 'FREE insulation quotes' at the front of my house while he was working here. The sandwich board had a small brochure holder containing flyers attached to it. I saw at least three of my neighbours take a flyer in the first hour of it being there. Not sure if it resulted in new business, but I hope so!

The Neighbourhood Drop

Here's another idea for a mobile business that extends the sandwich board strategy (see preceding section) just a tad.

Carly's Carpet and Upholstery Cleaning Service had a lightbulb moment recently. Every time Carly now gets called to a job, she takes five minutes to drop a flyer about her services in the ten letterboxes surrounding the home she's just been to. Carly also asks her clients to let their neighbours know if they're happy with her work (if they're not they can come and tell Carly). She's even thought of approaching people in the street to tell them about her services too.

The Client Bonus

For this strategy, you most likely need to have a business that pays well per service, or you could tailor the offer to suit the service price.

A web developer I worked with decided that his current customers were the most likely source of new business referrals, so, instead of simply asking each of them for a referral, he sent them a letter with a $500 bonus voucher. The bonus voucher offered them the opportunity to redeem the $500 for anything their heart desired for any new referrals that resulted in business.

The Magnet

Marketing your business can happen in the most unlikely places and at the most unlikely times, even when you're out shopping.

A mortgage broker I know had her car branded with her company logo, phone number and website. She also had magnets made up with a simple message and call to action. Each Saturday when she did the grocery shopping, she would drive her car to the local shopping centre, park in the spot that got the most walk-by traffic and then stick her brand magnets all over her car. The car obviously attracted lots of attention as people gingerly began to pick off the magnets, and lots of new business enquiries resulted. Can you think of ways you could be marketing while you're doing the shopping?

The Sampler

This idea is particularly good for businesses selling food, from the butcher to the baker, and even the chocolate maker!

While in Melbourne recently, I passed by a new chocolate shop that was opening for its first day of trading. Instead of handing out boring flyers, they were giving away samples of their chocolates in little boxes with an 'Opening Today' special offer only valid for that day. Hoards of people gathered around of course.

The Sausage Sizzle

Another way to tempt the tastebuds of your prospects and tempt them to open their wallet too.

Everyone loves a snag in bread with sauce. Len the Butcher has decided to have a fundraiser sausage sizzle out the front of his shop asking for small donations for the local school, while offering customers a free branded meat-cooler bag with every purchase.

The Dress-Up

Dressing up isn't just for kids. If you're brave and a bit whacky, take a leaf out of Richard's book.

One of my favourite stories about Richard Branson tells of when he launched Virgin Bride. The day the business launched, he opened the doors in a beautiful white wedding dress and full make-up. Do you think the media loved that one? If you've got the gumption to do something outlandish and dress up for your audience, go for it. It will definitely get people talking about you.

The Doorknock

Yuk! I must say I personally can't stand it when people knock on my door to try to sell me something. However, the life insurance industry and Encyclopaedia Britannica were built on the good old doorknock tactic.

The good folk at Grants Real Estate became tired of knockbacks over the phone, so they decided to try the doorknock approach, offering a free on-the-spot valuation to homeowners. Everyone loves to know what their house is worth even if they have no intention of selling! And the personal touch that comes with striking up a face-to-face conversation brought Grants some new business.

The Long Lunch

The long lunch has been one of my personal favourites when it comes to talking business. I really enjoy connecting with other professionals, customers, business owners, speakers and writers over a fantastic meal and a glass or two of wine. It's a great way to get to know other people personally and to discuss how we can help each other to achieve our business goals. If you're going to host a lunch, think carefully about the invite list and how each person will benefit from being there, and be sure to allow everyone their time in the spotlight!

One of my favourite customers offers travel services targeting women with a common love of travel. She hosts different themed lunches or dinners every month where she brings travel experts along to talk about different countries and travel options. She's held Spanish flamenco nights, yum chas, tapas nights and more. Her customers love them and always bring a friend.

The Showcase

Depending on the kind of business you're in, showcasing your work in places with lots of walk-in traffic can really work. Almost any product can be showcased without you having the expense of your own shop.

My local café showcases the work of local artists for a month or two and collects a commission from any art sold. A jewellery designer I know places her fine pieces in hairdressing salons and clothing stores, and pays a commission on sales.

Part VII
Appendixes

Glenn Lumsden

*'Not only is it eye-catching,
but it cost peanuts!'*

In this part ...

Planning and budgeting are two of the most critical (and most often painful) aspects of marketing. A simple plan keeps you on track. A budget makes sure you don't overspend or waste money. And it helps you measure your performance.

Here you find two simple templates to follow to help you write your marketing plan and create your budget.

If you're still having trouble writing a plan, you may want to find a marketing consultant to help you get it right. The marketing plans I write for my customers can end up around ten pages long and generally include a written plan, a simple budget, a step-by-step action plan and an annual marketing calendar.

Appendix A

Marketing Plan Template

- -

*P*reparing a marketing plan is one of the best things you can do for your business. It makes sure you understand how your company is positioned now, what your expectations are for its progress and how you're going to get there.

Review Chapter 4 for an insight into the importance of planning and what to consider. If you're just starting out or your skills in this area are a little rusty, you may find it worthwhile to engage the services of a marketing consultant. A web search should throw up heaps to contact.

Follow this simple ten-step marketing plan template to help you set up your plan. At Step 3, you need to go back to Chapter 2 to answer the ten questions posed in the customer value proposition model and check Chapter 19 for some hypothetical answers. When you get to Step 10, Appendix B provides a budgeting template to help you.

Creating Your Marketing Plan

Step	Outcome	What to Consider	Your Plan and Notes
1	Personal goals	Where do I want to be in 1, 5 and 10 years? How will I know when I have achieved these goals?	
2	Business vision and goals	What is the purpose of my business? What do I want to achieve financially in terms of revenue, profit, income, business value? What number of leads do I need to generate? How will I measure success?	
3	Customer value proposition (CVP)	What is the value I offer? (Check the CVP model in Chapter 2.) How will I position my business? What products or services do I offer? Who is my target market? How will I price my services or products? How will I be different from my competition?	
4	Environment and marketing SWOT	What outside forces may affect my business — economic, political, technological, global, competition? How will I deal with them? What are the strengths, weaknesses, opportunities and threats to consider?	
5	Branding	What is my business name? What will my business brand stand for? What will my brand look and feel like? What will my personal brand reputation be?	
6	Marketing materials	What marketing materials do I need to support me in marketing my business — website, business stationery, brochures, product packaging, advertisements, banners, letters, giveaways and so on?	

Step	Outcome	What to Consider	Your Plan and Notes
7	Marketing tactics	What marketing tactics will I select to create new business enquiries? What marketing will I do to retain customers and keep them coming back? Select three to six tactics from this book and then write a ten-point action plan for each.	
8	Selling	What direct sales force do I need? How will they approach prospects? What training and support do they need?	
9	Systems, processes and service	What systems do I need to ensure new business is handled efficiently and effectively? Consider a database, service standards, product ordering and delivery, technology requirements and more.	
10	Resourcing	What budgets do I need for marketing? What staff do I need to help market and run my business? How much time will we devote to it? What professional support do I need?	

Appendix B
Marketing Budget Template

- -

*P*reparing a great marketing plan and not having the financial resources to carry it out is an exercise in frustration. You need to really get down to the nitty-gritty to cost out what your planned activities require and how you may modify your plan to suit your budget, or vice versa.

When you've settled on your budget, keep your spending in check. And, by setting your expected outcomes, in dollar terms if possible, a budget helps you measure your performance and the effectiveness of your marketing activities.

If numbers seem to wash over you in the helter-skelter of getting on with business, make sure you have good financial advice and consider hiring a marketing consultant to help you with your marketing budget (a quick web search should give you a decent list to choose from or, of course, you can contact yours truly).

This template gives you a ten-step checklist of costs you may want to consider to help you work out how much you need to spend on marketing. Some of the costs don't relate to marketing directly and some you may not need or want. The best approach is to go through the process of finding out what each of them costs and then make the decision to eliminate or include them in your budget. Check back to Chapter 4 for more insights into the budgeting process.

What you should spend on marketing and what you actually have in the bank to spend are very likely never the same amount. Work out what you should spend and then what you can really do without, or get creative to find ways you can source these things without them costing big bucks!

Creating Your Marketing Budget

Step	Area	What to Consider (Add your own!)	Notes	Budget	Expected Results
1	Professional support and staffing	Business coach Marketing consultant Marketing project manager Image consultant Salespeople Service staff			
2	Customer value proposition	Copywriter			
3	Branding	Graphic designer			
4	Marketing materials	Stationery Sales brochures Giveaways Banners Car decals			
5	Advertising	Creative agency Media buying agency Ad placement costs			
6	Publicity and public relations	PR or publicity agency Media training			

Step	Area	What to Consider (Add your own!)	Notes	Budget	Expected Results
7	Relationship marketing	Networking Entertainment Gifts Sponsorships Events Exhibitions and expos Direct mail			
8	Website	Website developer Website hosting URL registrations Designer Copywriter			
9	e-Marketing	Directory listings Google AdWords Affiliate advertising Email marketing Video production			
10	Miscellaneous	Postage Photocopying Catering Equipment hire Travel Accommodation			

Index

Notes

Notes

Notes

Notes

FOR DUMMIES®

Business & Investment

Starting an
Online Business
FOR DUMMIES

0-7314-0991-4
$39.95

Small
Business
FOR DUMMIES

1-74216-853-1
$39.95

Investing for
Australians
ALL-IN-ONE
FOR DUMMIES

0-7314-0838-1
$54.95

Superannuation
FOR DUMMIES

0-7314-0715-6
$39.95

DIY Super
FOR DUMMIES

1-74216-943-0
$39.95

Investing in Real Estate
FOR DUMMIES

0-7314-0724-5
$39.95

Online Share
Investing
FOR DUMMIES

0-7314-0940-X
$39.95

Tax for
Australians
FOR DUMMIES

1-74216-859-0
$32.95

Leadership
FOR DUMMIES

0-7314-0787-3
$39.95

Freelancing
for Australians
FOR DUMMIES

0-7314-0762-8
$39.95

Australian
Resumes
FOR DUMMIES

1-74031-091-8
$39.95

Debt
Repair Kit
FOR DUMMIES

1-74216-941-4
$36.95

FOR DUMMIES®

Reference

0-7314-0723-7
$34.95

0-7314-0699-0
$34.95

1-74216-945-7
$39.95

0-7314-0909-4
$39.95

1-74216-925-2
$29.95

0-7314-0722-9
$29.95

0-7314-0784-9
$34.95

0-7314-0752-0
$34.95

Technology

0-7314-0985-X
$39.95

0-7314-0761-X
$39.95

0-7314-0941-8
$39.95

1-74031-159-0
$39.95

FOR DUMMIES®

Health & Fitness

1-74216-946-5
$39.95

1-74031-140-X
$39.95

0-7314-0596-X
$34.95

1-74031-094-2
$39.95

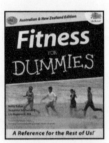

1-74031-009-8
$39.95

0-7314-0760-1
$34.95

1-74031-059-4
$39.95

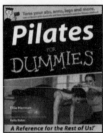

1-74031-074-8
$39.95

1-74031-011-X
$39.95

1-74031-173-6
$39.95

0-7314-0595-1
$34.95

0-7314-0644-3
$39.95